T0365079

Mayhem at the Manor

P.A.Fenning

Order this book online at www.trafford.com
or email orders@trafford.com

Most Trafford titles are also available at major online book retailers.

Print information available on the last page.

ISBN: 978-1-4269-1925-1 (sc)

Trafford rev. 01/20/2023

www.trafford.com

North America & international
toll-free: 844-688-6899 (USA & Canada)
fax: 812 355 4082

The True life Adventures of Amy Brown

Also available:

Sleeplless in Soho
Bedlam in a Bedsit
Ralphy to the Rescue!
Baby on a Barge
Chaos in the Computer Room

This book is dedicated to the memory of
Yvonne MacDonald.
She was one of a kind and sadly missed.
Her spirit burns brightly within these pages.

For Amber, Alex
and future generations.
This book presents an insight
into their grandma's life as a teenager in 1963.

Introduction

This book takes the reader back to daily life during 1963, which had one of the coldest winters on record and generally endured without the luxury of central heating. This year Sir Alec Douglas-Home became Prime Minister, and President John F. Kennedy was assassinated.

The Mod scene was burgeoning, but schoolgirl Amy Brown and her friends, with no money to spend on the latest fashions, improvised and made the clothes themselves. The Beatles were idolised as they reached giddy heights with their music. Beatle haircuts and jackets were a must for any self-respecting teenage Mod boy.

Amy approaches her sixteenth birthday, feeling persecuted by her family and teachers but appreciates the support and comradeship offered by her friends.

One day this book may prove to be of historical interest. Meanwhile, hopefully, it will offer some entertainment as Amy Brown attempts to cope with the many dilemmas and disasters that befall her.

The story is taken from a diary about real people and events, with most names changed to protect their identity.

Mayhem at the Manor

1963

Contents

< ***Life is a learning curve that never quite forms a perfect circle*** >

Chapter One

New Year
A Bad Start

The church bells resounded down the Welsh valley, ringing in the new year. The Brown family stood tired and shivering on the deserted platform waiting for the midnight special excursion train to take them home. This had been a flying visit, hurriedly arranged, to say a final farewell to Gran.

The Browns had left home at 6.30 am on New Year's Eve, and the round trip from Kent to Wales and back would take just twenty-four hours. Mum, Dad, teenage daughter Amy and younger brother Ray were each wrapped up in their own thoughts. Amy's thoughts were preoccupied with the impending trial.

As the last peal faded away, the silence of the still, crisp night returned. The dark sky twinkled with myriads of stars as though reflecting the freshly fallen snow sparkling on the hillside opposite. The only sound breaking the silence was the occasional jingle of a sheep's bell as they roamed in search of shelter.

That sound, almost tuneful, jogged Amy's memory back to happier times enjoying childhood holidays when she first discovered the touching and somewhat bizarre friendship her gran had fostered with a mountain sheep.

Gran lived in a small Welsh mining village, where, on a steel grey winter's day the oppressive mountains and slag heaps towered menacingly over the rows of slate-roofed terraced cottages. Yet in summer, when the mountains were decked out with lush green grass sprinkled with wildflowers, they became irresistibly welcoming – daring to be climbed to their heady heights. Amy loved to clamber to the summit and fill her lungs until they felt like bursting, revelling in the purity of the refined mountain air. To roll down the steep grassy slopes, out of control and gathering speed, screaming with delight and dizziness, heedless to the dangers lurking in the deep, hidden crevasses, was a wonderful childhood experience. Aunt Dot would arrive with a hamper of freshly prepared food and spread a blanket on a rocky outcrop for a panoramic picnic. This carefree summer holiday fun Amy had once shared with her best friend, Katy, who had been allowed to accompany her.

Each evening a tap on her gran's front door announced the arrival of her four-footed visitor. She would greet the sheep like an old friend as it trotted in bold as brass and lay down on the rug by the fire to warm itself. Gran always found it a titbit to nibble on, and after half an hour or so, it would stagger to its feet, bleat farewell, and head back to its mountain friends. There had been an invisible yet tangible bond between them: the sheep trusted Gran, and she enjoyed the brief daily visits that relieved her loneliness.

Grandad had died ten years earlier when Amy was five years old. Now she had only vague memories of him. Dad had often told her how, being an accomplished pianist, Grandad used to play the piano at the local cinema to liven up the silent films. Aunt Dot, Dad's eldest sister, and her husband, Uncle John, lived a few doors down from Gran and now looked after her as best they could. A lifetime spent working down a dusty coal mine had taken its toll on Uncle John's lungs, so now the slightest exertion left him gasping and wheezing.

The freezing wind chilled to the bone on that draughty platform causing Amy's eyes to water. It numbed her head but not her thoughts as she realised with deep sadness that she would never see her gran again. They had found her lying in bed, frail and faded, propped among the feather pillows, waiting to meet her Maker. She looked so very poorly, barely able to speak. A tear trickled down her pale parchment-like cheek, delicately etched with countless wrinkles, as Dad gave her a farewell hug. He was the baby of her family and had always been her favourite. Amy's sorrow intensified into gloomy depression as her reflections shifted to the prospect of returning to court in a few days to plead not guilty against her wishes.

The Christmas shopping spree that she and her schoolfriend Vie had embarked upon at the large town, half an hour's train ride from home, had started full of fun. As they headed for the large department store, each sported a sprig of mistletoe in their hair. Amy bought a grey flannel hipster skirt, while Vie fell in love with a beautiful brown suede pinafore dress.

"Just look at this soft pile," Vie said wistfully, running her fingers longingly up and down the rich suede panels. "If only I had the money I'd treat myself to this as my very own Christmas present." Vie's parents struggled to make ends meet. Her school uniform was well-worn, but being one of the gang, her other five mates didn't judge her.

Amy and Vie stood by the clothes rail discussing tactics and finally came up with what they considered was a foolproof plan to get Vie the dress of her dreams. They took three identical pinafore dresses into the changing room, put one in the bottom of Vie's bag and returned the other two to the rail. Their plan worked well, perhaps too well, because when Vie's eyes alighted on a leather hipster skirt, they decided to try their luck again. But their plan didn't go quite so smoothly this time.

The shop assistant interrupted by popping her head around the changing room door. "Is everything all right?" she asked, eyeing them suspiciously. "Do you need any assistance?" Vie assured her they were fine, but after she had gone, they lost their nerve and returned the three skirts to the rail.

As they sauntered nonchalantly, towards the exit, out of the corner of her eye, Amy spotted a woman trailing along behind them in a fairly obvious way. She nudged Vie. "Don't look now, but I think we're being followed," she whispered. They panicked and dashed out into the High Street, where they were quickly pounced on by the shop assistant and the other woman who turned out to be a store detective. Amy and Vie had no idea that shops employed such devious people.

They were unceremoniously frog-marched up to the manager's office for questioning before the police arrived to cart them off to the local police station. A policeman put them in a room where they were left to wait for several hours while their parents were contacted. Their fathers were then compelled to travel by train to collect them.

The longer Amy waited, the more the butterflies in her stomach made her feel sick with fear at the thought of facing her parents.

Vie remained calm and collected, fidgeting on the hard wooden chair.

"I don't know about you, but I'm getting a numb bum!" she complained. "It's not fair of them to blame you too, Batty, since the dress was obviously meant for me. It wasn't even your size, and they found it at the bottom of my bag."

"Don't be daft, Vie, it was as much my idea as yours to take the risk. It's a shame the plan wasn't as foolproof as we thought. We didn't allow for a snooping store detective to be involved. That gloating old bag was our undoing!" Intense hatred welled up as Amy recalled her sneaking along behind them around the shop.

"Apparently, if we'd dropped the dress inside the shop before leaving, they couldn't have touched us," Vie said ruefully.

"Yeah, if only we'd known. It's downright dishonest to inform us of the rules once it's too late and we've been arrested," Amy said, slumping in her chair. She felt as if the worries of the entire world were weighing her down. How could they have been so stupid? They both felt pretty ashamed of their master plan that had gone so horribly wrong. "You must swear never to utter a word of this to the others when we see them again at school," Amy declared. "You must promise, Vie."

"You can trust me, Bat, it will remain our dark secret," Vie solemnly asserted.

The nickname, Batty, had come about some years earlier when an impatient form teacher asked Amy to fetch a chair from the far side of a crowded classroom during registration. At this school, berets had to be worn until after assembly.

"Do hurry up, Batty Brown, we haven't got all day!" she yelled as Amy tried to pick her way between the desks wielding the chair above her head. She dislodged several berets, nearly causing one or two cauliflower ears, as she struggled to cope. The rest of the class had erupted in laughter at her antics, and the name Batty had stuck ever since.

Their fathers finally arrived at the police station, and the girls were formally charged. Amy copped the inevitable lecture from her dad on the train home. "You've been brought up to behave decently, my girl, and now you have gone and blotted your copybook," he remonstrated. On the opposite seat, Vie's diminutive dad reminded Amy of a pixie, with large pointed ears and a woollen bobble hat. He beamed cheerfully and didn't have a single harsh word for his daughter.

Arriving home, Mum was in a predictably foul mood and gave Amy the anticipated ear bashing. "You've brought shame and disgrace on this entire family!" she bawled as Amy set foot through the front door. "I know it's all that awful Vie's fault, leading you astray." She refused to listen to Amy's protests as her ranting gained momentum. "You're never to go to that girl's house again, do you understand?" Amy just nodded, feeling utterly miserable. Then as an afterthought, her mother added: "In fact, I forbid you from seeing her altogether since she obviously has a bad influence on you."

Though she would never admit it, Mrs Brown was a bit of a snob, despising the trappings of poverty. She had never really taken to Vie with her unruly hair and worn-out clothes that gave her a somewhat unkempt appearance. Amy suspected that this had a lot to do with her unreasonable outburst.

On the day after Boxing Day, Amy and her mother endured a sluggish unheated train journey followed by a long trudge through deep snow and then a nervous wait for two and a half agonising hours in a numbingly cold basement at the Juvenile Court.

"Now, don't you forget my girl – you are the innocent party and must plead not guilty," Mum insisted. She completely ignored Vie and her mum sitting opposite and kept repeating to anyone within earshot: "My daughter is completely blameless, a victim of circumstance." Amy just wanted the floor to open and swallow her up. She felt she was betraying her friend; all her protests had fallen on deaf ears. Her mother was adamant.

She didn't dare incur the full force of her mother's wrath by rebelling, so she obediently followed her instructions and pleaded not guilty. The court instructed her to return in two weeks to face a second full-blown trial. Meanwhile, Vie just pleaded guilty and was given a conditional discharge. Her ordeal was now over, while Amy's continued unabated. Her Christmas had been ruined by this black cloud hanging over her. Now her gran's illness had heaped sadness onto her already depressed frame of mind.

The journey home from Wales was miserable, sitting in an icy cold carriage in sub-zero temperatures. One other lady sat in a corner of the compartment gazing out of the window into the darkness. Amy watched abstractedly as her brother amused himself by playing with the lady's reflection. He patted her on top of her head, tickled under her chin and picked her nose. It occurred to Amy that if she could see what her brother was doing, the lady could too, though she showed no sign of being aware of his antics. Amy thought about telling him to stop but concluded that was her parents' job, and they had their eyes closed, trying to get some sleep.

Unable to get comfortable or warm enough to sleep, Amy found a scrap of paper and a pencil in her handbag. After much soul-searching, she made a list of New Year's Resolutions for 1963:

1) Get a Saturday job – I need the money.
2) Find a cure for my horrible freckles.
3) Try to be nicer to my brother – (tricky!)
4) Study harder, as next year's GCEs are looming.
5) Keep on the right side of the law.

After trudging uphill from the station for a mile through snow a foot deep, the Browns finally arrived home at six o'clock in the morning. Their house, with icicles hanging from the front porch and gutters, looked less welcoming than an abandoned igloo.

They had lived in the Crescent for as long as Amy could remember. Like the Browns, all the families who lived around the green in their corner of the Crescent had been there since the houses were built after the war. Theirs was a close-knit community, and apart from the odd exception, they all got along pretty well together. The Williams family, who lived across the green, were also Welsh and valued their friendship with the Browns. Dad and Gordon were good mates who enjoyed a friendly rivalry over who could grow the best vegetables on their adjacent allotments. The Williams family looked after the Browns' pets whenever they went on holiday and kept their plants watered. The Browns returned the favour when the Williams went away on holiday – usually to revisit relatives in the valleys.

As Mrs Brown pushed open the garden gate, Dennis Denton came out of the house next door wearing tight jeans, a black leather jacket and his mum's knitted tea cosy on his head as was his wont. Dad had given him the nickname Dennis the Menace after the cartoon character when he was a small, naughty boy. It had stuck, especially since his older sister was called Beryl, so she naturally became known as Beryl the Peril. He was a couple of years older than Amy and an avid Rocker, which caused a lot of friction between them as Amy considered herself a definite Mod.

"Happy New Year, Dennis," Dad called out with a wave of his hand.

"Huh, not when your old lady threatens to kick you out," he muttered.

"I suppose you came home drunk again," Mum said reprovingly.

"Anyone would fink it's a crime to celebrate," he grumbled and slouched off up the street through the snow.

Mum unlocked the front door, and they trooped through the hall into the kitchen, shivering. "I'm knackered!" Ray exclaimed, "couldn't sleep a wink on that freezing cold train. Trust Dad to find a cheap excursion that doesn't run to heated carriages."

"Mind your language, Ray," Mum said sharply. "Since it's only six o'clock we might as well get a few hours of sleep." She opened the dining room door, and a black streak of fur flew by, doing a complete circuit of the room without his paws touching the floor once. Toots leapt from table to chair to curtains to sideboard, knocking over a vase of flowers and sending a bowl of fruit crashing to the floor in his frenzied excitement. This was their black cat's mad way of welcoming them home as if they'd been gone for months instead of just one day.

They were all exhausted from the long journey and tramping home uphill through the snow because no taxis were waiting at the station at such an unearthly hour. Everyone was happy to take Mum's advice and go straight to their beds armed with hot water bottles. Amy loved her little bed with its dent in the middle caused by sagging springs. It seemed to hug her as she snuggled down into the dip.

After a fitful sleep, Amy got up in the middle of the afternoon, still tired and fed up, to find herself alone in an empty house. On the kitchen table, a note explained that they had all gone shopping. Amy decided to make the most of the situation and cheer herself up by sampling some spirits stored at the back of the pantry for special occasions. Not being a drinking family, some of the bottles were pretty ancient. She poured herself a tipple of whisky but nearly choked as the strong drink hit her throat, causing it to constrict. She quickly gulped down a glass of sherry to take away the taste of the whisky and followed this with a large brandy. Finding this nearly as bad as the whisky, she drank another glass of sherry. She soon began to feel quite light-headed, having eaten nothing, which quickly turned to nausea.

The drinks didn't succeed in cheering her up but fortunately, that evening, no-one noticed how quiet she had become in her inebriated stupor. Her parents assumed she was still recovering from the arduous journey. Amy lay on the settee feeling sorry for herself. She felt ostracised – the black sheep of the family. Outside, further heavy snowfalls were contriving to make life difficult. The fuzzy weatherman on the nine-inch screen of the upright television in the corner of the living room, promised more of the same.

Amy awoke with a bit of a hangover in the morning. On top of the crockery cupboard in the kitchen, a rhythmical, loud squeak proclaimed that Ruby the hamster was still running flat out in her exercise wheel. Despite being nocturnal, she remained wide awake. Amy thought she looked bored, so she took her out of her cage to enjoy the freedom of her favourite run around the skirting boards in the lounge. Unaware that the hamster was loose, Ray walked in, followed by Toots, the cat, and pandemonium broke out.

"Look what you've done, you idiot," Amy yelled, grabbing Toots by the tail as he lunged for the plump tasty-looking hamster. Ruby fled in terror under the settee. Ray quickly gathered up Toots and beat a hasty retreat leaving his sister on her knees, trying to coax Ruby out with a piece of digestive biscuit.

Dad came in carrying the newspaper and sat down in his armchair. "Ray hasn't forgiven Ruby for stealing his gobstopper last week," he said as Amy stood up with Ruby safely cupped in her hands.

"Well, it serves him right for leaving it lying around," she retorted.

Dad chuckled. "There was Ray frantically hunting for his missing gobstopper while Ruby staggered past with a pronounced list to starboard."

Amy smiled. "Yeah, that huge bulge in her cheek was a bit of a giveaway."

"Ray was livid – he's very partial to his gobstoppers," Dad said, opening up his paper.

That evening, the weather was the main topic of interest on the television news. Amy was full of admiration for the forecaster's precision when he confidently predicted a blizzard for midnight.

Dad received a letter from his sister, Dot, the next morning telling him that their mother was now gravely ill as her life drew to a close. He had to go to work, so Amy volunteered to walk to the Council offices where her Aunt Ruth worked to let her know.

Being Dad's older sister, the sad news naturally caused her great concern. She took Amy to the staffroom and made them both a cup of tea. She listened attentively as Amy described every detail of the brief trip to Wales. Amy often confided her problems to her aunt when she couldn't discuss them with her mother, but there were limits, and her current brush with the law was definitely, one of them. She knew she would only get a further reprimand. Her aunt sensed she was edgy and dispirited but concluded it was probably due to her gran's declining health, so she changed the subject to try and cheer up her niece. "How would you like to have Alwyn's piano?" she asked, "it's such a shame to see it sitting there unused in my front parlour when you could make good use of it. I'm sure your dad would be only too pleased if you learnt to play it properly."

Alwyn was Aunt Ruth's only son, and she doted on him. In her eyes, he was a genius, playing the piano like a hybrid of Grieg and Winifred Atwell. Since his marriage and relocation to the south coast, the piano had been abandoned to gather dust.

The offer surprised Amy, but she found the idea of learning to play the piano quite appealing once she had given it some thought. "That sounds great, but I'd better check with Dad first to see if it's OK," she said as she got up to leave.

After lunch, she called round to see her friend Coral, who lived at number one, the first house on the Crescent. She persuaded her to walk into town and help carry home the weekly groceries, a chore Amy detested.

Coral had the misfortune of inheriting her father's looks. She was tall and plain with a hooked nose. Her greasy, lank dark hair and acne did nothing to improve her appearance. She was rather straight-laced and spoke with a slight lisp made worse by the brace she wore to straighten her front teeth. This caused occasional projectiles of spittle to punctuate her speech, which was unfortunate if she happened to be facing you at the time. She attended church three times every Sunday and sometimes weekday evenings too. She had long since given up trying to persuade Amy to accompany her – much to Amy's relief.

They had been in the same class at four schools since primary school, though now, at Technical High School, they studied in separate classes because Coral had opted for commercial training towards a career in office work while Amy had chosen the technical course because the last thing she wanted to do was sit behind a desk all day. She had yet to decide what she actually wanted to aim for, career-wise. She assumed she would probably work with animals as they had always been a prominent part of her life.

"I might be getting my cousin's piano," Amy informed her friend as they reached the outskirts of town. She knew Coral would be dead chuffed at this news because she was already taking piano lessons.

"That's wonderful, just think – we could spend our evenings practising scales and helping each other," Coral said enthusiastically. Suddenly the idea of playing the piano lost some of its appeal for Amy.

Coral also owned a pet hamster called Fred. Amy's hamster was a ruby-eyed cinnamon – hence the name Ruby, whereas Fred was a more common golden hamster. "Fred has gone into hibernation,"

Coral announced, much to Amy's surprise. "You'd think it would be too warm to hibernate in our kitchen with the boiler in the corner." Amy envied Coral's cosy kitchen. How she longed for a boiler in their chilly kitchen on a bitterly cold winter's morning. Yet, even without any heat, Ruby had remained wide awake and active.

Pam Tibton came strolling along the High Street towards them. She was one of Amy's best friends, one of their gang of six at school, and they hadn't seen each other since before Christmas – an unusually long time for them, so they stopped to chat for a while.

Pam's Christmas sounded as though it had been as dull as Amy's. "My parents insisted on dragging me with them to spend Christmas over at my aunt's maisonette in the East End of London," she moaned. "Just because they'd arranged a get-together with the relatives. I told them I'd be fine at home, but they wouldn't hear of it. They didn't trust me – flippin' cheek! They thought I'd throw wild parties as soon as their backs were turned." She tossed her long dark hair over her shoulder in contempt. "Chance'd be a fine thing! Anyway, once we got there, the drinking started, and before long, they were all a bit merry. This didn't last, once my uncles got onto their favourite topic of football – then the sparks began to fly over which was the best team - West Ham or Millwall. It ended up in a free-for-all with mince pies whizzing across the room. I had to take cover under the dining room table. Aunt Bessie eventually restored order by threatening them with a helping of her awful sherry trifle."

"Well Tibby, at least your relatives have a bit of life in them," Amy said with a sigh. "My lot would just sit around diagnosing and comparing their latest aches and pains while nibbling on a sausage roll."

Coral hovered impatiently in the background. She didn't really approve of Amy's new set of schoolfriends since attending the Tech., so she dragged her off at the first opportunity.

"That Pam, will get you into trouble if you're not careful," she said primly as they entered the supermarket, "she's always after boys."

"Oh, that's not true," Amy protested, jumping to Pam's defence, "she's a good mate, and we have a right laugh together."

Coral shook her head, but refrained from further comment, not wanting to fall out with her friend.

The day of Amy's second court appearance dawned. She awoke with yet more butterflies flitting around her stomach, making her feel miserable. Amy and her mum arrived at the court late because the predicted midnight blizzard had finally arrived over a day late. All the trains were delayed, but this time they didn't have to wait so long in the dismally cold basement.

Amy was called into the courtroom and instructed to address the old man on the bench as 'Your Worship'. This sounded silly, so she called him 'Sir' instead, which appeared to irritate his minions immensely.

The store detective launched into what Amy felt was a blatantly biased attack. "Your Worship, I saw this young lady and her friend hovering suspiciously near a clothes rail."

'Bullshit!' Amy thought and bit her lip, fuming, 'I know perfectly well that our actions looked completely natural.'

After due consideration, 'His Worship' passed sentence and awarded her a conditional discharge, the same as Vie had received.

A furious Amy rounded on her mother as they left the courtroom. "What an utter waste of time this has all been - and it's all your fault! If only you'd let me plead guilty in the first place, as I wanted to, then I could have avoided this second gruelling ordeal." Mum ignored Amy's outburst and took her hanky out to dab her eyes. She was inconsolable that her bid to clear her daughter's name had failed.

Outside, the blizzard had blown itself out, and the fresh air helped Mrs Brown regain her composure. She suggested they walk to the nearby High Street to look for a new winter coat. Amy wasn't in the mood for shopping, but she did need a new coat, so she grudgingly agreed. As they walked along the snowy pavement, the dreaded department store, the cause of all her troubles, loomed ahead of them. Suddenly what little interest Amy had in shopping evaporated altogether. Mum tactfully suggested they settle for a quick cup of tea and a bun back at the station before catching the train home.

Indoors, Amy found Dad engrossed in his hobby of rag rug making. Oblong bits of material were scattered all over the dining room table. He sat humming as he deftly thrust the hook through a large square of sacking and tied the pieces, forming coloured patterns as he worked. Rag rugs were slowly spreading throughout the house. So far, they had infiltrated the bedrooms and kitchen. He seemed to be in a good mood, so Amy broached the subject of the piano.

"Sounds like a good idea," he said, "I'll see if I can arrange for Alwyn to deliver it next Sunday in his van when he visits his mum, though we'll have to make room for it in the lounge." He realised Amy had been through a harrowing ordeal in court, so he avoided the subject. Instead, he tried to cheer her up. "You remember you asked, a while ago, about having your ears pierced?" Amy nodded. "Well, you can have them done for your sixteenth birthday. How does that suit you?" He beamed at her, pleased with his offer.

"That'll be terrific, Dad," she said and impulsively gave him a hug.

The following morning, she lay in bed feeling depressed. Her criminal record lay heavy on her mind. Would it affect her job prospects? She eventually got up at one o'clock and wandered into the kitchen to receive another lecture from her mother.

"Ray must not find out about your lawbreaking activities. As far as he's concerned, we went shopping yesterday. Say nothing to nobody - the fewer people that know, the better. Now, hurry up - your father is waiting for you."

The snow had now melted, so Dad had offered to take Amy into town on his ex-GPO motorbike, affectionately known as his pop-pop. She had to get her school skirt out of the cleaners and buy a pair of stockings ready for the new term. The pop-pop was designed to seat the driver only but Dad had created a makeshift pillion by covering a lump of foam with imitation leather and sticking it to the rear mudguard. There were no springs to soften the bumps on the road and no footrests. Great care was needed to avoid sustaining third-degree burns from touching the hot exhaust with a bare ankle. Amy hated the motorbike - it simply wasn't fitting for a Mod to be seen riding on such a frumpy machine. She suspected her dad enjoyed adding to her embarrassment by wearing his old black beret pulled down tightly over his bald patch and held in place by a pair of yellow-lensed, fur-edged goggles. To complete his ghastly outfit, he wore huge leather gauntlets that came up to his elbows, and a heavy-duty mac, several sizes too large, that reached his ankles. As they walked along the High Street, Amy tried to keep a low profile, fervently hoping she wouldn't meet anyone she knew. Luck was on her side today.

"Don't ever meet me from school in that get-up because I shall definitely disown you," she told him as they emerged from the cleaners.

Dad smiled, removed his beret and goggles and stuffed them into his huge mac pocket in a vain attempt to appease his daughter.

Feeling a little brighter by the morning, Amy knuckled down and finished knitting her chunky, bright yellow jumper. She was very proud of the intricate cable pattern she had created.

"I'll sew it together for you if you like, dear," Mum offered, to Amy's surprise. As much as Amy enjoyed knitting, when it came to sewing up the seams, they usually refused to match up for her. Mum rarely offered to help her, so she quickly accepted before she changed her mind.

After lunch, Amy helped Dad take down the Christmas decorations because Mum had started to panic. "We have quite enough bad luck in this house without invoking a load more by leaving the decorations up after the twelfth night!" she wailed.

Christmas was steeped in tradition, and the Browns' decorating ritual was no exception. Every year the paper chains had to be hung strictly according to the detailed plan drawn to scale by Dad in the dim and distant past. Each coloured paper chain was numbered, and there were always four gigantic balloons in four bright colours - one for each corner of the lounge ceiling. The operation was carried out with military precision. Amy usually got roped in to judge when the loops were equal so that Dad, balancing on top of the stepladder, could finally push the drawing pin into the ceiling. Dad regarded it as a serious business with plenty of bad-tempered cursing on his part - until the final manoeuvre when the four balloons were inflated. He got Mum in a complete tizz by blowing them up to bursting point, ignoring her frantic pleadings with him to stop. "You tie off the balloon while I steady it," he instructed her, winking at Amy. As Mum struggled to tie the enormous balloon, he squashed it between their corpulent bellies until Mum's nerves gave way and she ran shrieking from the room. Dad thought this was a huge joke, and Amy suspected that Mum did too since they played this same charade every Christmas.

Now the decorations needed to be taken down, and each paper chain carefully vacuumed before being rolled up and stowed in a shoe box along with the plan, ready for next year.

"It would be nice if, just for one Christmas, we could vary your design," Amy said as she steadied the stepladder for her dad.

"This plan for the paper chains is carefully calculated to make four equal loops per chain so that they all meet up in the centre around the lampshade," Dad said from the top step as he pulled out a drawing pin and let the paper chain and balloon float to the floor.

"Why not live a little? Put the balloons in different places, or even splash out on a fifth balloon to compensate for the lack of a Christmas tree," Amy said with a touch of sarcasm.

"Christmas trees and their baubles are a waste of money," Dad said, coming down the steps. Amy sighed. She knew she was fighting a lost cause against her dad's tight-fisted attitude of make-do and mend. This was her father's philosophy on life, and he firmly believed in practising what he preached.

"Bah, Humbug!" she muttered as Mum came in carrying the vacuum cleaner.

"Let's get these dusty paper chains vacuumed and put away," she said briskly, "I want this room returned to normal."

The piano duly arrived Sunday afternoon in Alwyn's van and Dad helped to trundle it around the green and up the garden path, arousing curiosity from some of the neighbours who didn't bother to watch discreetly from behind twitching net curtains but opted to stand in their gardens and gawp openly.

Alwyn was a terrible bighead from all the years of praise heaped on him by his adoring mother. He sat on the piano stool and confidently launched into a rendition of boogies and rags. Amy had to concede he was a terrific pianist (probably inheriting his talent from his late grandfather) but she wouldn't dream of telling him as much.

That evening, Mr Hamilton arrived to collect the Browns in his latest car as they had been invited to tea. The two families had been friends for many years now. Mr Hamilton owned several garages selling new and used cars, so he changed his car nearly as often as he changed his socks.

As they were leaving, Mum whispered urgently in Amy's ear: "Whatever you do, don't mention anything about your brush with the law."

"As if I would," Amy said scornfully.

"Well, this is one skeleton that must be kept firmly locked away in the cupboard," Mum reminded her.

Amy suspected her mother suffered from the delusion that the sun shone from the Hamiltons' orifices. In Mrs Brown's eyes, they were the ideal family, living in a big posh house in a snobby area and attending church every Sunday. Mrs Brown tried to emulate them by putting on her upper-class telephone voice and giving herself airs and graces in front of them. Amy almost expected her to drop a curtsey to Mrs Hamilton who was a dead ringer for the Queen, even speaking like her.

During the war, before Mrs Brown married, she nursed at the same hospital as Mrs Hamilton's sister, Gladys. They shared digs and kept in touch long after they went their separate ways. When the Hamiltons moved to a nearby town, Gladys introduced them to the Browns, and their friendship blossomed.

The Hamiltons had three daughters, much to Mr Hamilton's disappointment. He desperately wanted a son to inherit his garages, so consequently, he was always fussing over Ray. He sometimes seemed jealous that Dad had a son and he didn't. Amy got the distinct impression that being a mere girl, in his eyes, she was persona non-grata. Kathleen, Rosamund and Annette were home for the hols from their boarding school. Amy hated the idea of being packed off to a school hundreds of miles away. She was surprised to discover that they didn't seem to mind or even bear a grudge against their parents for sending them there. The sisters all looked the image of their father, sporting short straight boyish haircuts, and they all spoke with well-rounded vowels. Amy was a little older than Kathleen, the eldest, with whom she corresponded when she was away at school but Amy didn't really consider her to be a close friend.

Comfortably seated in the Hamilton's lounge after tea, they exchanged belated Christmas presents. Amy received yet more hankies. Was everyone under the impression that she was extra vulnerable to colds? She also received a selection box of chocolates to share with Ray, which she knew would lead to arguments over who had what.

Mr Hamilton suggested a game of Newmarket. "Go and fetch the tin of buttons, please, Ros," he said as he rummaged in a cupboard until he found a pack of playing cards.

After an hour, Dad had accumulated a pile of buttons in front of him, and everyone else looked a trifle fed up. "I seem to be on a winning streak tonight," Dad said, beaming as he shuffled and dealt the cards.

"Anyone would think we were playing with money instead of buttons," Amy whispered to Kathleen as play commenced again. A pile of buttons had accumulated on the King of Hearts. Play slowed to a halt as everyone studied their hands.

"Oh, do come on! Someone must have the Queen of Hearts," Ray said impatiently.

"Well, I know it's not in the dummy hand, so someone's onto a winner," Ros said, looking around at everyone. Then she started to giggle. Amy looked up to see her toothless father grinning and gurning with the Queen of Hearts stuck to his bald patch. She let out a groan.

Mum blushed with embarrassment. "Oh, Lou, stop messing about and play the game properly."

"I think we can safely say that Dad has won," Ray said, throwing down his cards. Everyone agreed, and Mrs Hamilton went off to the kitchen to make the coffee.

Mrs Brown's supercilious ideals were usually reinforced after a visit to the Hamiltons. No sooner had they returned home than Amy became embroiled in a bitter barney with her mother over the subject of Vie yet again. She stormed upstairs to her bedroom with her mother yelling after her: "I mean what I say, young lady, you will have nothing to do with her this coming term, because she is not the right sort of person to have as a friend."

'What a flippin' cheek my mother has got!' Amy fumed, 'I'll show her! I shall have nothing whatever to do with *her* instead. She's a snooty, mean old cow!'

The following morning, Amy wanted to get out of the house, so she decided to walk around the

Crescent to Coral's. Dad stopped her as she was leaving. "Would you pop over the bridge to Smith's and get me an ounce of Old Holborn and a packet of green papers while you're out?" Amy scowled as he thrust a ten-shilling note into her hand. She found herself lumbered with this trip to the local sweet shop near Coral's at least once a week and felt she did more than her fair share. "You can buy yourself some sweets with the change," he bribed. Amy sighed and put the money in her pocket.

Coral was out, so she went across to the phone box near Coral's house to ring Yvonne, her scatty Scottish friend, for a chat. Yvonne sounded her usual cheerful self and promised to tell Amy about her new boyfriend at school the next day. Then Amy tried ringing Jean, another schoolfriend, but got no answer. She walked across the railway bridge to the shop and bought Dad's tobacco and a quarter of rhubarb and custard sweets for herself. She reluctantly returned home and spent the rest of the day avoiding her mother by staying in her bedroom. The last day of the holidays had arrived, so she packed her satchel ready for school and checked that each piece of uniform had her name sewn on it.

Chapter Two

January
Back to School

The first day of the new term caused Amy to plummet to new depths of depression. The mere act of crawling out of her cosy bed into an icy cold bedroom was grim at such an ungodly hour.

Part of the school occupied a large Grange where Amy arrived at her form room on the first floor. Pam and Fluff had been so bored during the holidays that they were glad to be back at school. Fluff was a wheezy, mumsy girl, the eldest of a large family. Her out-of-school activities were limited to the occasional trip to the cinema because her spare time was commandeered for babysitting duties with her younger siblings.

Yvonne arrived in a fluster, late as usual; her bouncy dark locks windswept and her clothes more dishevelled than usual. Schoolbooks hung out of her bulging satchel. She had been raised in Dundee by her very strict gran and had only recently arrived in England to live with her mother and new stepfather. Her strong Scottish accent, though pronounced, was usually comprehensible, except where Mrs Butler, their form mistress, was concerned.

Amy helped to sew name tags onto Yvonne's uniform while she told Amy all about Alex, her latest. Yvonne could win the heart of almost any unsuspecting boy she chose with her effortless banter and captivating face. Like Pam, she was another dark-haired beauty with large expressive green eyes tinged with sadness and fringed by long, black, curling lashes. Amy envied her flawless complexion but not her well-proportioned figure, which lacked any semblance of elegance. Her gait was reminiscent of an old sea dog with a wooden leg. She was self-conscious of her ankles, or to be more accurate, her lack of them because her legs joined her feet without acknowledging any discernible shaping. At least one of her legs had the plausible excuse of being run over by a bus many years ago when she was lucky not to lose the leg altogether. Every winter Yvonne was a martyr to poor circulation when her hands and feet turned a blotchier shade of purple than usual. Despite these handicaps, Yvonne was one of the most popular girls in the entire school, with her easy way of befriending people. She attracted new friends like a flower to bees and was generous to a fault. She would gladly lend a friend her last penny though she demanded the same generosity in return - only far more frequently! Yvonne's boundless energy led to an exhausting friendship, that could wear Amy to a frazzle.

"Ooh Bat!" she exclaimed, bubbling over with excitement. "Just wait 'til you meet Alex. He's tall, slim, blonde and such a dish! In fact, he's terrific. This time it's the real thing. I'm madly in love, and he's told me how much he loves me too! Life at the moment is just perfect." She lapsed into a daydream and then gave a sharp cry of pain as she pricked her thumb on the needle, jolting her back to the present. "By the way, Batty," she said after removing her sore thumb from her mouth, "you're invited to my sixteenth birthday party at Alex's house in a fortnight's time, so you'll be able to tell me what you think of him."

Jean came in red-faced and puffing from the climb up the sweeping main staircase in the Grange, followed by Vie. Jean caught the tail end of the conversation as she flopped down next to Amy. This prompted her to announce her own news, to try and impress the others. "Guess what, girls, we held a wild New Year's Eve party at our house that lasted for two days. It was fantastic!"

"So, how come none of us was invited?" Amy demanded, her voice charged with disbelief. The girls had learnt to take Jean's stories with a good pinch of salt.

"Er, well, it was only arranged at the last minute. There wasn't time to let you know," she stammered, flushing slightly, unsettled by Amy's scepticism.

Amy leaned across and gave Vie her belated Christmas present of stockings. "Mum has forbidden me from seeing you," she whispered.

Vie just shrugged. "Well, we can hardly avoid seeing each other since we're in the same class," she remarked.

Amy grinned. "Mum obviously didn't think it through."

The door opened, and a diminutive Mrs Butler hurried into the room to take registration, her arms full of books which she dumped on her desk.

"Good morning, girls. No doubt you are all glad to be back and can't wait to start work again," she said wryly, tugging the register out from the bottom of the pile. This was greeted with a unanimous groan. Being young and easygoing, she was very popular with the girls in her class. Yvonne dashed up to her desk and asked for a change of address form as her mum and stepfather had just moved house. Mrs Butler frowned, looking perplexed and demanded: "What on earth is a 'forrum'?" This caused a burst of giggles from her class. "All right, girls, settle down. After registration, I shall check every piece of uniform to make sure it is correctly named." A second groan went around the room, accompanied by a flurry of activity as clothes were carefully scrutinised.

The new term offered the exciting prospect of brand-new purpose-built classrooms. Class 5G2's first lesson was geography in the New Building that had just been completed in the grounds of the Grange. No-one liked Miss Finley, the new geography mistress who had quickly earned the nickname of Frog-eyed Freda because of her bulging eyes though she was more like a scraggy-necked vulture as she hovered up and down the aisles waiting to swoop on some unsuspecting victim.

This term, for the first time, they could enjoy the luxury of eating lunch in comfort as the New Building housed a proper canteen next to the main hall. No more pushing desks together in classrooms in the Grange and across the road in the Manor House. No more lukewarm meals ferried in from goodness knows where. The Manor kitchens in the basement were too old to be used for preparing meals. Mrs Host, the art mistress, had requisitioned them for her pottery and craft classes, so the only ovens in there were the pottery kilns. The kitchen in the Grange had been a makeshift domestic science room since the school opened five years ago. At last, they now had a large super-equipped domestic science room in the New Building.

There just remained Mrs Snake's octagonal music room to be constructed this year on the farther side of the Grange, and then the school would be complete. At present, only third to sixth-year students attended the school, but the autumn term would see the school expanding to take in first years from the Eleven Plus exam. Amy definitely was not looking forward to that. She liked the school the size it was now, with the youngest being thirteen. She didn't relish an influx of silly little eleven-year olds who would need mollycoddling.

At breakfast the following morning, Amy sat at the dining room table eating a bowl of cornflakes and trying to ignore Ray, who was pulling faces at her across the table. Mum sipped her tea and gazed out of the window down the garden path. "I can see Snowy in his cage throwing his food bowl into the air. Have you fed those guinea pigs this morning, Amy?"

"He's Ray's guinea pig, so he should feed him. How come I get lumbered with feeding and cleaning out his rotten guinea pig?" Amy asked indignantly, feeling hard done by.

"It's just as easy for you to look after three guinea pigs as two," Mum replied firmly.

"Not when one is an albino rat with an amputated tail masquerading as a guinea pig. He won't even touch the rabbit pellets, and when I tried to give him a carrot the other day, he bit my finger!"

Ray stuck out his tongue. "He's just a fussy eater."

Amy leaned across the table. "So how come my Bobby and Patsy have pretty, chubby faces and your Snowy has an ugly, pointed snout and beady pink eyes? And, come to think of it, I've never heard him squeak like a guinea pig."

"He's probably a mute guinea pig," Ray reasoned.

Amy gave a triumphant: "Ha!"

Dad came into the room clutching a letter and looking troubled. "Listen, this is the news we've all been dreading. Your gran has passed away. Me and your Aunt Ruth will have to go to Wales to attend the funeral." The guinea pigs were forgotten as the sad news sank in.

"Thank goodness we made that brief trip to her bedside at New Year. I think she was hanging on to see you, dear," Mrs Brown said, trying to impart some comfort to her husband.

"If you go on your old pop-pop, it'll take several days to get there, and Aunt Ruth won't ride on that pillion," Amy said as she gathered up her satchel and school coat.

"No, I don't think my motorbike is up to that length of journey. It'll have to be the train again,"

Dad said, with a sigh, shaking his head. "And no cheap excursion rates this time," he added ruefully.

Arriving at school, Amy strolled through the Manor gates, her thoughts still wrapped up with happier times back in Wales. Suddenly her recollections were rudely interrupted by a loud horn honking behind her. Short-sighted Ton-Up Slater, their eccentric old English teacher, was about to mow her down with her moped. She looked ridiculous in her leather peaked pilot's hat clamped down tightly around her bespectacled face. Her pebble-stone glasses made her eyes appear twice their normal size. A long trench coat flapping about her welly-clad ankles completed her appalling ensemble. Amy wondered how she ever mastered the basics of driving when her brilliant academic mind was always busy calculating complex conjugations to the exclusion of all else. The mundane mechanics of life seemed to have passed her by. Tied to the parcel rack of her moped were several tins of cat food to feed the tabby mother cat and her kittens who had taken up residence in the Manor stables. Could this be proof, perhaps, that somewhere beneath her vague and cold facade, there beat a humane heart?

With the previous night's homework still to do, Amy headed for the Manor cloakroom. Each morning, a crowd could be found huddled on the benches under the rows of coats and berets with books spread out, trying to catch up on their homework before the teachers arrived. The girls found it quieter to work here and more discreet than in the openness of the New Building cloakroom. The rules were simple: The first girls to finish had to pass their exercise books around for copying and then keep guard for marauding teachers.

Once assembly was over, the continuous round of boring lessons dragged on through the day. After school, Amy met her mother in town so she could be fitted out with a new winter coat while the sales were still on. Their tastes in fashion being miles apart, it was tricky to find a coat they both liked. More importantly, one with a price tag, small enough to keep her father happy. As they browsed together in the clothes shops, Amy got the impression her mother was trying to call a truce and make up for being so nasty about Vie. Mum tried in vain to coax a little conversation out of her daughter. Amy was still annoyed with her mother, so didn't bother talking. She just gave the odd grunt in response to any questions. They finally agreed on a brown corded velvet coat at the Co-op costing seven pounds and fifteen shillings.

Later that evening, Amy was forced to revise her opinion when they fell out again. Mum had just finished sewing up the seams on Amy's yellow jumper.

"I think I'll wear it to the Vets tomorrow night - it'll go with my new grey hipster skirt," Amy said, holding the jumper up to inspect the finished article.

"Your father and I have agreed that you cannot go to the Veterans Club tomorrow evening," Mum announced in her no-nonsense voice. "Or any other Friday evening, for that matter, because we know it's a favourite haunt of that Vie's." She liked to drag Dad into her side of the argument for moral support, even if he hadn't been consulted.

Amy quickly countered by trying to reassure her with a small fib. "Vie told me she's not going there anymore, so you've got nothing to worry about." Amy wasn't very good at lying, especially to her mother. She had a way of staring hard at her until she blushed from head to toe with guilt, even if she had told the truth. Amy suspected that she hadn't managed to convince her.

Friday evening had been Veterans Club night for some time now. The weather had worsened with freezing winds, so Amy was glad to be wearing her warm new jumper. Pam called for her, and they didn't hang around in case Mum put her foot down and forbade her from going. They dashed out of the front door with Amy tossing a "see ya," over her shoulder to her glowering mother before making the treacherous one-mile trek along icy pavements.

Outside the club, they met up with Vie and Lynn. Lynn had remained friends with Vie since they all split up after junior school and went to their various secondary schools. She was a short chubby girl with a round rosy face and a cheerful disposition. She lived in the next road to Vie and often came out to the club with her. Pam was a tall captivating brunette, so she usually had the pick of any boys they met up with. Amy rarely took preference over Pam unless the boy happened to favour a blue-eyed blonde with a speckled face. Amy hated her freckles and was convinced they put her at a distinct disadvantage.

The Veterans Club was the only option, with nowhere to go locally on a Friday evening. It was held in a shabby memorial hall on the outskirts of town. The harsh, unflattering strip-lighting did nothing for a girl's complexion, but at least the entrance fee was cheap.

Jean was already there as she only had a short walk from her house. She sat with her ample posterior spilling over the edges of a wooden chair in the corner. An overweight, somewhat unhealthy dollop, she had attached herself to Amy when she could find nobody else to befriend at school. She suffered from an inferiority complex which she tried to compensate for by making herself appear more interesting. She habitually told whoppers to impress, but nobody was fooled anymore. It singularly failed to have the desired effect of making her more popular. The other girls tolerated her, but their patience wore thin at times. Jean lived so much of her life in a make-believe world that she seemed afraid of facing up to the real world. The girls always invited her to their social outings, but despite promising faithfully to meet them, she rarely turned up. The Veterans Club was the exception because she was dragged there by her older next-door neighbour, Sheila. Jean had confided to Amy that although Sheila was her friend, she was free and easy with her affections where boys were concerned. Jean believed she was only one step away from prostitution. Amy was shocked by this news. Surely she wouldn't tell such lies about a friend. Sheila did come across as being a bit coarse, but nonetheless, she seemed a likeable, lively girl.

Tongue in cheek, Amy tapped Jean on the shoulder. "There's a dance at the town hall tomorrow night. The Searchers will be playing, so it should be a great night. D'you fancy coming?"

Jean beamed, pleased to be invited. "'Course, I'll come. Wouldn't miss a chance to see the Searchers in person."

"O.K. I'll meet you outside the town hall at seven-thirty," Amy said, knowing that Jean probably, wouldn't be there.

Amy, Pam and Vie danced together all evening as there was a shortage of decent boys. Jean, Sheila and Lynn sat huddled at the back of the hall, discussing and comparing the clothes worn by everyone else. From a corner of the stage, the Dansette record player bravely blasted out 'Locomotion' by Little Eva at full volume, doing its best to make up for the lack of a live group. The girls formed a long train, singing and shunting themselves around the hall while the bemused boys just looked on, too self-conscious to join in.

As they were leaving at the end of the evening, Vie gave Amy her late Christmas present. Amy pulled off the wrapping to discover a bottle of lavender water. "Oh, how lovely Vie," she said, trying to sound enthusiastic, but she doubted she would ever use it.

Pam caught a bus to her home in the next town while Amy walked home with Vie and Lynn. On their way, disaster struck when one of Amy's stilettos skidded on a patch of ice, sending her sprawling. She yelled as her face hit the pavement, making her nose bleed. She could taste the warm blood and realised she had also split open her lip, but she was more concerned about looking a mess. Lynn and Vie grabbed an arm each and helped her to her feet. Amy managed a gory smile causing the girls to recoil in horror, not so much at the blood, as

Amy assumed, but at something far worse - a gappy smile! A piece of her front tooth had snapped off.

Amy was totally devastated. Her tongue explored the new gap confirming her worst fears. “What on earth am I going to do?” she wailed, “I can’t even smile until I get it fixed.”

“Oh, don’t worry, Bat, it really doesn’t notice that much, and you’ll soon get it fixed,” Vie assured her. They tried to make light of it, but Amy was inconsolable. At home, her mother, being an ex-nurse, brought out her trusty first aid box and launched herself into nursing mode. She was too busy trying to staunch the bleeding to quiz Amy about whether she had been out with Vie.

Saturday morning dawned, and Amy was still trying to come to terms with her broken tooth. She wrapped a scarf around her face to protect her sore mouth from the cold wind and walked to the end of the road to ring Jean from the phone box by Coral’s house.

“Just checking that you’re still coming tonight, Jean.”

“Sorry, but I can’t make the dance - I’ve got a splitting headache.”

“Well, it’s lucky that I rang then!” Amy snapped irritably and hung up, wondering, not for the first time, why she bothered with Jean.

The temperature dropped dramatically that evening, falling below freezing. Amy went down the garden to feed her guinea pigs, and the icy wind shot agonising pains through the exposed nerve of her broken tooth. She was thankful she didn’t have to go out to the dance after all.

Amy hated the long dark winter evenings when everyone was confined to one room, and the rest of the house imitated the North Pole. The Browns sat huddled around the small coal fire in the lounge, watching their upright, monochrome television. They scorched the front of their legs while the draught on their backs remained icy cold.

Amy was busy cleaning her guinea pigs' cages Sunday afternoon. Dennis, wearing his mum's tea cosy again, leaned on the fence, annoying her. "Bet you'd like to see my latest tattoos," he said.

"I'm really not interested. I got more than I bargained for last time when you dropped your trousers to show me a fox disappearing down a hole," Amy said, pausing to scowl at him.

Dennis grinned. "Ah, but these tattoos are a must for any self-respecting Rocker." He held out his clenched fists. "Look, I've got L O V E across the knuckles of my left hand and H A T E on the right hand. I cuddle my girlfriend with my left arm and use my right fist for a good punch-up."

Amy glanced at his knuckles, unimpressed. "You're obsessed with fighting," she said.

"Better than your mamby pamby Mods who can't knock the skin off a rice pudding!" Dennis countered derisively.

"There's more to life than fighting, you know."

"Come off it. What could be better than rounding off an evening at the pub with a good punch-up."

Amy spotted Kathleen coming down the garden path looking immaculate in her best, though somewhat frumpy, clothes.

"Hello, Amy. We've just arrived to have tea with you. Mummy, Daddy, Ros and Annette are indoors. Can I give you a hand?" she offered.

Amy looked at her clean clothes dubiously. "Well, if you really want to."

Dennis had been eyeing Kathleen up and down. "Aren't you goin' to introduce us?" he asked, grinning lasciviously at Kathleen.

"Er, Kathleen, this is my slob of a neighbour, Dennis. Feel free to ignore him."

"Charmin'!" Dennis said indignantly. "Nice to meet you. Would you like to see a fox disappearing down a hole?"

"Don't you dare!" Amy snapped, "Kathleen has led a very sheltered life."

Kathleen glanced around vaguely. "Is there a fox near here?"

Amy quickly thrust a bucket and shovel into her hands. "Well, if you don't mind, perhaps you could shift that pile of fresh manure over to the main heap."

This wasn't exactly the sort of help Kathleen had meant. She smiled bravely and showed willing, carefully tiptoeing around, trying to keep her Sunday best clean.

"I think I'll take my fox indoors then if you're not interested," Dennis said, stretching and giving a yawn. Amy ignored him, so he ambled off down his garden.

Mrs Brown called out to the girls from the back door to come in as tea was ready. Kathleen turned, lost her footing and slipped, landing face-first in the smelly heap.

"Oh, blimey!" Amy gasped and hurried over to pull Kathleen up. She picked bits of straw from her hair and grabbed a handful of clean straw to try and clean the mess off her clothes.

"What am I going to do?" Kathleen wailed, looking miserable, "Mummy will be furious if I ruin my best clothes."

"It's a good job they're dark, so the marks don't show," Amy said, trying to reassure her, "maybe your mum won't notice." She produced a tissue and wiped Kathleen's face.

Indoors, everyone sat around the dining room table. It was laden with cold meats, salad, fruit and cakes. Dad was smiling with a full set of teeth on display. Amy guessed that he had been nagged by Mum to wear them. Now and then, a pungent aroma wafted across the table whenever Kathleen moved.

Mrs Brown looked a little agitated. "Er, it's a little stuffy in here. Would you open the window, please, dear," she said, looking earnestly at her husband, who was happy to oblige.

"Once the girls are back at boarding school, I shall be going to Norfolk to visit my sister, Gladys," Monica said between mouthfuls of ham.

"Will you be going to Norfolk, Harry?" Mum asked as she offered him the plate of bread and butter.

"Far too much work at the garage, Cis, I can't possibly get away."

"But how will you manage for meals?" Mum sounded concerned.

"Oh, I'll muddle by somehow," Harry said vaguely.

"Nonsense! You must come and stay here with us," Mum insisted, "mustn't he, Monica?" She looked across the table for support from Harry's wife.

"It's very kind of you to offer, dear," Monica said, "if you're sure it won't inconvenience you."

"It'll be no trouble at all. Harry can have Amy's room - I'm sure she won't mind."

Amy forced a smile while fuming under her breath.

"Bless you, I'd love to come and stay," Mr Hamilton said, beaming with pleasure, oblivious to Amy's seething at his acceptance, "it's most kind of you."

When Mr Hamilton wasn't looking, Amy glared at her mother. She knew this would mean having to share a bed with her - a daunting prospect. Her father would be moving in with Ray because he had a double bed all to himself. Amy often pondered over the unfairness of why her brother had the big bedroom with its double bed, and she, the eldest, was relegated to the cramped box room and her single bed. She was well aware of the fuss her mother always made over Ray. She concluded that the reason was obviously favouritism.

Dad switched on the television after the Hamiltons had left. The latest weather forecast showed that Saturday had apparently deteriorated into the coldest day for seven years, with Sunday just as bad. Temperatures had reached minus 29 degrees Fahrenheit which Amy considered was seriously COLD!

"You kids must wrap up well for school in the morning," Mum advised as she banked up the fire with more coal. "A pity you don't still wear liberty bodices like you did when you were little - they kept you really warm." Amy groaned, recalling the fleecy-lined bodices she was forced to wear with their rubber buttons down the front. At least being older had some compensation.

Monday morning, Amy's classmates were curious to see her broken tooth and offered their commiserations. She felt self-conscious about her tooth, so she was relieved when their interest proved no more than a fleeting diversion.

In English Literature, Mrs Slater had the class read Lark Rise by Flora Thomson. Most of the class found it an excruciatingly tedious exercise. Amy, however, revelled in its pleasant rusticity. Perhaps because it reminded her of carefree childhood summer holidays spent at her maternal grandparents' cottage in the depths of Suffolk. They each took turns reading a paragraph to the rest of the class. As she waited for her turn, Amy's gaze wandered around the room and came to rest on Mrs Slater's no-nonsense grey short straight hair. 'I bet she cuts it herself to save on hairdressers fees,' Amy thought, 'judging by the way it's lopped off dead straight just above her earlobes. It's as if she's stuck a basin on her head as a template.' She found it impossible to believe that any self-respecting hairdresser would willingly cut her hair in such an awful style.

Amy and Coral usually travelled to and from school together. Today Coral had to go to her piano lesson after school. As Amy alighted at the bus stop, she met up with Pissy-nicks Parks, the youngest daughter of the large family who lived next door, so she had no choice but to walk home with her. Amy saw very little of her these days. All her life, she had worn endless hand-me-downs from older brothers and sisters. They were a large family of ten, so they couldn't all sit at the table together for a meal. They ate at two sittings, reminiscent of school dinners. Amy wondered if, these days, Pissy-nicks had gained better control over her bladder. Many years ago, Amy had allowed her to borrow her little red bike only to have it returned later with a very soggy saddle!

The following morning class 5G2 attempted to make princess sponges in domestic science. Jean shared a large wooden table with Amy. They gathered all the necessary equipment and carefully weighed their ingredients. Jean tucked a stray lock of hair under her cap, managing to dab flour on her face in the process.

She leaned across and whispered to Amy: "How would you like to come to my house on Sunday afternoon? I'll ask Mum if you can stay for tea. If Barry, my next-door neighbour, is in, I'll introduce you to him. He's tall and good-looking. I'm sure you'd like him."

Amy agreed to go but was well aware that if Jean was true to form, she would come up with an excuse by the weekend to wriggle out of the arrangement.

Jean's sponge went wrong and came out of the oven flat as a pancake, so Miss Snodgrass insisted that she make another one. Then, while they were washing up, Mrs Slater popped her head around the door, peering vaguely through her pebble-stone specs. "Can I leave this meat in one of your fridges until after school, Miss Snodgrass?" she asked. Without waiting for an answer, she promptly opened an oven door, shoved the wrapped meat onto a shelf, thanked Miss Snodgrass and left. Miss Snodgrass scolded the girls for giggling. She quickly rescued the meat and put it in the fridge.

Jean shook her head and sighed. "Modern appliances are like alien contraptions to poor old Ton-Up," she declared.

"I wonder how on earth she copes in her own home," Amy said, handing Jean a soapy mixing bowl to dry. "I bet her long-suffering husband must have plenty of patience - or ulcers!"

Amy came rushing out of school, thankful to be ahead of the crowds, when she saw her dad had come to collect her. He was still in his uniform, standing next to his ambulance, which he had parked in front of the main Grange gates. "Let's go," she panted as she hurriedly clambered up into the cab. Amy wasn't ashamed of her dad being an ambulance driver. Nevertheless, he had a knack for unintentionally embarrassing her in front of her mates far too often for her liking.

"Not so fast," he said, "we might as well wait for Coral and give her a lift home too." Amy groaned and tried to hide by sliding down, out of sight, below the dashboard. As the girls walked past, they peered through the windows, curious to see who had been taken ill. Finally, Coral arrived, and Amy squeezed up on the seat to make room for her friend.

"Other parents collect their daughters from school in a more normal mode of transport like a car," she grumbled to Coral. Unlike Amy, she didn't mind in the least as she was pleased to be getting a lift home since her dad only possessed a push bike.

At home after tea, Mum showed Amy a pattern for a striped pom-pom hat she had bought. "I thought perhaps you might like to knit this for Ray," she suggested, "since you've finished your yellow jumper and have nothing to knit at the moment."

"Very considerate, I'm sure," Amy remarked sourly. "He'd better wear it if I go to all the trouble of making it for him," she added with a scowl.

The following morning, Dad packed his bag, ready to leave for his mother's funeral. In Wales, the tradition was for men only to attend funerals. The women stayed home to prepare the food for the gathering afterwards. Customs there were far slower to change and move with the times.

Mr Smith, who owned the sweet shop and tobacconist across the bridge, was always in demand for his taxi service. He loaded Dad's suitcase into the boot, and the rest of the family waved Dad off as he left to collect his sister en route to the station, with the snow falling thick and fast again.

Amy had an appointment with Miss Stevens at the start of the lunch hour to receive a ticking-off as she had only completed half of her science homework. This made her late for lunch, and, in her rush, she forgot to sign in the late book.

Miss Catting caught her trying to creep in. "Come here, Amy Brown," she ordered angrily. "Just where do you think you are going?" She glared at her down the length of her shiny nose.

"Sorry, Miss Catting, I've been to see Miss Stevens," Amy said, trying to look suitably humble by staring hard at the floor.

Miss Catting eyed her suspiciously. "Get to your seat quickly, and don't forget to sign the late book."

"No, Miss." Amy meekly turned to go.

Miss Catting stopped her in her tracks with: "Just one moment!" She felt an iron grip on her shoulder. "What denier stockings are you wearing?"

Amy's heart sank. "Er, fifteen denier, Miss," she mumbled.

"I thought as much," Miss Catting trumpeted, "you know perfectly well that the school rules stipulate that only thirty denier or more are permitted in this school."

"Yes, Miss, but I laddered the only decent pair I have," Amy said lamely. This was the best excuse she could think of on the spur of the moment.

"You will wear regulation thirty denier stockings, and if you don't have any, then it's back to ankle socks. Is that clear?"

"Yes, Miss Catting." Amy finally escaped from her clutches and headed for her dinner table.

"Yoo-hoo, Batty!" Yvonne called out, waving her over.

Amy sat down and scowled at Yvonne's smiling face. "What a bloody awful day! I hope it doesn't get any worse," she muttered.

"Oh, don't let old Catty get you down. Her bark's a lot worse than her bite, you know," Yvonne said blithely. "Here, I've saved you a large helping of meat pie." She piled up Amy's plate with pie and vegetables. Amy tucked in, waiting to see what Yvonne was after as she wasn't usually so unstinting where food was concerned.

"Hey, Bat, do me a favour," she pleaded, giving Amy's arm a tug which caused her intended mouthful of pie to end up on the floor. "Can you lend me eight pence for my bus fare home? I've been and spent all mine on tuck and don't fancy struggling home on foot for miles through the snow." Amy hadn't the heart to refuse her.

Jean was conveniently absent from school the next day. "I bet she contrives to be absent tomorrow too. Then I can't make arrangements to go over to her house on Sunday," Amy told the others as they lounged on the straw bales in the Manor stables during their lunch break. Jean spent a lot of time absent from school - far more than anyone else. The girls often discussed Jean amongst themselves, speculating why she was so reticent about her home life.

"It's just not worth making any arrangements with that girl," Vie said, shaking her head. "I don't know why you bother."

"Well, I like a challenge, and getting inside Jean's house is definitely that!" Amy declared, absently stroking a kitten curled up on her lap.

"I reckon she's got some dark secret that she doesn't want the rest of us to know about," Fluff said with an air of mystery, and the others nodded in agreement.

Yvonne jumped up. "I'm taking a leaf out of Jean's book. I've wangled the whole afternoon off with a hospital appointment to see a specialist about my painful verrucas," she said, glancing at her watch. "Time I was gone - see ya tomorrow."

"You jammy devil!" Amy yelled after her.

Friday arrived - but at school, Jean didn't - as Amy had anticipated. The jive session in the gym during the lunch break was the highlight of the school week as far as the girls were concerned. Suddenly their energy was boundless as they jived and twisted around, despite dancing in their grotty plimsolls to prevent damaging the wooden floor.

Amy arrived home from school to be presented with a new pair of thirty denier stockings as she walked in the back door. "I had to dash out to the shops especially to buy these today," Mum told her.

"You needn't have bothered," Amy retorted, turning them over and glaring at them.

"You know your dad and I, don't approve of you breaking school rules," Mum said crossly, "just make sure you wear them." This didn't please Amy, who had no intention of wearing them if she could help it.

Mum turned to take a pie out of the oven. Friday was her baking day, but things hadn't been going well. "Just look at this crust – it's burnt!" she exclaimed crossly, adding somewhat illogically, "and it's all your father's fault!" Amy quickly vanished up to her bedroom before she could be blamed too.

That evening she met up with Pam and Vie en route to the Veterans Club. Her mother didn't bother arguing with her this week, but Amy realised she wouldn't give up the fight so easily.

They arrived at the club, but there was no sign of Jean. Vie went to chat with Gary, a greasy, leather-clad Rocker who lived near her. Pam and Amy danced together for most of the evening until they heard a yell. "Hiya Bat, Hiya Tibs," came across the hall announcing the unexpected arrival of Yvonne. She had brought along her much-adored Alex to show him off. With his tall, sleek, blonde-haired, blue-eyed good looks and immaculate silver mohair suit, he was every bit as suave and handsome as Yvonne had described. But at twenty, he was quite a bit older than them.

Yvonne and Alex smooched off around the floor, totally wrapped up in each other. A scruffy boy walked over to Amy and introduced himself as Arthur, a friend of Gary's. He pestered her for a dance, so she eventually agreed in the hope that he would then leave her alone. But his keenness increased by the end of the dance, and he asked if he could walk her home. Pam was getting a lift home with Yvonne and Alex, so Amy reluctantly agreed as Gary was accompanying Vie home and she didn't fancy playing gooseberry.

Once she got chatting with Arthur on the way home, she discovered what a complete drip she was lumbered with. She refused to hold his arm to prevent herself from slipping over, despite a freezing wind blowing practically at gale force. She didn't want to give him the wrong impression that she liked him. Amy glanced across at Vie. She was whispering and giggling with Gary, looking like she enjoyed his company.

Amy left Vie and Gary at the end of the Crescent. On reaching her front door, she quickly thanked Arthur for bringing her home. She dashed indoors, grateful for the scarf wrapped tightly over her mouth, which prevented any chance of a goodnight kiss. 'I should've just given him a gappy grin,' she thought wryly, 'that would've frightened him off.'

Indoors, her mother was looking agitated. "They have just made an announcement with a special bulletin on television stating that Hugh Gaitskell, the leader of the Labour party, has died suddenly," she said, wringing her hands. Amy had no interest in politics, so the news of his death meant little to her.

"His name does sound vaguely familiar," she acknowledged, relieved that the news distracted her mother from interrogating her about which friends she had been out with.

Dad and Aunt Ruth arrived home from Wales late on Saturday morning. He brought the mandolin that he used to play as a boy. "I thought you might like to learn how to play it," he said, giving the leather instrument case to Ray. "After all, if Amy can learn to play the piano, I don't see why you can't learn to play the mandolin."

Amy felt a little miffed because her dad hadn't brought anything back for her. "He'll never play that - he hasn't got a single musical note in his whole body!" she scoffed.

Yvonne arrived after lunch, her cheeks and nose glowing from the cold. She and Amy exchanged late Christmas presents. Amy gave her an address book, and Yvonne gave Amy face powder. Mum had often told Amy how much she liked Yvonne. Amy realised this was because Yvonne could switch on her irresistible charm and her mum fell for it every time. If her mum had an inkling of just how scatty Yvonne could be, Amy knew, without doubt, that she would ban her from seeing Yvonne too.

The recent heavy fall of snow didn't deter Yvonne from dragging Amy around the Crescent to the phone box so she could ring Alex. She chatted and giggled with him for over an hour while Amy fed coins into the box. Her feet were completely numb from the subzero temperatures and the icy wind that blasted in through the broken panes of glass in the phone box. Yvonne appeared immune to the intense cold despite her poor circulation.

'Just goes to show what love can do,' Amy mused as she listened, a trifle enviously to all the billing and cooing. Yvonne finally hung up once the money had run out, and they floundered home through the snow to catch up with their homework.

Amy obligingly did some of Yvonne's French homework for her and lent her English homework for Yvonne to copy. These were Amy's two best subjects, so Yvonne took advantage of them.

Half an hour later, Yvonne jumped up. "Look at the time! I've got to dash - I'm meeting Alex this evening."

"I don't suppose you can let me have the eight pence I lent you the other day?" Amy asked half-heartedly.

"Sorry, Bat, I've no money left after feeding that phone box. I'll pay you back next week, I promise."

It occurred to Amy that the phone money had been acquired by raiding the stash of threepenny bits in the plastic, pink elephant, which her mother kept hidden behind the scales in the pantry. She refrained from pointing this out to Yvonne.

Sunday morning, Amy awoke to find a steady rain dissolving away the snow. By the afternoon, the temperatures had dropped sharply, and the rain had frozen over, making the pavements and roads enormous ice rinks. Ray persuaded Amy to go outside and help him make a long slide the whole length of the pavement in front of their house.

Just as they got into the swing of sliding, old man Parks came shuffling out and put a stop to their fun by chucking a bucketful of ash all over their slide. "A bloomin' danger to life and limb," he muttered, "you ought to know better." He shook the empty bucket at them, then went back indoors, still grumbling.

"You rotten old spoilsport!" Amy yelled after him. "Why don't you mind your own business and throw your rubbish outside your own front door." She didn't notice a car draw up, and Mr Hamilton get out, suitcase in tow. He looked a little disconcerted at the altercations in progress. Ray hurried across the green to carry his suitcase. Amy just glared at him before stomping indoors. She was in no mood to be turfed out of her bedroom. She felt hard done by - life was dealing her more than her fair share of bad luck lately.

She arrived early at school on Monday morning to finish Yvonne's and her own French homework in the Manor cloakroom. Jean was still absent, which was no surprise to Amy or any of the others, either.

During assembly, Clara Hardacre, the headmistress, announced that bouffant hairstyles were forbidden in school again that year.

"What she really objects to, is the way berets can be folded up, pinned to the back of the head, and then almost totally obliterated by a good bit of back-combing," Pam whispered to Amy. Miss Hardacre had enlisted her faithful band of prefects from the upper-sixth to spy on the girls as they travelled to and from school. Detentions were handed out with monotonous regularity to any girl caught deviating from her strict school rules.

Having overslept that morning, Yvonne brought her breakfast to school with her. She and Amy sat at the back of the classroom, sharing the croissants and marmalade during Religious Knowledge and Geography, balancing them on their knees beneath the desks. Unfortunately, Miss Finley caught Amy with a mouthful of croissant and gave them both detentions.

On the way home, Amy called at the local fish shop for some smoked haddock, which she needed for domestic science the next day.

At home after tea, Mr Hamilton got off on the wrong foot with Amy by criticising her lack of help with the washing up. She noticed that he ignored

Ray's bone idleness, and neither did he offer to dry the dishes himself. Amy felt relieved to escape to the kitchen and boil the haddock and an egg ready for the cookery lesson. She stood at the cooker, mulling things over and concluded that Mr Hamilton was plainly a Male Chauvinist Pig. Her darling brother could do no wrong in his eyes.

Dad had been busy enquiring about a good dentist who specialised in crowning teeth. Since his own diabolical experience some years ago, when he had all his teeth removed in readiness for dentures, he was taking extra care to find the right one for Amy. His bungling dentist had smashed the nerve endings in his gums. It was now uncomfortable for him to wear dentures for more than a few minutes as his gums quickly became painfully swollen. He would have no option but to remove his dentures then and there, regardless of where he might be, which usually caused the maximum embarrassment for Mum. He eventually gave up wearing his false teeth altogether. But Mum still tried persuading him to wear them whenever they had company. The lack of teeth didn't stop him from eating virtually anything except lettuce and nuts. Having no teeth meant he could pull marvellous faces when the mood took him. He'd have Amy's friends in fits of laughter with his facial contortions that could easily win a gurning contest.

He walked into the kitchen to find Amy packing her ingredients into a tin, ready to take to school. "I've finally tracked down a dentist near London specialising in crowning teeth. He comes highly recommended, so I've arranged an appointment for you."

"The sooner, the better, as far as I'm concerned," she remarked. Amy was already fed up going around with her top lip buttoned down firmly over her teeth. "If I go on much longer like this, I'll end up with such a complex that I won't be able to open my mouth, let alone smile."

At school the next day, there was still no sign of Jean. "She's overdoing the avoidance bit," Amy commented to Pam as they headed for the domestic science room. Today the recipe was kedgeree, using the haddock and egg. Amy's finished effort reminded her of what Toots had brought up the previous week after eating the remains of Ray's chicken curry.

Afterwards, a new coloured student from the local P.E. College took the class for a ballroom dancing lesson in the gym. She started, full of enthusiasm but soon realised she was wasting her time trying to get the girls to glide gracefully around the floor. Their plimsolls and fleecy-lined maroon sugar bags masquerading as knickers vanquished every last vestige of elegance.

After tea that evening, Amy let Ruby out of her cage for her usual run around the skirting boards in the lounge. On reaching the fireplace, she would pause to consider. Should she take the shortcut inside the fireguard and across the tiled hearth? Or opt for the longer route around the fender and along the edge of the rug. Tonight, unfortunately for her, she chose the latter course.

Mr Hamilton, unaware of Ruby's perambulations, stood on the rug, puffing importantly on his pipe. "You know, Lou, with business doing so well, I'm considering investing in another garage. Ray could do worse than come and work at the garage when he leaves school. I could arrange an apprenticeship for him."

Dad beamed at Harry from his armchair. "That's very generous of you, Harry. I'm sure Ray will jump at an opportunity like that."

To Amy's horror, Mr Hamilton stepped back just as Ruby darted across the rug behind him. Amy yelled, but it was too late. Ruby shrieked in pain and Mr Hamilton jumped forward as if he had been shot up the bum by a red-hot clinker. Ruby ran to her favourite refuge under the settee. Amy saw that one of her hind legs was dragging uselessly behind her. Mr Hamilton, choking on his pipe, was full of profuse apologies, but Dad would have none of it.

He glared at Amy. "It's all your fault," he shouted, "how was Harry supposed to know that Ruby was creeping around behind him? You should have warned everyone that she was loose."

"But you know that Ruby usually has a run after tea," Amy protested.

"Yes, but Harry doesn't – though he does now!"

Amy eventually succeeded in coaxing Ruby out. "She hasn't had much luck on her outings lately; she could end up a very neurotic hamster," she said, stroking Ruby and gently checking her damaged leg. "Her back leg is sticking out at an odd angle, so I'm sure it must be broken. I'll have to take her to the vet and get it examined."

Amy put Ruby back in her cage and took herself off to bed, feeling irritable and depressed. Nothing was going right for her or Ruby at the moment.

Wednesday morning, there was still no Jean at school. Vie was absent as she had to attend her nan's funeral.

"It must be the exceptionally, cold weather causing so many old people to drop like flies," Amy whispered to Pam during registration. She rummaged through her desk, searching for her plimsolls. Unable to find them, she resigned herself to the prospect of running around in bare feet during P.E.

At the morning assembly, Clara Hardacre made the unpopular announcement that, unlike other sensible schools, her school would not close down because of the extreme weather conditions.

In the gym, Amy stubbed her toe on the springboard as she ran to leap over the vaulting horse and then limped over to the coconut mats where Fluff was trying to balance on her head. "This is no joke on the cold gym floor," Amy moaned, sitting down and rubbing her throbbing toe, "and there's the distinct possibility of getting splinters too."

Miss Catting's shrill whistle sounded, signalling the end of the lesson. The girls quickly returned the equipment to the storeroom at the rear of the gym before enduring a lukewarm shower in the changing rooms.

"It's all right for Clara," Amy grumbled as they hurried to get dried and dressed. "She's tucked up in her cosy study in the Grange with a huge log fire roaring in the grate behind her desk, keeping her nether regions roasted. I bet she never had to run around a freezing cold gym barefoot!"

"Never mind, I've heard it's fish and chips for lunch today," Fluff said, trying to cheer up her friend.

After school, Coral offered to accompany Amy to the vet with Ruby. The vet confirmed that

Ruby's leg was indeed broken. He gave Amy some antibiotic tablets for Ruby because the leg was swollen and too small to put in a splint.

That evening Amy discovered it was impossible to persuade a hamster to swallow a tablet. Ruby took it eagerly enough, pushed it into her cheek pouch and then ran off to her larder, where she expelled it and then ignored it. Amy tried crushing it and mixing it into her food, but Ruby wasn't fooled that easily because she just refused to eat.

Dad insisted that Amy had been conned by the vet. "I've never heard of a tablet curing a broken leg before," was his much-repeated opinion. Amy had to agree with him – the tablets did seem pretty useless, so she finally gave up on them.

On the way to school in the morning, Amy's nose began to bleed copiously. She had been suffering from repeated nose bleeds since an accident during a gym session at her previous school when she was hanging upside down on the ropes. She let go hoping to land on her feet but lost her sense of direction and landed on her nose. To this day, a large blood stain remained on the gym floor.

She had no choice but to do her geography homework in the Manor toilets. A plug of toilet paper hung out of her left nostril, which didn't help her concentration. At least she found the toilets quieter than the cloakroom and less likely to be invaded by teachers. Fortunately, her nose stopped bleeding by the time she went across to the New Building for assembly. Jean was still absent. 'Perhaps she'll never come back,' Amy thought as Mrs Snake began pounding out 'Fight the good fight' on the piano.

After the break, the girls headed for the geography room in the New Building. The phone on the wall in the corridor started to ring. They saw Mrs Slater lope past, eyeing it suspiciously. Once she realised nobody else was going to answer it, she reluctantly returned and gingerly lifted the receiver as if expecting it to bite her at any moment. The girls giggled as they heard her shout repeatedly: “Hello, hello, who’s there?” into the earpiece. Hearing no reply, she hung up in exasperation and stomped off, muttering angrily.

“Can you believe that!” Amy gasped, and they all fell about laughing.

“It’s about time she joined the twentieth century!” Pam said as they entered Miss Finley’s domain.

That evening, Ray finally got to wear his first pair of long trousers and not before time, with the severe winter causing problems for everyone.

“At least your knees will be cosier,” Amy told him. “It’s unfair that girls aren’t allowed to wear trousers to school. They would be far more practical and definitely warmer than skirts.”

“Seems pretty fair to me,” Ray said with a grin as he walked up and down the lounge getting accustomed to the feel of material flapping around his calves.

Yvonne was the first girl in their class to reach sixteen. Friday morning, she began her birthday by strolling into school an hour late and charmed Mrs Butler with a load of old flannel to avoid getting another detention.

The five girls sneaked into the domestic science room during their break because Yvonne had brought some coffee, bread and butter. They made themselves piles of buttered toast and basins of hot coffee because they couldn't find any cups. Mrs Slater nearly caught them, but they spotted her through the glazed door, her bent figure loping along the corridor. They hid the steaming basins of coffee in the cupboards and ducked down behind the benches. Mrs Slater opened the door and peered short-sightedly around the room before leaving. Any other teacher would have noticed them quite easily.

Yvonne and Amy stayed behind after school to write a boring essay entitled: 'Why food should not be consumed during lessons' for their detention. They caught the bus to Amy's house afterwards, so Yvonne could change her clothes. Alex was treating her to a slap-up meal instead of the intended party, which she had to cancel at the last minute. Her mum had forbidden her from holding a party at Alex's house as she was convinced it would turn into an orgy.

"Once Mum gets an idea in her head, it's impossible to shift it," Yvonne said, with a sigh, as they climbed the stairs to Amy's bedroom, "so I just gave in gracefully." Amy thought Yvonne's mum had sex on the brain, but she refrained from saying so.

Yvonne stood in front of the mirror in Amy's cramped bedroom, admiring herself while Amy struggled to get her zipped into her new red dress.

"D'you think I'm getting too fat? This dress is definitely a bit on the tight side."

"Well, maybe it wouldn't hurt to lose a few pounds," Amy said. She heaved a sigh of relief as she finally persuaded the zip to reach the neckline. This wasn't what Yvonne wanted to hear.

She enjoyed her food far too much to contemplate dieting.

A knock on the front door announced the taxi's arrival, which had come to take Yvonne in style to the station where she had arranged to meet up with Alex. After she had gone, Amy got herself ready and sneaked out the front door before her mother could stop her. She met up with Pam on the way to the Veterans Club.

Vie appeared for a while during the evening before leaving to go to a Mormon dance with Lynn.

"I'm a bit worried about Vie getting involved with the Mormon church," Pam confessed as they headed for the ladies to freshen up.

"Oh, they're a pretty harmless bunch," Amy declared. "You don't see the Church of England going to the trouble of arranging dances for teenagers."

"Well, I think it's Lynn who's influencing Vie to go," Pam said, tugging a comb energetically through her sleek dark hair.

Amy tried to reassure her friend. "Lynn's a fairly sensible person, so I'm sure there's nothing to worry about."

They returned to the hall and spent the evening inventing a Mod dance with lots of intricate steps, so they needed total concentration as it involved a lot of counting.

Amy came downstairs Sunday morning and nearly tripped over a ladder, lying in the hall. She was sure it hadn't been there when she went to bed the night before.

At breakfast, her mother scowled at her. "You caused us a lot of trouble last night," she snapped.

"I don't see how because I just went to bed as usual," Amy protested defensively.

"Yes, that's just it! Out of sheer habit and no doubt being tired too, you went up to the toilet and locked the door, then went to wash in the bathroom, also locking the door. Finally, you went to bed in my room and automatically locked the bedroom door too! By the time I came up to bed, you were sound asleep. No amount of knocking and calling could rouse you. I didn't fancy sleeping on the settee, so your poor father had to go across the green to the Williams' house and borrow their ladder. He had to climb onto the porch roof and clamber through the bedroom window, which, as luck would have it, had been left slightly open. He unlocked the bedroom door, and you never stirred once!" Amy could hardly believe that she had slept through all the commotion.

Feeling lethargic, she spent the afternoon knitting Ray's pom-pom hat, but with just the pom-pom left to make, he wasn't showing much enthusiasm for it.

Monday began badly for Amy as she knocked timidly on the heavy wooden door to Clara Hardacre's study. She clutched the dental note excusing her from afternoon lessons which required Miss Hardacre's signature. She looked up at the box on the wall containing a red and green light. The green light flashed, and a buzzer sounded, indicating that she could enter. Miss Hardacre, her precisely permed grey hair looking immaculate as usual, sat straight-backed behind her enormous desk and looked sternly at Amy over the top of her glasses.

"Ah, yes, Amy Brown isn't it? Come in and close the door." She took the note that Amy thrust towards her and glanced at it before continuing.

"I ought to tell you that I have been asked by the court to write a report on you and your friend Vie."

Amy felt devastated that the school had been notified of her misdemeanour. She stood there enduring yet another lecture, too mortified to attempt any defence. The last thing she wanted was for her headmistress to be dragged into her court case. Amy knew that Clara, furious at having her school's reputation besmirched, would now have cause to pick on her.

'I'll be doomed to a school life of victimisation,' she thought as she made her way to her first lesson.

Mrs Brown met Amy from school after lunch. The thaw had set in with water, slush and mud everywhere, making walking difficult. However, it didn't prevent them from catching the train to the new dentist who had been recommended to Dad.

Amy had a morbid dread of dentists since she was seven when her mother dragged her to the masochistic school dentist. It seemed to Amy that he drilled and filled almost every tooth she had aided by his heavily made-up old bag of an assistant. Mum had described her as mutton dressed as lamb. The dentist didn't bother to numb her gums and smacked her on the legs if she whimpered with pain. Amy had tried complaining to her mother afterwards as she rinsed her mouth in the dingy corridor outside his surgery. She had to use a cracked mug chained to a deep dirt-ingrained sink. But her mother had refused point-blank to believe her.

Now she sat in the hot seat once more, a nervous wreck with her palms sweating. The dentist took a long look at her chipped front tooth and grunted. "I won't touch that until it has stopped growing," he announced. "It'll take at least another year."

Horror of horrors! 'How on earth am I going to cope for that length of time without smiling or talking properly?' Amy wondered, feeling panic-stricken. A depressing thought flashed into her head: 'Bang goes any hope of getting a boyfriend until it's fixed.'

The dentist continued to probe around the rest of her teeth and found a small cavity, which he filled, then and there without bothering to numb her gums.

"You look pretty brave to me," he told her, revving up his drill, but Amy was unimpressed by his flattery. 'Shows how little he knows,' she thought bitterly. 'Another masochistic bastard!'

Mr Hamilton returned to his own home that evening. Amy was relieved to get her little bed back again. She discovered the comforting dent now dipped even deeper.

Tuesday, as usual, was domestic science, with steak and kidney pie on the menu. Amy brought an extra pie dish for Yvonne at her request, as her mum didn't seem to own one. Vie didn't bring any meat because her mum couldn't afford it, so she pretended to be ill, and Miss Snodgrass packed her off to the medical room to lie down all morning.

Mrs Slater caught Yvonne clucking during English, so she made everyone stay in after school as a punishment for Yvonne's chicken impression. The class protested about the unfair treatment but to no avail. No-one thought to ask Yvonne why she had a sudden urge to start clucking, but then, for her, odd behaviour was considered normal.

Amy arrived home from school to find her father furious with her mother. A door-to-door salesman had sold her a magnifying glass on straps to hang over the nine-inch screen of their television. "He assured me it would make the picture much bigger," she protested, desperate to justify her uncharacteristic impulse purchase.

"Come off it – you've been well and truly conned!" Dad bawled. "All it gives is a distorted picture, greyer than ever and definitely no bigger."

"Well, I was fed up peering at that tiny screen, and I thought it would improve the picture quality," Mum said defensively with a sniff and then stomped off to the kitchen in a huff. She hated being criticised for her lack of judgement.

"What we want is a new telly with a bigger screen," Amy piped up.

Her father just gave a derogatory snort. "There's plenty of life left in this set," he said, walking towards the door.

"Yeah, there is, and it's nesting amongst the valves!" Amy muttered as Dad left to go and visit his mate, Gordon. She knew she was wasting her breath because her father would never fork out for a new telly while some vestige of a picture remained on their old upright.

Amy's nose bled again during Wednesday's lunch break, so she went to lie down in the medical room for a while until it stopped.

On her way home from school, the temperature dropped sharply, and snow began to fall again. Over tea, Mum threatened to make an appointment for Amy to see the doctor about her nose bleeds, but Amy didn't care if she did. She was far more concerned about her chipped front tooth. She sat in front of the mirror in her room that evening, practising talking while covering her top teeth with her lip. After many failed attempts, she achieved an acceptable result. Then she concentrated on her smile, bringing her bottom lip up so that her smile just revealed the undamaged part at the top of her tooth. A hideous grimace looked back at her. She sighed, feeling fed up, and went downstairs to start on her art homework.

She sat on the wooden chair in the kitchen and drew a pair of her dad's old boots, surprising herself by achieving what she considered to be one of her best pictures. This helped to cheer her up for the rest of the evening.

Thursday morning, the school was buzzing about an attack. A man had accosted Cindy Morton, a quiet girl in Coral's class, as she took a shortcut across the heath on her way to school. She had managed to escape from him with just an enormous black eye to show for her ordeal. After being interviewed by the police, she was sent home.

Miss Hardacre immediately announced a new rule during assembly: All pupils were forbidden to walk to or from school unless they were in twos or threes.

"Whose daft idea was it to put a girls' school in the middle of a heath where all the local perverts hang out?" Amy said as she and the rest of her gang lounged on the straw bales in the stables discussing the attack while playing with the kittens during morning break.

"Yeah, I'm surprised this hasn't happened before now," Pam said, "I've seen some very dodgy-looking geezers hanging around when I walk from the bus stop to school."

"I expect some of them could be patients from the nut house since it's not far from that bus stop," Yvonne said. "They can be pretty scary when they shamble past ranting away to themselves."

After lunch, Yvonne left to go to the hospital for further treatment on her verrucas. Because of the new rules, Amy and Pam volunteered to accompany her to the bus stop.

Before Yvonne hopped on the bus, she slipped a fag into Amy's satchel. "My last one – you have it, Bat. I'll get some more in town."

At home, after tea, Amy ducked into the toilet for a quiet smoke which entailed standing on the toilet seat so she could reach to puff the smoke out of the little window high up behind the toilet. Great care was needed to foil her mother's sharp nose.

That evening, Amy stood in the bay window gazing at the large snowflakes swirling down and blanketing the ground once more. Although the end of January had arrived, winter still dragged on interminably. Spring seemed a lifetime away. Upstairs she could hear the muffled sound of Ray plinking on his mandolin. He was attempting to teach himself to play it, but Amy didn't hold out much hope of him succeeding. Behind her, in the lounge, she could hear Mum still trying to persuade Dad that the thick magnifying glass hanging over the television screen hadn't been a waste of money. "It really does improve the picture," she insisted. But her words fell on deaf ears.

"I tell you – you were conned, my dear," Dad repeated for the umpteenth time.

Chapter Three

February
A Swim in The Font

The snow had been falling heavily all Friday, so school closed ten minutes early. With no buses running, this wasn't much help. Coral and Amy found themselves trudging for three miles through deep snow, their feet wet through and numb, before they were halfway home.

Amy refused to be deterred from going to the Veterans Club, even though the snow continued to fall thick and fast. She had no option but to borrow her mum's frumpy fur-lined boots with zips up the front. She plodded along, weighed down by the heavy boots, carrying her own shoes to change into.

Vie and Lynn met up with her on the way, but when they staggered through the double doors at the club into the small, dimly lit entrance hall, all three felt like drowned rats. Their drenched hair clung to their heads like soggy seaweed. None of them owned an umbrella or had bothered to wear a scarf. The luxury of a mirror had now been installed in the cramped shabby cloakroom. They huddled together and back-combed frantically, trying to resurrect a bit of life into their hair. They eventually moved out into the hall and hovered around the single heater near the stage, gently steaming themselves dry, which took most of the evening.

Jean wasn't there, but Arthur, the same scruffy boy from the previous week, once again tried his luck by asking to take Amy home.

This time she wasted no time being polite. "Get lost!" she snapped and turned her back on him. He just shrugged and wandered off.

Vie grinned. "I think he got the message."

"Why do I seem to attract such nerds?" Amy demanded crossly.

"Well, there's always more nerds around than decent blokes; it's just a case of weeding them out."

"Huh, is it worth it?" Amy gazed dismissively around the harshly lit room with its bare strip-lights hanging down from the high ceiling. She preferred dimly lit places that hid her freckles.

Not many people had braved the elements to get there that night. Five or six girls sat at the far end giggling and eyeing up a group of boys who hovered by the Dansette record player on the corner of the stage. They were engrossed in sorting through the 45s and arguing over what to play next. A few couples shuffled around on the floor, smooching to 'Sealed with a Kiss' by Brian Hyland.

Amy sighed. "I can't see this getting any better, so I think I'll start the long slog home because the snow will be pretty deep by now." Vie and Lynn agreed, so they all returned to the cloakroom to get into their coats and tug on their boots before bracing themselves to battle the freezing silent night air thick with large snowflakes.

Throughout Saturday, a strong wind developed, blowing the snow into deep drifts. Amy stayed indoors and indulged in an afternoon of baking because the oven warmed up the kitchen, making it feel quite cosy for a change. She made a birthday cake for Aunt Ruth using the recipe she had used for the Christmas cake since everyone had said how delicious it tasted. She also attempted a batch of vanilla slices that turned out quite well, considering she had used shortcrust instead of puff pastry.

Saturday teatime was routinely spent eating banana sandwiches while watching the Lone Ranger. Today the television went on the blink just as Tonto and his masked friend rode off into the sunset. Amy fervently hoped her tight-fisted father would reconsider and fork out for a new telly that received the ITV channel. But her dad wasn't giving up on the old one that easily. He coaxed it back to life with a deft thump on the side and another on the top.

"You see – I told you there's still plenty of life in these old valves," he said gleefully. Amy just grunted disconsolately.

As she strolled home from the bus stop Monday afternoon, daydreaming, as usual, a rat with half a tail scuttled across the pavement in front of her. She didn't realise what it was at first and stopped to let it go by. The rat shot down an alleyway that led to the smelly Smith's scruffy house, next door but one to Coral's. As the horrid truth sank in, Amy shuddered and quickly walked on, wondering whether the health department ought to be informed. Perhaps the whole Crescent was in danger of becoming overrun with vermin.

Her thoughts were rudely interrupted when the Park's mangy mongrel leapt out as she passed their gate. It tried passionately to lick her face, nearly knocking her over. Amy pushed it away and shouted at it as she hurried down the alleyway and through the back gate.

She flounced into the kitchen and flung her satchel on the chair. "I've run the gauntlet trying to get home safely down this street today," she snapped angrily at her mystified mother. She was busy ironing sheets on the kitchen table with its ungainly blocks of wood nailed to the feet of its neat lathed-turned legs. Mum had once complained to Dad that bending over the table while making pastry or ironing made her back ache. Being resourceful, he had solved the problem by raising it, oblivious to the tasteless style he had created. This wasn't the only item of furniture to be on the receiving end of his attention. His armchair irritated him because it propelled him back each time he sat down. Being in a particularly crotchety mood one day, he took his saw to it and hacked off the ends of the front legs to lower it, ignoring Mum's pleas to stop ruining a good Parker Knoll chair. He alone appreciated his handiwork.

Domestic science on Tuesday morning entailed concocting Madeira cake and egg mornay. Surprisingly, most of the class managed to cook them successfully though nobody fancied eating the egg mornay.

Afterwards, they endured a boring maths lesson in their form room with Mrs Butler. Yvonne livened things up by using her ruler to catapult a twist of paper containing flour across the room in Amy's direction. She ducked just in time. It hit the notice board beside her, bursting above her head. The next time Mrs Butler turned to write on the blackboard, Amy retaliated with a similar flour bomb. Yvonne used her desk lid as a shield, hiding behind it to quickly make more ammunition. After the flour supply was exhausted, they started on the egg mornay. Several others joined in the fun, but Mrs Butler soon became suspicious of the odd noises and giggles coming from the rear of the class.

"Now what's going on back here?" she demanded crossly, marching up the centre aisle to investigate. Her foot skidded on a piece of egg mornay, and she grabbed hold of a desk to stop herself from falling. The evidence was strewn all over the desks and floor. She was far from amused by their antics, especially when she spotted a piece of egg mornay hanging from a light fitting. The entire class were ordered to spend their lunch hour cleaning up the mess. Fortunately, Mrs Butler was in a good mood, so Yvonne managed to sweet-talk her round to ensure that all thoughts of detentions were forgotten.

After school, Coral invited Amy indoors when they reached her house so she could show off her knowledge of chords on the piano. She even lent Amy a music book so that she could get some practise in at home. Coral went into the kitchen and poured them each a glass of milk.

"While you're here," she called out, "d'you think you could come and check on Fred for me? I'm getting a little worried about him. He's still in deep hibernation, only now there seems to be a bit of a pong coming from his cage."

"Er, yeah, of course, I will," Amy said dubiously and climbed up on a kitchen chair to reach his cage. She carefully lifted it down from the top of the larder and gingerly pulled back the bedding covering him. She gently touched his lifeless body; he was stone cold and stiff as a board. She wrinkled up her nose; the smell was pretty pungent. She realised Fred would not be waking from this deep sleep. Poor Fred must have died at the beginning of winter. Coral had just assumed he had gone into hibernation. Amy tried to break the sad news gently, but it still came as a bit of a shock to her friend. Common sense dictated that he needed to be buried as quickly as possible. They performed an impromptu burial service and dug a grave as best they could in the frozen ground by the garden shed. Coral, being religious, insisted on saying a solemn prayer. With the ceremony over, Amy tactfully withdrew and went home, leaving Coral to grieve privately.

At morning registration, Yvonne was bubbling with excitement over a Stephanie Bowman outfit she had ordered from a catalogue. "It's the answer to my prayers!" she proclaimed. "I'll be able to lose weight without having to actually diet. It'll be a doddle!"

Fluff was more pragmatic. "Sounds too good to be true," she commented, "how does it work?"

"Well, it looks like a large plastic bag with elastic at the wrists and ankles. You wear it while you sleep, and it acts like a sauna. It'll be so much easier than dieting. Just think, one month from now, I could have an hourglass figure." Yvonne stroked her sides which showed little sign of curves at the moment, while the others, unconvinced, just grunted non-committally.

"I'll come over to yours on Saturday, Bat, so we can revise. If it's OK with your parents, I'll sleep over and bring my Stephanie Bowman outfit to show you how it works."

"I'm sure my mum won't mind – she thinks you're a lovely girl," Amy said with a wry grin."

"She's truly a woman of good taste," Yvonne said piously and burst out laughing.

Coral arrived at Amy's house after tea to collect her music book. She suggested a quick duet on the piano. They sat together on the stool, hunched over the keyboard, concentrating on their finger positions. They found it difficult because several keys kept sticking down, which didn't make for very harmonious music.

"Are you getting over Fred's death yet?" Amy asked tentatively between chords.

Coral shook her head. "It's going to take a while to come to terms with the loss of poor Fred. He was such a lovable little chap," she said in a hollow voice.

"Perhaps another hamster might help to fill the emptiness?" Amy suggested.

Coral looked shocked. "I need time to grieve for Fred. If I get another hamster too soon, I will feel as if I am being unfaithful to Fred's memory."

Amy struck a wrong chord and muttered a swear word under her breath. "I think that's enough for today," she said, closing the music book with a snap.

"You really must get those keys sorted out if you want to play properly," Coral advised primly as she left.

"I expect that'll be a job for Dad," Amy remarked.

After Coral had gone, Amy busied herself in the kitchen, rolling out the marzipan. She laid it carefully on Aunt Ruth's birthday cake and then set about making the flat icing, only she made it too thin, so it ran off the cake and onto the table. She quickly scraped it up and mixed in more icing sugar to thicken it, and then it stuck to the marzipan perfectly. As she worked, she listened with frustration to Radio Luxemburg. The music faded in and out from the old Bakelite wireless on the windowsill, its round illuminated dial glowing warmly like a friendly face, the pointer its smile. She was convinced that the signal always faded just as a good record was being played.

The weather forecast cut into the program, with the weatherman predicting a thaw was on the way. He pronounced that this winter of 1963 was now officially worse than that of 1947. This news didn't surprise Amy, who felt like she had been trudging through snow for months in sub-zero temperatures. Thanks to the ice, her smile was now ruined by a broken tooth. "Sometimes I think life has got it in for me," she murmured with resignation as she carefully put the iced cake in the larder to set.

Thursday morning, Jean was finally back in class. Yvonne was absent at the hospital again, this time having her varicose veins examined as they had been causing her a lot of pain.

During art, Jean and Amy shared a daffodil with instructions from Mrs Host to paint it in fine detail on a black card. Amy had barely spoken to Jean since returning from her extended absence. Jean realised she would have to work hard to win Amy around. She tried in the only way she knew how. "You'll never guess who I've had a letter from," she whispered excitedly.

"No, you're right, I won't," Amy said in a bored voice.

"Well, it's from my uncle who lives in the States. I don't think I've told you about him, have I?" Amy absorbed herself in her painting, making it plain that she wasn't in the least bit interested in Jean's uncle.

But Jean wouldn't be put off. Instead, she continued with her excitement mounting. "You've heard of Lorne Green, the actor who stars in Bonanza, haven't you? Well, he's my uncle! I've been invited to the States to visit him for a holiday!"

Amy could barely control the smirk that threatened to burst into laughter at any moment. This was one of Jean's best stories yet. "Oh, come off it Jean. D'you really expect me to believe that you've got a famous American actor for an uncle?"

Jean flushed. "But it's true, I tell you," she protested, "what's more, I've got the letter to prove it. He's even promised to introduce me to Elvis and Michael Langdon – won't that be fantastic! I'll try to get Michael Langdon's autograph if you like." Jean adored Elvis, and she knew Amy had a big crush on Little Joe in Bonanza. Amy was sure it was all a figment of Jean's vivid imagination. If she allowed herself to believe for a moment that it might be true, she would be at the mercy of enormous pangs of jealousy.

Amy could feel her anger rising hot inside her. "Do you think I was born yesterday?" she whispered crossly, "or perhaps I just look extremely gullible!" How dare Jean deliberately try to make her feel envious.

Jean shifted uncomfortably in her seat. "I told you I can prove it," she persisted. "I promise I'll come to your house this evening and bring the letter to show you."

"Seeing is believing!" Amy retorted and returned to her picture.

At home, after tea, needless to say, Jean failed to show up. Amy set to work decorating Aunt Ruth's cake. The red lettering was barely decipherable, but the finished result looked almost good enough to eat. She hoped it would taste as good as the Christmas cake.

Mrs Brown came into the kitchen smiling. She was in a good mood for a change because she had indulged in a rare treat and bought herself a new black handbag with the money Dad had given her for Christmas. "Do you like it?" she asked, thrusting the handbag under Amy's nose, eager to have her choice endorsed by her fashion-conscious daughter. Amy examined the plain, eminently functional bag and diplomatically gave it her seal of approval. Mum appreciated this as she usually lacked confidence in her own judgement. She paused to admire the finished cake before leaving and refrained from criticising the uneven lettering.

Ray didn't have to go to school the next day because they had run out of coal for the boilers.

"You lucky turd! I wish our school was as incompetent," Amy muttered in his ear as she heaved her bulging satchel onto her shoulder.

Ray grinned. He rarely scored a point over his sister. "I shall be in the cinema watching 'Bridge over the River Kwai'," he said, "while you're slogging away at lessons."

Mum came in and spoilt the moment for him. "If you're going out, make sure you wear the pom-pom hat that Amy knitted for you and pull it down over your ears to keep them warm." Ray scowled, and it was Amy's turn to grin as she slouched off to catch the bus to school. She had a pretty good idea how much he hated that hat and knew he would only wear it under protest.

During registration, Amy sat next to Jean and deliberately ignored her. She hadn't forgiven her for yesterday's pack of lies.

Jean leaned across and smiled sheepishly at her. "How do you fancy a great day out at Wembley seeing the Record All stars Show? There'll be masses of stars performing, and what's more, Cliff Richard will be topping the bill!" She hoped this would win her round as she guessed that Amy wouldn't be able to resist the opportunity of going to see her beloved Cliff.

"Of course, I'll go if Cliff is going to be there. But I'll only believe you're coming with me once you have put your money where your mouth is and paid for your ticket," Amy said cagily. She wondered if she was losing her marbles by expecting Jean to turn up for once. Jean beamed with delight. Success at last!

Yvonne, broke as usual after spending all her money on tuck, exuded her charm on Amy to wheedle a further sixpence out of her for the bus fare home.

"Don't forget you now owe me one and tuppence," she reminded Yvonne as she grudgingly thrust the money into her hand.

"Och, you'll get the money back, I promise." Yvonne flashed her a smile of even white teeth. "By the way, Mum has agreed to let me stay over at yours tomorrow night, so we'll be able to get plenty of revision done."

Amy harboured some doubts, but at least she hoped Yvonne would cheer her up, as she felt in need of it.

After school, Amy went to the doctor about her persistent nose bleeds because Mum had kept her word and made the appointment.

Doctor Lawrence peered short-sightedly up each nostril with the help of a small torch and grunted. He didn't have much to say - just muttered about making an appointment for her to see an ear, nose and throat specialist at the hospital. Amy didn't like the sound of that.

With exams looming the following week and loads of revision, Amy gave the Veterans Club a miss that evening to revise.

Saturday was Aunt Ruth's birthday, so Amy put the cake in a tin and carried it to her house. Aunt Ruth lived in an Edwardian semi-detached house. She was delighted to find Amy on her doorstep when she answered the door. She led her along the hallway past the front parlour, which was only used on special occasions, and into the back room where she and Uncle Henry lived. A fire crackled brightly in the grate, but Amy's spirits sank when she saw Aunt Ruth's simpering granddaughter,

Nicola, sitting on the sofa. She was visiting her nan, much to Amy's dismay.

Amy put the tin on the table and removed the lid.

"Oh, Amy, my dear, what a lovely looking cake!" her aunt exclaimed, "you must have put such a lot of work into making it. I'll get some plates, and then we can all have a slice with a cup of tea." She trotted off to the kitchen while Amy sat on a chair by the table, revelling in the compliments her cake had received. It was short-lived as her eyes came to rest on Nicola's red face, which nearly matched her hair. Her jealousy was thinly veiled as she puffed herself up.

"I've bought Nan a beautifully engraved silver frame to hold a photo of me," she boasted, "and she's promised to keep it by her bedside so that she can see me first thing each morning when she wakes up."

'How nauseating!' Amy thought and jumped up. She called out to her aunt: "Sorry but I've got to go. I've just remembered that I'm expecting Yvonne anytime now." She found it impossible to stay a moment longer in the same room as the obnoxious Nicola.

Yvonne arrived at teatime complete with schoolbooks, jim-jams and her Stephanie Bowman outfit. Amy swapped bedrooms with her disgruntled brother so that she and Yvonne could share his more comfortable double bed.

Yvonne sealed herself up in her plastic outfit at bedtime and rustled noisily every time she moved during the night.

"It's like trying to sleep next to a giant carrier bag," Amy complained but only received a snore by way of a reply.

She was rudely awakened early in the morning. An exuberant Yvonne was bouncing up and down on the bed, beating her about the head with a pillow. "C'mon, Bat, let's have a pillow fight. I've just weighed myself, and I've lost two whole pounds overnight. Isn't that great?" Amy had no choice but to defend herself or be battered mercilessly. This was definitely not her idea of a good start to the day!

After breakfast, Amy headed off down the garden armed with a shovel and scraper to clean the guinea pigs' cages. She left Yvonne to ingratiate herself with her mum. She made all the appropriate responses that adults like to hear as Mrs Brown droned on about the soaring price of bread and bus fares. She batted her long dark eyelashes over her large, expressive eyes, affecting a picture of engrossed interest that fooled Mrs Brown.

"I wish you could be more attentive, like Yvonne," Mum said to Amy when she came indoors. Amy shook her head dismissively as she washed her hands at the sink. She knew only too well what a Jekyll and Hyde character Yvonne could be. The sound of Roy Orbison singing in the lounge told her that Yvonne was playing her records.

They spent the afternoon doing more revising, their books spread all over the dining room table. After tea, Amy taught Yvonne the new Mod dance she and Pam had invented. Yvonne danced around the lounge like a fairy elephant while Amy desperately tried to avoid having her toes flattened. At nine o'clock Yvonne plodded off through the snow to catch her bus home.

She paused at the gate and called out to Amy: "Don't forget to ask your dad if you can come to the dance in London on Saturday. It should be a hoot." Amy just nodded and waved, feeling drained of energy.

Monday morning began badly for Amy when Miss Hardacre stopped her after assembly and told her to go to her study at lunchtime.

The first lesson was English language, where Mrs Slater gave them a challenging exam. Amy read through the paper and found she had to choose three of the five questions to answer. As she studied them, her gaze drifted from the paper and came to rest on the four tins of cat food on Mrs Slater's desk. Two of them were open.

"Do you think she's been feeding the school cats or having an early lunch?" Amy whispered across the aisle to Vie, who started giggling. The cats were supposed to catch their own food in and around the Manor and its outbuildings. Mrs Slater regularly supplemented their diet, making them fat and lazy. Amy became aware of a cold, steely glare from behind pebble-stone glasses boring into her. She quickly put her head down and began scribbling.

Jean had brought a brown corduroy jerkin to school as she thought Amy might like it. During the morning break, Amy tried it on in the small upstairs cloakroom of the Grange as it was usually quiet in there.

"Oh, it fits you perfectly, Bat," Jean gushed as Amy stood on tiptoe to see it in the mirror that hung on the wall over the hand basins. "It was far too tight for me to wear."

"It's really nice of you to bring it in for me," Amy said in a muffled voice as she struggled to pull it off over her head.

"Well, you can pay for it by weekly instalments, making it easier since we're saving up to go to Wembley."

Amy stopped half out of the jerkin. 'What a tight-fisted cow!' she thought. She liked the jerkin but didn't expect Jean to charge for her second-hand, unwanted clothes.

"Oh, that reminds me, I've got the money here for my ticket." Amy was stunned. Could this mean she was really intending to go? She was so amazed when Jean handed over the money that she agreed to buy the jerkin from her in instalments after all.

With lunch over, Amy knocked timidly on Miss Hardacre's door, wondering what she had done wrong now. The green light flashed, and the buzzer sounded, so she turned the large brass door knob and entered.

"Ah, Amy Brown. Come in and close the door," Miss Hardacre said, glancing up from a pile of exercise books. "I need to discuss your GCE subjects with you as your parents have an appointment with me tomorrow."

"Oh," Amy said, breathing a sigh of relief. She had forgotten about the appointment Mum had mentioned a while ago.

"Do you have any preference on what subjects you would like to take?" Miss Hardacre pulled a notepad towards her.

"Well," Amy hesitated, wishing she had been given more time to think about it. "I enjoy cooking, so perhaps I could have a go at domestic science?"

Miss Hardacre waved her hand dismissively. "I think you need a couple of good solid subjects; I suggest you take science and biology." Amy was speechless, stunned by the awful prospect of studying such boring subjects. Miss Hardacre didn't bother to justify how she arrived at this conclusion. She made some notes and then dismissed Amy.

'So much for democracy!' she fumed as she stomped back to her class in a huff. 'More of a dictatorship than a discussion!'

Mum and Dad pootled up to the gates of the Grange on Dad's pop-pop motorbike the following morning, so Amy naturally kept well out of their way. Fortunately, everyone was in class, so they missed the spectacle of her dad in his diabolical get-up. Amy had given him strict instructions at breakfast to remove his goggles, beret and gauntlets before showing himself in the Grange.

The biology exam in the afternoon was a nightmare. Amy had drawn bone structures on a piece of blotting paper which the girls furtively slid along the bench to each other, but it didn't help much. Pam had diagrams inked up her arm, which she could only share with Yvonne, who sat next to her. When she discreetly pushed her sleeve up, the ink smudged and made the diagrams hard to decipher.

Towards the end of the exam, Fluff began to panic when she discovered she had come out in a red rash.

"It's probably just a nervous rash caused by worry over that exam," Vie reassured her as they walked to the Grange for Mrs Slater's English lesson. "After all, it's an important exam if you want to be a lab technician someday." Fluff's keenness to become a laboratory technician was a mystery to her friends. To be on the safe side, everyone gave her a wide berth in case her rash was contagious.

Miss Hardacre strode into the English class to give Mrs Slater a note just as she was writing the English language exam results on the blackboard. Miss Hardacre waved the girls back to their seats after they had all jumped to their feet, as they had to do every time she walked into a room. Amy was convinced that Clara deliberately ignored the exam results listed on the blackboard because hers were top of the class. Miss Hardacre merely left as abruptly as she had entered.

"That's one in the eye for Clara!" Amy muttered with satisfaction to Pam.

"I think you're getting paranoid about Clara disliking you. At least you got good marks. I only just passed by the skin of my teeth."

"You can hardly blame me for getting paranoid when she dictates what grotty subjects I should take for GCE!"

The Browns' ex-neighbours, Mrs Bullen and her daughter, Katy, paid them a surprise visit that evening. They belonged to the original group of neighbours, like the Browns and Williams. They moved into the Crescent when the houses were first built after the war. Katy and Amy had grown up together and become best friends. Although Katy was eighteen months older than Amy, they had attended the same junior and secondary schools until Amy went to Technical High School. Katy had shared family holidays with the Browns in Suffolk and Wales. Sadly Mr Bullen died of leukaemia when Katy was twelve. Since then, she and her younger brother, Charlie, had looked on Mr Brown as a surrogate father.

"Mr B," said Katy, (The Bullens always called Amy's Mum and Dad Mr and Mrs B.) "I want to ask a big favour of you." She took a deep breath. "Would you be kind enough to give me away at my wedding? Only I can't ask one of my uncles to do it without offending the others, so I've decided to ask none of them."

"I'd be proud to," Dad said, looking dead chuffed at being asked. She also wanted Amy as a bridesmaid, which pleased Amy immensely because she had never been a bridesmaid before. Katy had been engaged to Keith for quite a while, and they had become inseparable. The wedding would take place in eighteen months, in September 1964, which seemed like an eternity to Amy.

The Browns' old upright television finally gave up the ghost the next day. They were the first family in their street to have a television. This had its disadvantages because each evening, all the children would queue at their front gate to come in and watch Children's Hour. They'd sit agog, in rows, cross-legged on the floor in the Browns' lounge. Amy and Ray found themselves relegated to the back of the room, where they had difficulty seeing the tiny nine-inch screen.

The televising of the Queen's coronation caused the same problem. Amy, then five years old, had never seen so many neighbours crammed into their lounge. Every seat and chair arm was occupied, with the children having to sit on the floor.

At least with a new telly, they would have a choice of channels to watch now that ITV was well established. Amy suspected that the only reason Dad had agreed to get a new set was to watch wrestling. Every Saturday afternoon, he made some excuse to pop over to the Williams' house, where he knew his mate Gordon would be glued to the box. They'd get excited and involved, yelling instructions to the wrestlers and advice to the referee, cursing him when their pearls of wisdom were ignored.

Amy posted the postal order for the Wembley tickets on her way to school Thursday morning. Fluff was absent; everyone assumed she was getting her rash diagnosed.

Jean was very excited about the forthcoming show. She couldn't stop talking to Amy about the show during the morning break in their form room. Grey clouds cast gloomy shadows, and the rain spattered relentlessly against the windows.

Yvonne was yelling and chasing Fat Frudge around the form room because she had sneaked a jam butty out of Yvonne's desk while she was in the cloakroom washing her hands.

Suddenly Miss Hardacre burst into the room, her face flushed with anger. "I am trying to mark exam papers downstairs, but it is nigh impossible with the racket coming from up here," she shouted. "You sound like a herd of demented elephants stampeding around. Much more of it, and you'll all be crashing through the ceiling into my room. Please remember that this is an old house. It should be treated with respect." She glanced out of the window. "The rain has nearly stopped, so you can all go outside and get some fresh air for the short time that's left before your next lesson." She promptly turfed everyone out into the cold.

"What a mean old bag," Amy grumbled as she and Yvonne donned their coats and headed for the freezing outdoors. "Just our luck to be lumbered with a form room directly above the head's study."

They wandered across the road to the Manor courtyard, where the cobbles looked like stone islands among all the puddles. The girls huddled into the stables to shelter from the cold. They flung themselves down on the bales of straw, and Pam pulled a Valentine's card out of her satchel.

"Look what I got in the post this morning. It hasn't been signed, so I can't be sure who sent it." She proudly handed it around for the others to admire.

"Oh, come off it, Tibs," Yvonne said, "you know it must be from the love of your life - the gorgeous Dan." The others all grunted in agreement.

"I expect you're right," Pam said sadly, "we'd still be together now if my miserable mother hadn't forced me to stop seeing him." Her lips quivered into a thin defiant line; her eyes flashed with anger. "I shall never forgive her for interfering in my life!" Dan was a topic that could still bring emotional turmoil erupting to the surface at the merest mention of his name.

"She had no right to say you were too young for a steady boyfriend," Amy said fiercely. "How diabolical of her to make you pack him up. Such a terrible shame since you were so well suited and totally besotted with each other."

"Parents are always trying to ruin or run your life for you," Yvonne declared with a toss of her head. "Mine are just as bad. Because of them, me and Alex plan to elope to Gretna Green."

"What!" everyone gasped in unison, gawping at her with eyes boggling, totally flabbergasted.

"Are you stark raving mad?" Vie demanded.

"You're not serious," Pam said, disbelief written all over her face.

"We have no choice," Yvonne continued, "because if we don't go, my parents will try to break us up. They've made it clear they disapprove of Alex - they think he is far too old for me and a bad influence."

"Why are parents so flippin' interfering?" Amy said crossly. "They always think they know what's best for us - as if we totally lack any vestige of judgement and can't be trusted!"

"If I had been old enough, then maybe that's what me and Dan would have done," Pam said with a sigh.

That evening, Amy watched the snowflakes floating past the kitchen window as she listened to Radio Luxemburg. The earlier rain had now turned to snow. Mum came in to show her the powder compact she had bought for Coral as a birthday present from Amy.

"Well, at least she'll have no excuse now for having a shine on that large hooked nose," Amy observed rather unkindly.

As Mum turned to leave, she paused. "By the way, Dad has reluctantly agreed to let you go to the St Valentine's dance in London on Saturday, but only because it has been organised by the Mormon church."

"I suppose that makes it respectable in his eyes," Amy said. Despite Yvonne's keenness, she suspected it would be a dull evening, but she didn't want to miss out on a late night up in town with her mates.

Coral's birthday arrived, so Amy gave her the compact as they travelled to school together on the bus.

"Oh, this is really lovely," she gasped, beaming with pleasure as she examined it. Amy smiled, thinking, 'Mum must have good taste after all.'

Fluff was still absent at registration. Pam leaned across the gangway. "I called at her house on my way to school, and her mum told me she's got measles. I expect she caught them from one of her younger siblings."

"I hope she stays away until they're completely gone," Amy said. "Freckles are bad enough without measles as well."

Amy, Pam, Vie and Lynn arrived at the Veterans Club that evening to find Yvonne, Alex, Jean and Sheila there already. Amy and Pam were enjoying a dance when Amy's heart sank as she saw a familiar face coming through the door. Dennis the Menace, her next-door yob of a neighbour, swaggered in. He was still wearing his mum's knitted tea cosy. She tried to ignore the Rocker, but he spotted her and sauntered over.

"How yer doin' Amy?" he asked, grinning broadly, aware of her discomfiture. "I didn't know you haunted this dump." Amy just gave him an insipid smile. "Aren't yer goin' to introduce me to yer mates?" He leered across in Yvonne's direction as she emerged from the ladies toilet.

"Yvonne's here with her boyfriend, so don't even think about it," Amy snapped, turning her back on him. As she sought to disown him, she noticed a gorgeous boy who she hadn't seen there before.

He was the classic tall, dark and handsome. Amy felt sure he smiled in her direction – or was it just wishful thinking on her part?

A fight broke out on the road outside as they left the club at the end of the evening. Alex somehow ended up in the middle of the affray, as the police arrived on the scene, and he was carted off to the police station. Yvonne, almost hysterical, rushed off along the middle of the road chasing after the police van, waving and yelling frantically. Dennis had left the club before the fight started. Amy was sure he would have been in the thick of it, as he loved to brag about how much he enjoyed a good punch-up.

Early Saturday evening, a minibus arrived to pick up Amy and her mates from the car park at the local shops to take them to the St Valentine's dance at the main hall of the Mormon church in London. Pam, Vie, Lynn, Yvonne and Alex all turned up but, as expected, Jean didn't. Alex was subdued, having just been released on bail pending his court appearance.

"Please don't mention last night's fracas in front of the Elders," Yvonne begged the others as they crowded onto the bus.

The American Elders were three clean-cut young men who introduced themselves as George, Randy and John. George drove the minibus while the other two strummed their guitars and urged everyone to join them, singing folk songs to pass the journey. Yvonne needed no encouragement to sing her lungs out. She almost drowned out everyone else who were trying to keep in tune. Vie and Lynn had been seeing quite a lot of the Elders lately. Amy wondered, somewhat cynically, if their interest lay in the Mormon church or with these rather dishy young men.

Arriving at the large modern building in South Kensington, they were ushered inside. They deposited their coats in a cloakroom before entering the large ballroom opposite. A group was playing on a stage at the far end. The room was already fairly crowded, and they were soon enjoying themselves dancing to the music. The twist had been banned because the Mormons thought it far too promiscuous.

The highlight of the evening came when a large tent was erected in the middle of the dance floor where couples could enter to get 'married' and receive a 'marriage certificate'. Having no partner, Amy eyed up a shy-looking boy. He was loitering near the entrance to the tent.

She screwed up her courage and walked over to him. "Excuse me but do you have a partner to marry?" she asked nervously. The boy blushed, shuffled his feet and shook his head. Feeling emboldened by his timidity, Amy gave him a warm smile. "How'd you like to marry me? After all, it's only a bit of harmless fun."

She grabbed his hand and dragged him inside before he had time to think about refusing. Only after the certificate had been completed did they discover each other's names. His was Brian, and though he seemed quite a nice boy, after they had danced together briefly, Amy concluded he was far too quiet and shy so she made an excuse to leave with no intention of seeing him again.

Vie got 'married' to a drip called Doug, who she found lurking out by the cloakroom and collared for the ceremony.

"There's no need for you two to elope now you're married," Amy said, grinning at Yvonne and Alex as they emerged through the tent flaps.

Yvonne was clutching a marriage certificate in her hand. "If only this was the real thing," she said with a sigh and squeezed Alex's arm.

Later in the evening, Yvonne and Amy decided to go off and explore the rest of the building. The front part of the ground floor was occupied by the ultramodern church.

"This just doesn't feel like a proper church to me," Amy said, her voice echoing as she gazed around at the shiny new wood. "Real churches should be old with woodworm and smell of damp and mouse droppings to give them character and soul. This squeaky-clean auditorium is more like a concert hall. It lacks a reverent atmosphere – or any atmosphere, come to that."

Yvonne shrugged. "I don't really care one way or the other. A church is a church to me, regardless of its age. Come on, let's go for a ride in the lifts." She grabbed Amy's arm and dragged her off to the entrance lobby.

There were several lifts to the many floors, but one floor looked pretty much like another: long straight corridors with loads of doors. However, down in the basement, they discovered the dimly lit baptism room. It was a very eerie place where the centre of the floor consisted of a small oblong pool with steps leading down under the water.

"This must be where the converts come to be dunked," Amy said irreverently and shuddered as she peered down into the still, gloomy water lying cold and silent.

It didn't have the same effect on Yvonne. "This is great!" she whooped, "I could just do with a swim to freshen up." She began to peel off her clothes.

"Yvonne, you can't," Amy gasped in horror. "What if someone comes in and catches you? The Mormons definitely won't appreciate you wallowing naked in their font."

Ignoring Amy's protests, Yvonne dived in and swam two lengths of the font, then beckoned to Amy.

"Come on in, Bat, it's not too deep for you."

As a non-swimmer, Amy had no inclination to join her friend. "You really must come out now," she begged.

"Oh, all right, you spoilsport." Yvonne sighed and reluctantly hauled herself up the steps. She struggled to button herself back into her clothes, with no towel to dry herself.

"What about your hair?" Amy asked.

"Oh, it'll soon dry if I stand near the radiator in the hall," Yvonne said as she wrung out the excess water.

A relieved Amy led her back to the bright lights and music in the dance hall, where Yvonne received some odd looks – not that she cared.

At a quarter to midnight, everyone clambered back into the minibus and sang all the way home.

The following afternoon, Yvonne arrived at the Browns' house with her mum and dad for a surprise visit. They brought along their noisy and excitable boxer dog, who slobbered and barked constantly. This definitely didn't please Amy's Dad, who was in bed trying to sleep as he was working night shifts. He got up in a foul mood and glared at the dog when it tried to chew his slipper. Amy was sure her mum didn't think much of Yvonne's parents – especially her neurotic mother. She always managed to steer the conversation around to sex no matter what the subject under discussion happened to be. This topic was strictly taboo in Mrs Brown's prudish household.

Amy took Yvonne to her bedroom to listen to records, leaving the adults to chat among themselves. Perhaps she shouldn't have been surprised when Yvonne confided that she had a half-brother and half-sister in Scotland, each with a different father from her own. Also that her mum's new husband was her first husband! Amy was sure that if her snobbish mum had any inkling of the colourful past enjoyed by Yvonne's mum, she would ban her from the house – along with her husband and noisy dog. Amy couldn't help wondering what Yvonne's stepfather saw in Yvonne's mum, knowing her background.

According to Yvonne, he wasn't a particularly nice man. "He's very quick-tempered and always so strict with me," Yvonne complained.

"I can't say that his strictness has had any noticeable effect on you," Amy remarked with a grin, "and let's face it, you do need a lot of controlling at times."

"Och, Bat, how can you say that?" Yvonne protested, pretending to look hurt.

On Monday morning, Miss Hardacre announced the results of the French exam.

"That old cow has deducted marks from my paper for poor handwriting. Now I come second by half a per cent to goody-goody Gardner – her flippin' favourite!" Amy whispered in Vie's ear. "I knew she'd be picking on us for dragging her precious school through the court, and this biased marking proves it!"

The girls gathered at the summerhouse in the Manor grounds for a change during the break. The tuck was duly divided up as usual.

Yvonne swallowed a mouthful of crisps and then casually announced: "Me and Alex have talked things over and postponed eloping for the time being. We're hoping my parents will give up their hostility towards him."

"Probably just as well," Amy said, "I can easily imagine the ructions that would break out if your mum discovered you had run off to get married."

Pam giggled. "Knowing your mum, she'd have forty fits!"

Yvonne and Amy sneaked out during the lunch break to walk the half-mile to the local village shop to buy sweets. While there, Yvonne made a quick phone call to Alex to make arrangements for meeting him that evening, and then the girls strolled back to school, munching their sweets.

"Any chance you can get me a roll-on corset the same as yours the next time you're near that shop in your town?" Amy asked.

"'Course I can," Yvonne mumbled, stuffing a flying saucer into her mouth, "they're a good buy at four and eleven pence, but you'll have to give me the money first as I'm stony broke." Amy dug around in her purse and handed over five shillings which Yvonne quickly pocketed. "I'll get you a roll-on the next time I go into town," she promised. Amy wondered whether she would ever see it.

At that moment, Miss Catting and Miss Snodgrass came into view, walking in their direction, deep in conversation. To avoid being caught, the girls quickly ducked behind a large bush to hide until the teachers had passed by; then Yvonne crept out and checked the coast was clear.

"It's OK, Bat, you can come out now." Amy emerged cautiously, and as they walked on, Yvonne confessed to Amy that she had given up on the Stephanie Bowman outfit. "I found that any weight I sweated away in the night was replaced when I had a drink at breakfast."

"So much for easy slimming, eh?" Amy laughed and tactfully refrained from adding, "I told you so." They lapsed into telling each other bad jokes for the rest of the walk back to school.

"Right, Bat, what's green and goes up and down?"

Amy grinned. "I know that one. It's a gooseberry in a lift."

"Wrong!" yelled Yvonne gleefully. "It's this...." She gave a loud snort, and Amy pulled a face.

"That's disgusting! All right, if that's how you want to play. What's brown and comes steaming out of cows?"

"Er, cow pats?"

"Wrong! It's the Isle of Wight Ferry," Amy said triumphantly.

Yvonne burst into hysterical laughter, rolling on the ground and kicking her legs. Tears streamed down her cheeks as she shrieked at the top of her voice: "Oooh Bat, I'm going to pee me breeks!"

Luckily no-one saw her, and Amy eventually succeeded in calming her down. "Yvonne, you're nutty as a fruit cake and far too easily excited. It wasn't that funny."

Back at school, in the changing rooms, Yvonne swapped her soggy nylon panties for a pair of fleecy maroon knickers. She rinsed out her panties and hung them to dry on a radiator.

"If Catty Catting sees them, she will probably confiscate them," Amy warned her.

Yvonne thought for a moment. "I think she's taking 5G1 for history this afternoon in the Manor. With any luck, she shouldn't come over here."

"Hurry up, you two, or you'll be late for Frog-eyed Freda's class." Pam had popped her head around the door. "I thought I heard your voices. Bet you haven't saved me any of your sweets," she added with a grin.

Amy awoke in the morning with griping stomach pains and a pounding headache. Mum relented and allowed her to stay at home. She lay back on her pillow and heaved a sigh of relief. Her symptoms, although unpleasant, had come to her rescue. She had no idea what ingredients to take for domestic science. In addition, she had a religious knowledge exam which she hadn't bothered to revise for, so she was sure she would come bottom.

She got up at lunchtime feeling a little better. Later, after tea, there was a knock on the front door. Amy answered it and found Coral on the doorstep.

"I can't stop - I just popped round to see how you're feeling."

Amy assured her she was feeling a lot better. "I expect I'll be back at school tomorrow."

"I've had a word with my piano teacher. He's offered to give you lessons if you like," Coral said excitedly.

"Sounds great, but I'll have to ask Dad first." Amy suspected her dad wouldn't be too keen to pay out good money for piano lessons.

Coral turned to go, then paused. "Oh, by the way, Mum and Dad have bought me another golden hamster for my birthday to replace Fred. I've christened this one, Henry." Amy was relieved that Coral was finally out of mourning for Fred.

The Parks called Mrs Brown and her first aid box into action that evening when young Kenny fell off his bike and suffered a nasty gash to his knee. Most residents in the Crescent knew Mrs Brown was once a nurse, so she was called on to tend to any minor injury or ailment. Sometimes she grumbled about the cost of replacing bandages or ointments but she was flattered that her expertise was in such demand.

Some years previously, Dennis had suffered a bad accident while playing down on the disused Puffing Billy line, a favourite haunt with local children. Being inquisitive, he dropped a lighted match into a can that still had some petrol in it, to see what would happen. The can exploded, causing his face to look more like an extremely sore bum. Most of his hair and several layers of skin on his face burnt off. He rushed home and held his face under the running water from the cold tap in the kitchen until his mum came home and insisted on rubbing margarine all over his face. This made matters ten times worse. It was doubtful whether he would get his features back to normal again. He suffered such agony that the only person he trusted to dress his face properly was Mrs Brown. She had plenty of experience treating airmen with terrible burns during the war. The doctor was very impressed with her handiwork and happily agreed for her to carry on.

At least on this occasion, the doctor supplied the dressings because they needed to be changed every morning. Dennis had always remained very grateful to Mrs Brown for her patience when removing his bandages. She took immense care not to damage the new skin that was forming. As a result, he barely had a mark to show for his misadventure; even his eyebrows and eyelashes grew back again.

Feeling better by the morning, Amy returned to school, dropping straight into a mock GCE art exam, painting an imaginary picture. The topic had to be a sport, so Amy painted a tennis court with a kneeling girl using two racquets to check the net height. Amy considered the finished result diabolical and had no doubts that it would fail miserably.

While she slaved away with brush and paint, she thought of Ray, enduring his own living hell at the dentist, having several teeth extracted. Amy didn't have much sympathy for her brother because he had steadfastly refused to put a toothbrush near his teeth for years.

Ray looked miserable at teatime. "I had seven teeth out," he moaned. His swollen cheeks reminded Amy of Ruby with full pouches. Unable to eat a thing, he slunk off to his bedroom to mope.

"You can stay off school tomorrow as you have lost so many teeth all at once," Mum called out after him, "you'll need a while to recover."

After tea, Mr Brown absorbed himself in his rug making, so Amy thought this would be a good time to tell him about the piano lessons.

"But how much will they cost?" he asked suspiciously, as Amy knew he would. She mentioned the fee, and he ummed and ahhed while digging into the rag rug with his hook. "Sounds far too expensive," he said at last, "I shall look for a cheaper piano teacher myself." Amy just shrugged and left him to his rags.

'What a tight old bugger!' she thought as she gazed through her bedroom window. The snow fell thickly and silently, masking everything it touched and softening outlines. She knew there was no point in arguing once her father had made up his stubborn mind.

Yvonne arrived at school in the morning and shoved a tea caddy under Amy's nose. "It's a Christmas present from my mum and dad to your mum and dad," she explained, seeing Amy's puzzled look. Amy knew her parents wouldn't be pleased because they hadn't bought them a present.

Amy developed another stomach ache during breakfast the following morning, so she staggered back to bed until it had worn off. After lunch, Mrs Brown took her to the other side of town to keep an appointment at the hospital, with the ear, nose and throat specialist. He numbed her nose and stuck a hot needle up the offending nostril to cauterise the troublesome blood vessel. With great trepidation, Amy watched, boss-eyed, as the needle homed in and was thankful that she couldn't feel a thing.

They met Coral in town afterwards, and Mrs Brown suggested she accompany them to help Amy choose a pair of new shoes for school. Amy eventually found a black pair of moccasins that they could all agree on. Mrs Brown inevitably had to compromise because her choice would have been frumpy, clumpy shoes with thick heavy soles that never wore out.

Amy didn't go to the club that evening because her nose had begun to thaw out, and it felt like a throbbing Belisha beacon. The cold deep snow looked inviting to her hot hooter, so she grabbed a handful and held it on her nose until it melted, but it only gave a brief respite from the throbbing.

Saturday morning, Amy was propped up in bed enjoying breakfast laid out on a tray, courtesy of her mum, which made a pleasant change. Her mum had taken pity on her suffering due to her hot, uncomfortable nose. She languished in bed all morning and, by lunchtime, felt well enough to get up and tackle a spot of baking.

A recipe for a feather-light sponge that Amy had seen on the back of a packet of flour looked mouth-wateringly good, so she rose to the challenge. Unfortunately, the sponge didn't respond in the same way. It turned out flat and rubbery, but not wanting to waste it, she used it in a trifle instead.

The Hamiltons arrived for Sunday tea. Mr Hamilton presented Amy with a lamp to fix over her bed. She thanked him, wondering whether this was in recompense to ease his conscience for hurting Ruby. Or perhaps, he just wanted the convenience of having it installed, ready for his next stay with them.

Amy was dispatched to school Monday morning, bearing a set of cork table mats to give to Yvonne for her parents as a Christmas present from Amy's parents. Etiquette demanded that they couldn't accept the tea caddy without giving them a present. The mats were an unwanted gift that had lain in the bottom of an upstairs drawer for years. Such things did not enter Mrs Brown's repertoire as 'necessary items for the table.'

Yvonne used her charm to wheedle another sixpence out of Amy during the break.

"Do you realise you now owe me one and eightpence, a pie dish and a roll-on?" a somewhat peeved Amy reminded her.

Yvonne grinned and gave her friend a hug. "I haven't forgotten – really, I haven't," she assured her.

At home, Mr Brown spent the evening trying to mend the sticking keys on the piano in readiness for Amy's piano lessons. Despite much searching, he still hadn't tracked down a cheap music teacher.

Amy was in a good mood all the next day because it was Shrove Tuesday, and pancakes were her favourite food. She offered to make them for tea as Ray's friend, Ian, had been invited to stay. Amy thought this an excellent opportunity to show off her prowess in the kitchen. Unfortunately, the pancakes turned out hard and leathery, but Mr Brown saved the day by quickly whipping up a fresh batch. However, he ran into a spot of bother when he attempted to toss them. He got so cross with one for sticking to the pan that when he finally freed it, he gave it an almighty toss and, turning the frying pan over, made an impromptu bat. As the pancake flopped back down, he hit it for six, yelling: "Get up there, Cecil!" The pancake smacked against the ceiling and then hung there, refusing to budge or fall. A heated debate ensued with much arm-waving to decide who would climb up and scrape it off the ceiling. Everyone agreed that Mr Brown should be the one to get it down as he had stuck it up there, but he refused, point blank, to have anything to do with it out of sheer pigheadedness. So there it stayed, hanging just to the right of the lampshade. Ian found the whole pancake fiasco hilarious and giggled uncontrollably, causing Mr Brown to get even more irritable.

Amy tried to restore some good humour to the evening by volunteering to wash up, but a saucer slipped out of her soapy hands and smashed on the floor. She quickly hid the pieces in the dustbin before her mum noticed. She knew, before too long, Mum would realise she was a saucer down because she was forever counting and checking the crockery and cutlery.

"I reckon Mum suspects visitors of stashing crockery in their handbags and pockets when they leave," she commented to Ray. He had come into the kitchen with another dirty plate. "Don't be surprised if she frisks Ian as he leaves."

Ray grinned. "All parents can't be as odd as ours, can they? I'm sure Ian thinks Dad is round the bend!"

Class 5G2 was dispatched on a three-mile run during games the next day. "We shouldn't have to suffer like this in these freezing cold temperatures," Vie complained as she jogged along with Amy.

"You notice Catty Catting didn't come with us," Amy said between puffs, "I bet she stayed behind to put her feet up in the warm staffroom. This cruelty and injustice are hard to bear, and what's worse – I think I'm developing a touch of frostbite on my fingers!" She crossed her arms and tucked her hands into her armpits, trying to warm them up. This made jogging more awkward.

Yvonne and Pam lagged behind as Yvonne was busy matchmaking. She had arranged a date for Pam with someone she knew called Gordon. Pam was none too happy about going on a blind date despite Yvonne's assurances of his eminent suitability.

The school was closed for stocktaking the following day, which pleased the girls immensely. Coral accompanied Amy into town to help her choose some clothes as her mum had given her the money to buy an outfit for best. Finally, in a small corner clothes shop, she opted for a royal blue suit with a gold chain to fasten the jacket.

They crossed the road to visit Woolies. A pair of screw-on crucifix earrings took Amy's fancy, so she treated herself to them. "It won't be long until I get my ears pierced – unless I chicken out," she told Coral, who was pulling aside the curtains on the photo booth next to them.

"Come on, Amy, let's have our pictures taken," she begged and jumped into the booth. They each had a set of photos taken for two shillings apiece and couldn't stop giggling all the time the camera flashed.

"I don't know why I bother," Amy said with a sigh as she pored over the developed photos five minutes later, "I'm just not photogenic."

"You're being over-critical – they look all right to me," Coral said, comparing the two sets of pictures. Amy took small comfort from the thought that, compared to Coral's photos, hers didn't look too bad after all.

They continued along the High Street to the music shop. Amy had been desperately saving her pocket money so she could buy a copy of 'Please Please Me' by her beloved Beatles.

"Ray has given me the money to get him 'Looby Loo' by the Chucks as it's one of his favourite records," she told Coral as she entered the frumpy shop. It sold a lot of sheet music and pianos downstairs and housed the record department upstairs. The main reason Amy liked this shop was the dishy shop assistant who worked on the record counter. He was always smartly dressed in a suit and had dark wavy hair and brilliant blue eyes. When he asked what she would like, her knees turned to jelly, and she smiled, clutching the record counter for support. She wished she had Yvonne's forwardness to tell him exactly what she wanted, but instead, she merely asked for the records. He served her politely, seemingly oblivious to the emotional turmoil he was stirring up.

Chapter Four

March
Doughnuts and Detentions

The Browns were now the proud owners of a brand-new television which swivelled on three legs. It had sliding doors and an enormous seventeen-inch screen. It also received radio programmes, and with ITV in addition to the BBC, Amy appreciated sitting in her own lounge watching Robin Hood at Saturday teatime. She even found the adverts an enjoyable novelty. Previously, she had occasionally visited her friend, Diane, to watch ITV on her television. She lived further along the road, and they had once biked to secondary school together.

Amy met Vie's mum on Saturday morning as she walked to the other side of the estate to visit Vie. She was a large woman, who had a firm grip on the reins in her household, and domineered her diminutive husband.

"I'm just popping over to see Vie," Amy informed her. Reluctant to stop, she quickly said goodbye and hurried on to Vie's house, where she arranged to meet Vie and Lynn down town for an evening at the flicks.

They met up at 7.00 pm outside the cinema in the High Street. Amy felt like the proverbial bee's knees in her new blue suit. All three were devoted Cliff Richard fans, so they thoroughly enjoyed drooling over him through 'Summer Holiday.'

The picture over, they emerged to discover the gorgeous boy from the Veteran's club loitering outside the cinema with his mate on their motorbikes.

Vie gave Amy a nudge. "I know him," she whispered, nodding towards his mate, "his name's Steve, and I think his mate's name is Tony."

As they walked past, Steve yelled: "Hey, Vie, how d'you fancy a lift home?"

Vie grinned at him and pointed to her tight skirt. "In this skirt? You must be joking. Perhaps another time."

Tony sat on his bike studying his petrol tank with an attitude of what appeared to be shyness. Amy's skirt was nearly as tight as Vie's, but she wished Tony would pluck up the courage and ask to take her home too. She would have struggled onto his pillion regardless. But her hopes were in vain, as the offer never materialised.

As they walked along the High Street towards the Wimpy Bar, a bus went by, and Amy caught a glimpse of the lovely Ken sitting by the window on the top deck. She'd had a crush on him since the memorable day when Vie had briefly spoken to him as she and Vie had walked past as he waited at a bus stop in town. She had been annoyed with Vie at the time, for not introducing her to such a dishy bloke.

She grabbed Vie's arm, pointed at the bus and gave a dramatic swoon. "Oooh! Look Vie – it's that lovely Ken. You really must introduce me to him."

"But I don't know him that well," Vie protested, "he just happened to go to the same youth club that I used to go to occasionally. Besides, I thought you fancied Tony now."

"Well, I do – and incidentally, if you'd worn a looser skirt, I could be on his pillion right now!"

"We couldn't very well accept lifts and leave Lynn to walk home alone, could we?" Vie pointed out in a whisper.

Amy sighed. "No, of course not, but just because I fancy Tony doesn't mean I can't fancy anyone else, does it?"

She led the way into the Wimpy Bar, and they sat down at a table by the window and ordered coffees to revitalise themselves before the journey home. Each table was equipped with a jukebox selector, so they chose the Beatles' 'Please Please Me' followed by Cliff's 'Do You Wanna Dance'.

Lynn had been unusually quiet so far that evening. Now she leaned across the table towards Amy. "You'll never guess what me and Vie have decided to do," she said with an air of mystery and then looked at Vie. "Shall I tell her?"

"Tell me what?" Amy demanded impatiently. She hated being kept in the dark.

Vie just shrugged, so Lynn took a deep breath and continued. "As you know, me and Vie have been spending quite a lot of time with the Elders lately, especially George and John, helping them set up a Sunday school. They're good company and often call round in the evening for chats, over coffee. We've been having long discussions with them about their religion and beliefs. After careful consideration, we've decided to become Mormons!"

Amy's jaw dropped with surprise. "You're kidding!" she gasped, "I didn't think either of you was particularly religious." She knew they had been hanging around with the Elders but had assumed they were attracted to the young, clean-cut Americans with their guitars and folk songs.

"It's true," Vie chipped in, "we like their ideals, and we've talked it over with our parents, and they said they have no objections."

Amy sipped her coffee and gave the matter some thought. "So you could end up sharing a husband!"

Vie laughed. "I doubt it. Not all Mormons are polygamous."

"Well, I admire you both," Amy said, "you've obviously made up your minds, but I hope this doesn't mean you'll emigrate to America."

"It's a possibility – maybe sometime in the distant future," Lynn said with a smile.

"Well, they definitely won't be making a convert out of me, and they had better not try!" Amy declared stoutly.

The following afternoon, Kathleen Hamilton, home for half-term, came for a visit. Amy persuaded her to help clean the guinea pigs' cages again and was surprised to see her enjoying herself as she mucked out.

Mrs Brown invited her to stay for tea as she had made a large raspberry jelly in a mould and given it pride of place in the middle of the table. While she was in the kitchen getting the dishes, Mr Brown, being in a playful mood, livened things up. He picked up the serving spoon and smacked it down on the jelly, causing it to splatter. Everyone received an unwanted helping in the face and hair.

Mum came in and glared at her husband. "What an example to set the children!" she exclaimed, "you should know better, especially when we have a guest." Mr Brown looked suitably chastised but gave the girls a wink when his wife wasn't looking. Kathleen giggled uncontrollably, whereas Amy didn't find the sticky jelly in her hair remotely amusing.

Kathleen helped take the dishes out to the kitchen once the meal was finished. She glanced up and noticed the pancake hanging from the kitchen ceiling. She refrained from passing comment, as everyone else was deliberately ignoring it. She assumed this was another of Mr Brown's jokes that had gone awry.

After tea, Mr Brown took Kathleen home on the back of his pop-pop. She had never ridden on a pillion, let alone on a handmade one fixed to a mudguard. She managed a smile as she bravely clung on, for dear life, to the back of Mr Brown's mac.

Meanwhile, Amy helped her mum wash up the tea things, putting her in a better mood. Amy judged this to be an opportune moment to tell her about Vie's conversion to the Mormon church.

"It can only have a beneficial influence on her, I suppose," Mrs Brown said, "but I still don't approve of her as a suitable friend for you." Amy had hoped she might reconsider her opinion of Vie, but apparently, that was too much to ask.

When Mr Brown returned home, he fixed Amy's new lamp to the wall above her bed. She wished he had fitted it a little higher when she sat up in bed the following morning and received a painful crack on the head.

Vie was absent from school Monday morning. Jean, pleased to be back on friendly terms with Amy, ingratiated herself by giving her two pictures of Cliff. “I know you like to cover your bedroom walls with his pictures,” she said. Amy wondered if Jean was trying to turn over a new leaf but discovered she had an ulterior motive. “Er – perhaps you could lend me your ‘Please Please Me’ record? I promise I’ll look after it.”

“I suppose I could bear to be parted from it,” Amy said reluctantly, gazing dreamily at the pictures of Cliff.

“And I would love to borrow your Buddy Holly LP too sometime, maybe,” Jean added as an afterthought.

“You’re pushing your luck a bit,” Amy said and grinned, “but I’ll try to remember.”

She walked round to Vie’s after school and immediately put her foot in it with her mum, who thought Vie had been at school all day. Vie hadn’t arrived home yet, so Amy decided not to hang around for the showdown.

“Would you ask Vie to meet me at the Railway Tavern at seven-thirty?”

Vie’s mum scowled. “I might not let her out when she gets home,” she muttered. Amy thanked her and left quickly.

That evening she met up with Vie and Lynn as arranged. Amy felt guilty for dropping Vie in it with her mum. “Me and my big mouth. I didn’t realise you were playing truant.”

Vie laughed. “It’s OK, Bat. I only got a mild telling-off. Lynn took the day off school too, so I stayed round at her house.”

"Cor, if that had been my mum, she'd have hit the roof. I wish my mum was more lenient and would let me bend the rules occasionally," Amy said wistfully.

They had a smashing time dancing to live music from a terrible group. Tony and Steve were there, and Amy noticed Tony glancing across at her and smiling, so she plucked up the courage to smile shyly back at him. Towards the end of the evening, Steve sauntered over and asked to take Vie home. She was wearing a fuller skirt, so wouldn't have any problem sitting astride his pillion tonight. Amy's heart skipped a beat when she saw Tony making a move in her direction. At that moment, pesky Arthur from the Veteran's club suddenly appeared and started chatting to her. She told him impatiently to clear off, and he finally got the message and left. She looked around for Tony, but he had vanished. Amy was fuming.

Vie bounced into class Tuesday morning, looking flushed with excitement. "Steve is fantastic!" she gasped, sinking into her seat. "He came in for coffee, and we chatted for ages. We got on so well, he's asked to see me again tomorrow night."

"Great! But did you ask him about Tony?" Amy asked anxiously.

"Well, to be honest, his name only cropped up once, But at least I found out from Steve that his name is actually Bob, not Tony. They work together at the same factory."

"Oh, but he looks far more like a Tony than a Bob," Amy said, feeling unreasonably disappointed by this news. "It'll take a bit of getting used to."

Yvonne breezed in, waving something white above her head. "I've got your roll-on, Bat," she yelled.

"At last!" exclaimed Amy, and then, realising the entire class were grinning. "You might try being a little more discreet," she whispered.

Yvonne failed to see any need for discretion. "It's only a roll-on, not a naughty nightie. What's more, it only cost four and sixpence."

"I gave you five shillings to buy it, so you owe me sixpence change," Amy said, giving the garment a careful tug to test its elasticity. She made a mental calculation and added, "you now owe me two and tuppence altogether. Am I ever likely to get it back?"

"'Course, you will, Bat," Yvonne promised but didn't say when that would be. She quickly changed the subject. "Don't forget that you're meeting Gordon tonight, Tibs – I'm sure you'll like him."

"I'm not looking forward to this blind date – you know I hate them."

"Och, you'll enjoy yourself, you'll see," Yvonne said, trying to reassure her.

Shrewsbury biscuits were the recipe of the day in domestic science. They made a tasty snack to make up for the lousy lunch of cheese salad, which left the girls still feeling hungry. Mrs Slater was on duty in the canteen and hated to see any food wasted. She forced Amy to eat the watercress leaf she had left on her plate, which Amy had mistaken for a dandelion leaf. After she had closed her eyes and swallowed hard, she remained convinced it was a dandelion leaf.

After tea that evening, Mrs Brown started nagging her husband about the pancake on the ceiling because it had been hanging around for a whole week.

"Er, I must visit Gordon and sort out what vegetables we're going to grow on our allotments this year, love," he said and escaped out the back door.

With her dad gone, it was Amy's turn to be picked on by her mother as she helped with the washing up. "I heard there was a fight at the Veterans Club. Your father and I can't allow you to go to such rough places – they're not safe for young girls."

"But Mum, it was only one fight, and I didn't get involved," she protested.

"I should think not! Nevertheless, you mustn't go to that place anymore – especially if it's the sort of place that Dennis frequents."

Amy guessed the Menace next door had been telling tales.

At registration the following morning, Pam admitted that she had been unimpressed with Gordon, her blind date. "All he did was talk about himself all night," she complained, "he thought he was God's gift! Huh, he was anything but, being short, balding and deadly boring." Yvonne tried persuading Amy that perhaps he was the man of her dreams instead.

"Get knotted, Yvonne," she scoffed, "I'm not going to be fobbed off with Pam's rejects."

Yvonne shrugged. "It's your loss. You shouldn't listen to Pam – she's too fussy. Gordon is a really nice chap." Amy preferred to let Pam be the judge of that.

After an absence of three weeks, Fluff finally arrived back in class, minus her spots. Netball practise was the last lesson of the day, so she and Amy contrived to avoid the unwanted exercise by volunteering to be reserves. The ploy worked, and they relaxed on the sidelines enjoying the warm sunshine, which had almost melted the snow. Occasionally they cheered on the others as they leapt around the court in frenzied activity.

Afterwards, in the changing rooms, Yvonne begged Amy for the loan of her domestic science homework to copy. Amy felt she could hardly refuse after Yvonne had finally got her the roll-on.

Yvonne was absent the next day, so Amy was unable to hand in her domestic science homework before registration. "I'm sorry, Miss Snodgrass, but I left it at home by mistake," she told her, trying to sound contrite.

"It's just not good enough, Amy Brown. Have it on my desk before your next domestic science lesson, or you will be in detention."

Amy stomped off back to her form room, furious with Yvonne.

"Just wait 'til I see her – that's the last time I help her out with her homework," she whispered to Jean while rummaging around in her satchel. "By the way, here's 'Please Please Me'. I know I said you could borrow it, but only for a couple of days, and you must promise to take good care of it."

"Of course, I will," Jean assured her. She glanced at the empty desk in front of Amy. "By the way, do you know where Vie has got to today?"

"Yeah, she's got an appointment at the hospital this morning to have a whitlow on her finger removed. I expect she felt a bit self-conscious about it now that she wants to look her best for Steve."

Pam arrived late for registration, bursting to tell the others the news she had heard. "Guess what happened to Catty Catting on her way to school this morning," she whispered across the gangway to Amy and Jean. "She only crashed her Mini into a lamppost! Apparently, she swerved to avoid hitting a cat."

"Well, I hope she missed it," Amy said, adding as an afterthought: "Was she hurt?"

"No, she came out of it unscathed, but the poor Mini looks a bit sorry for itself. I saw it parked in front of the Manor gates as I came in just now."

Amy arrived home after school to find that her dad had finally succumbed to the pressure of constant nagging and scraped the offending pancake off the ceiling. There remained a large, greasy stain to tell the tale.

Pam arrived at school the following morning with more news, but it was somewhat disconcerting. Yvonne had apparently left home after a big row with her parents and had gone to live at Alex's house. "They found out about Alex's court appearance and forbade Yvonne from seeing him again."

"They should have realised that Yvonne, being headstrong, would do something like that," Fluff declared.

"I met up with her yesterday evening at a coffee bar," Pam continued, "and she told me she has no intention of returning to school. She wants to get a job instead."

"What a daft nit!" Amy blurted out. "I bet her mum will be furious with her over this. What's more, she had better come back, else I'll get a detention because she's got my domestic science homework."

Jean returned Amy's Beatles record and brought in some of her own records for her.

"Here's the Buddy Holly LP you wanted to borrow," Amy said, passing it over. She was relieved to get her Beatles record back. It occurred to her that there was a definite improvement in their friendship as they exchanged their records. Perhaps because Jean had refrained from telling her usual porkies.

That evening, Amy had to tell a porky when she told her mum she was going over to see Pam and then went to meet Vie and Lynn for their weekly soiree at the Veterans Club. They arrived to find the place in darkness, and the doors locked. A notice pinned to the door explained that it had closed due to nearby residents complaining about the fighting and noise.

Instead, they headed for the pub at the end of the street. They enjoyed a pleasant evening listening to music and telling each other jokes. They had to shout to be heard because they were sitting next to the jukebox. Vie proudly brandished her whitlow-less finger for the others to admire. During the evening, Amy drank six bitter lemons and had cause to regret it on the way home when she was busting for a pee and couldn't hang on any longer.

"What am I going to do?" she wailed, crossing her legs, "I'm desperate." The other two were no help and just fell about giggling. With no alleyway to duck into, she could do nothing but 'pee her breeks' as Yvonne would say. Vie and Lynn thought her predicament was highly amusing. Amy shivered as her warm soggy knickers and stockings clung to her and quickly chilled in the cold night air. Her shoes squelched, and she found it difficult to walk normally. She was thankful to reach home under the cover of darkness.

During Monday morning's registration, Fluff turned and whispered to Amy, sitting behind her. "I went to Pam's house yesterday, and she showed me a painful-looking blister on her heel. I expect that's why she's not turned up today."

"She's probably nursing it better, ready for tonight because I've arranged to meet her at the Railway Tavern," Amy whispered back.

But her dad scotched her plan over tea that evening. "I've heard a lot of worrying stories about that Railway Tavern," he said, wagging his butter knife in her direction. "I'm not having a daughter of mine frequenting a dive."

"But Dad, it's good fun there," Amy protested, desperate not to have another place put out of bounds. "We don't loiter or drink in the bar. We go straight through to the back room where the dances are held. They usually have great live groups playing there."

"Well, you're not going there tonight, but I'll make further enquiries about the place, just in case its reputation has improved of late." Her dad was adamant and remained immune to Amy's pleading, refusing to say where he got his information.

"I bet it's your cronies at work, who have been called out to a fight there at some time in the past," Amy said bitterly. "But it's not like that now." She jumped up from the tea table, grabbed her apple pie, drenched in custard, and stomped off to eat it in front of the television.

'Now I shall miss seeing the lovely Bob,' she thought grimly and then collided with her brother in the doorway. The dish flew out of her hand and smashed upside down in the fireplace.

"Why don't you look where you're going," she yelled.

"Don't blame him when you should be sitting at the table eating and not wandering around with a dishful of food in your hand," Mum said, coming to Ray's defence. "Make sure you clean up that mess properly."

Amy glared at the pie and custard splattered all over the fireplace. She resented the grotty job of cleaning it up since she didn't consider it her fault in the first place.

Feeling fed up, she expended her frustrations in the kitchen that evening. She made a large batch of coconut ice and then stuffed herself with it as a consolation until she felt sick.

'Life is so unfair,' she thought as she stomped upstairs to bed, 'I feel like clearing off. Perhaps Yvonne wasn't so daft after all when she left home. Even the flippin' rain is picking on me – it hasn't stopped all day, and it's pissing me off!'

Yvonne made an unexpected appearance the following morning when she honoured 5G2 with her presence. During the break, as they huddled in the Manor stables, she explained to the others that she had returned home because she and Alex had fallen out.

"He only had the cheek to go out drinking with his mates and expected me to stay home with his mum and sister, watching the telly. I might pack him up if he gets let off in court, but for the time being, I'm trying to make tentative peace with my mother. It's not easy, though; she can't help gloating because she thinks she's won now that I'm back home and not speaking to Alex."

Amy was pleased to see Yvonne. It meant she could get her domestic science homework back from her and onto Miss Snodgrass' desk in the nick of time to avoid a detention.

They concocted gingerbread finger biscuits in domestic science. As gingerbread was Dad's favourite, Amy hoped she'd be able to bribe him with them in order to change his mind about letting her go to the Railway Tavern.

Amy lacked a partner for the ballroom dancing lesson in the gym, so she had no option but to dance with the student teacher. Jean was permanently exempted from any exercise, so she sat at the side watching. Whenever Amy tried to find out from her why she must never exert herself, all she got were evasive answers. She gave vague references, sometimes to her liver or sometimes to her heart. The other girls were all inclined to think she was pulling a fast one, collaborated by her parents.

The teacher grabbed Amy firmly around the waist. Amy, feeling self-conscious, concentrated hard, her eyes fixed on their feet, afraid she might step on her teacher's toes.

The teacher soon tired of looking at the top of Amy's head. "Amy Brown, you will never get your man like this!" she said sternly, "I want you to look me straight in the eyes and smile."

"I have no intention of getting my man this way," Amy retorted with a scowl and promptly trod on her toes.

Pam was still absent with her blister the next day, so Amy concluded, with relief, that she hadn't made it to the Railway Tavern the previous evening.

During the lunch break, as Amy, Jean, and Yvonne sat on a bench in the Manor grounds, Jean confided to them wild tales of her colourful upbringing in an African village. She had returned to her irritating habit of letting her imagination run riot.

"I lived there with my parents until I was five when I was struck down with sleeping sickness. The resident witch doctor cured me by chanting loads of spells and giving me herbal remedies." Amy and Yvonne feigned amazement which pleased her immensely. She didn't notice them grinning at each other behind her back.

Amy returned Jean's records, but Jean annoyed her by hanging on to her Buddy Holly LP. "You don't mind if I bring it back on Friday, do you?" she asked, "only tomorrow I've arranged to go to the Ideal Home Exhibition with Fluff."

"Er, I suppose it's OK," Amy said casually, attempting to conceal her irritation. She wondered whether Jean would bother turning up to meet Fluff.

Mum had spent the day visiting Great Auntie Gertie. She returned home at teatime laden with gifts. A packet of tobacco for Dad and sweets for Amy and Ray. However, Mum received the best present when Auntie Gertie gave her a solid gold bracelet with an initial 'C' depicted in diamonds. It was an old family heirloom that she wanted Mum to have. Mum proudly clamped it around her plump wrist and was relieved to find it just fitted.

The following day Jean and Fluff were both absent, so the girls assumed they must have gone to the exhibition.

For most of the week, Coral had extra shorthand classes after school each evening, so Amy caught the bus home alone. She couldn't help noticing the rather dishy conductor. His piercing dark eyes twinkled as he gave her a ticket. He only charged her a threepenny fare. This was proof in Amy's eyes that he must fancy her.

Friday morning Jean and Fluff were still absent.

"Perhaps they got themselves hopelessly lost in London," Amy remarked to Yvonne. They were heading for the science laboratory in the New Building with the rest of the class to hear their exam results.

Amy only managed 33% and failed miserably, as did over half of the class. She was disappointed but surprisingly, Miss Stevens said she was satisfied with the overall results!

"It's not like her to be so easily pleased," Amy said to Yvonne as they packed away their books at the end of the lesson.

"She was in a good mood for once – maybe she's got herself a boyfriend, eh Bat?"

"She'd need to shave or pluck her bushy eyebrows before any bloke would look twice at her," Amy said with a grin, making Yvonne giggle.

They arrived upstairs at the Grange for their English lesson. Mrs Slater was in a foul mood and threw one of her famous fits, closely followed by the wooden blackboard rubber, aimed at Yvonne's head because she was giggling again. Luckily she ducked in time and it sailed harmlessly out of the open window at the rear of the classroom. It landed on the building site below, where the workmen were laying the foundations for the new music room. It plopped right into the middle of an expanse of wet cement to the surprise and annoyance of the workmen. Mrs Slater dispatched Yvonne to retrieve and clean it. Yvonne only had to bat her long eyelashes to have a workman willingly flounder through the cement to recover the rubber for her.

On the bus home, Amy was over the moon to find the same delectable conductor on board. He again only charged a fare of threepence. Amy gazed into his dark brown sexy eyes as she handed over the money. Did she imagine it, or did he hold her hand for a fleeting moment as he took the money?

She was supposed to visit a local piano teacher with her dad after tea. He had found one whose fees were quite reasonable, so he wanted to arrange some lessons. But his motorbike refused to start and demanded his attention. Amy chose the wrong moment to ask him if she could go to a dance in London with Yvonne the following night. His temper was frayed from trying to coax life back into his bike, so he promptly banned her from going.

"But Dad, it's at the Mormon church again, and you didn't mind the last time I went," she pleaded.

"You didn't get home until long past midnight if I remember rightly. That's far too late for you to be out at your age." Amy knew better than to press the point when he was in one of his stubborn moods, so she stomped off to sulk in her bedroom.

Saturday morning, Amy rang Yvonne from the phone box, at the corner of the Crescent to tell her the bad news. Yvonne sounded disappointed but cheered up when Amy offered to lend her some records.

Dad's motorbike was still out of action, so he and Amy walked for over a mile to get to the piano teacher's house that evening to book some piano lessons. Mrs Falco was an Italian lady with eyes as black as currants. They glinted as she scrutinised Amy closely from behind her rimless spectacles.

She wore her grey hair pulled back severely into a bun with only the odd wisp daring to escape and soften the hairline around her face. She charged Dad a reduced fee of thirty-five shillings a term as Amy was still at school, which suited him fine. She gave Amy a music book to study, ready for her first lesson the following Friday.

After they arrived home, Amy browsed through the book and concluded it would be a doddle.

Jean and Fluff returned to school Monday morning, safely back from their trip to London.

Amy pulled Fluff to one side. “Did Jean actually turn up for once?” she asked in disbelief.

Fluff laughed. “I was just as surprised when I saw her arrive at the station. We agreed it wasn’t worth coming back to school for one day on Friday, so we met up and went shopping instead.”

“That must be an all-time record – Jean turning up two days on the trot! Maybe there’s some hope of her turning up for our outing to Wembley next Sunday then,” Amy said with a grin.

Jean came over and tugged on her arm. “Here’s your Buddy Holly LP, Bat. Sorry I wasn’t able to return it Friday as I promised.” Once again, Amy wondered if Jean had finally turned over a new leaf.

Amy gave Yvonne the bag of singles she had brought with her.

“Thanks, Bat. I’ll look after them and return them by next Monday.”

“Well, I’ve included some of my favourite records, so I’d prefer it if you’d let me have them back Friday so I can listen to them over the weekend.”

"'Course I will," Yvonne assured her. Then she pulled out a screwed-up garment from her satchel. "What d'you think of this skirt I'm making?"

Amy gazed at the very creased dark blue material Yvonne proudly held up. "Er, yes – it should look great once it's finished and you've given it a good iron."

"That's why I've brought it in. I want you to give me a hand." Amy forced a smile, concealing her heavy heart.

During lunchtime, Yvonne stood on top of the mounting steps outside the stables in the Manor courtyard wearing the blue skirt. Amy marked with tailor's chalk where the hem needed to go and then pinned and tacked it into position, which wasn't easy with Yvonne unable to stand still for more than a moment.

"How about we try getting a Saturday job after school?" Yvonne suggested, hopping restlessly from foot to foot.

Amy was keen on the idea, so once school was over, she and Yvonne caught a bus into the next town and headed for the large department store in the High Street. The floor manager soon disillusioned them when he told them there were no immediate vacancies.

Disappointed, they made for a nearby cafe and ordered two consolatory cups of coffee, then discovered they had no money to pay for them. The lady behind the counter was very understanding after Yvonne batted her eyelashes and explained their predicament while oozing charm.

"You look like two honest girls; I'm sure I can trust you to bring the money tomorrow evening," she said.

They sat at a table by the window, and Yvonne produced a packet of cigarettes. They sipped their coffee, making it last while they smoked four cigarettes each. A man in a mac hunched over a cup of tea at a nearby table glared at them and muttered something rude about underage smoking.

Yvonne turned around and glared back. "If we want to put nails in our coffins, it's our prerogative and has nothing to do with you!" she snapped in a haughty voice she rarely used. Amy admired the way Yvonne was never lost for words. How she wished she could be more assertive. With their coffees finished, they got up and left for the bus stop.

As Amy was about to get on her bus home, Yvonne generously gave her the last cigarette in the packet. She saved it, to smoke in the toilet before going to bed. She took the usual precaution of standing on the toilet seat to puff the smoke out of the small window. She first removed her shoes so as not to mark the seat. As she flicked the fag end out of the window, she aimed it across into the Denton's garden. Suddenly, one foot slipped and splashed down into the pan. Before she could regain her balance, her foot became wedged around the bend. She struggled to extricate it, accompanied by much cursing.

Then her brother pounded urgently on the door. "Come on out and stop hogging the bog," he yelled through the keyhole. "Sounds as if you're having a bath in there."

Amy finally managed to free her foot. She unlocked the door and scowled at him before hobbling across the landing, leaving wet footprints on the lino.

She had arranged to go over to Yvonne's house Saturday evening. On the way, she popped in at the cafe to belatedly give the lady the money they owed for their coffees on Monday evening. As she turned to leave, she saw her bus go sailing past the window. At the bus stop, she studied the timetable, which informed her she had a half-hour wait for the next bus. Then the heavens opened up and the rain pelted down in stair rods. She wasn't dressed for wet weather, and the cold raindrops dripping down her neck rapidly made her feel chilly and depressed. When the bus failed to arrive, Amy, now drenched to the skin, gave up and went to find a phone box to ring Yvonne and explain why she hadn't reached her house.

Back at home, she changed into dry clothes and decided on a therapeutic bout of cooking to cheer herself up. She hunted through the food in the pantry and found a bag of fresh lemons, so she made some lemon curd. It looked good and smelt good, but she didn't like the flavour. She had forgotten she didn't like lemon curd.

In the morning, Miss Hardacre began interviewing girls who hoped to come to her school later that year. Amy saw them as she entered the Grange and headed upstairs to her form room to collect a book from her desk. She couldn't help feeling sorry for them, sitting in a row on the wooden bench outside Miss Hardacre's study, waiting to be summoned, their fingers nervously twiddling buttons. Amy could remember only too well the day she had sat there shaking in her shoes, hoping to make a good impression. Her interview had been remarkably mundane – even Miss Hardacre could barely conceal her boredom.

Then she stumped Amy by asking her what book she was currently reading. None was the truthful answer, but Amy felt sure this wasn't what Miss Hardacre wanted to hear and realised it wouldn't help her cause. She racked her brains until she recalled a stuffy book she had struggled to finish a while back. As soon as she mentioned the title, Miss Hardacre sat up abruptly and took a renewed interest in her.

"Oh, that's by Elizabeth Gouge," she gushed, her eyes lighting up, "one of my favourite authors."

Amy sighed, relieved that Miss Hardacre had heard of the author. She managed to relate a little about the story, which, fortunately, Miss Hardacre had read, so she promptly filled in any details that Amy had missed. A rapport appeared to be developing between them of a shared experience. Amy had always suspected that book was the sole deciding factor for her acceptance into Clara's exclusive scholarly enclave.

This morning Miss Hardacre didn't want distracting noises above her head, so 5G2's form room was temporarily moved to the old Manor. They were allocated an upstairs classroom at the end of a dark, creepy corridor, which was reputed to be haunted. Rumours were rife of a grey lady, sometimes headless, seen gliding along this corridor and through the closed door into the classroom. The corridor had a fusty smell, and the room was always cold – even on the hottest day. No-one dared to stay in there alone.

Unable to get out of double games, Amy and her gang were forced to spend the hour after assembly running up and down the hockey pitch brandishing their sticks like a bunch of demented beaters trying to flush out game. The unaccustomed exercise made Amy feel quite queasy.

Miss Catting, their sports teacher, had been in a bad mood since her car crash. When she spotted a necklace on Yvonne, she immediately confiscated it, much to Yvonne's dismay, as it had been a present from Alex.

Yvonne vowed to get her revenge, so at lunchtime, she composed a nasty letter to Miss Catting as she and the other girls lounged in the stables. "See what she thinks of that!" Yvonne declared as she finished writing.

"Serves her right for being so nasty," Amy said, "though I doubt the letter will make a scrap of difference."

"I'll take it home and type it out this evening. Then there won't be any incriminating handwriting," Yvonne said, carefully stowing the letter away in her satchel.

After registration the following morning, Yvonne had to leave for another appointment at the hospital about her varicose veins. Before she left, she managed to sneak the typed letter onto Miss Catting's desk in the Manor without being seen.

During the lunch hour, Jean and Amy sat in the creeper-shrouded summerhouse on the terrace, which overlooked the murky pond in the Manor grounds. They discussed when and where to meet on Sunday for their outing to Wembley.

Once they had agreed on their plan of action, Jean announced: "I've got a dark secret that I've not told anyone before, so you must promise not to breathe a word to a soul." Amy duly promised, harbouring some misgivings. Jean continued:

"The fact is, way back in my ancestry, there lurks an African chieftain, and in each subsequent generation of my family, there is always one throwback showing some Negroid feature." She paused, taking a deep breath for dramatic effect before playing her trump card. "In my generation, I am that throwback!"

Amy couldn't stop herself from bursting into laughter at this ridiculous claim. She stared hard at Jean's annoyed face. "Well, I suppose your nose is slightly podgy. But there's certainly nothing Negroid about your fair hair, blue eyes or pasty complexion," she said, trying to sound serious.

Jean grew increasingly irritated with Amy's apparent scepticism at the momentous news she had just divulged. "Since you don't believe me, I'll prove it to you," she said peevishly. She untucked her blouse, tugged it up with a triumphant flourish and revealed a large area of dark skin covering her rotund paunch. Amy gazed at it in amazement, lost for words. Of course, it could just be an extra-large birthmark. After pondering over Jean's ludicrous story, Amy was inclined to think that was what it must be. But for Jean's benefit, she said: "OK, maybe that does prove there's a grain of truth in your story." Jean smiled, pleased that Amy believed her story for once.

Amy arrived home to find Dennis the Menace's parents, the Dentons, standing by the kerb scrutinising a second-hand old banger they had just bought. Mrs Denton would make an ideal stand-in for Peggy Mount any day. Her deep voice could be heard bellowing through the adjoining wall from next-door when she was berating her poor diminutive husband, Art. He was a good-humoured little man who accepted his lot stoically.

Amy felt sorry for him. She recalled, as a five-year-old, how she would run outside to meet him as he arrived home from work and begged him to show her one of his tricks. Her favourite trick was his apparent ability to remove the top half of his thumb without a drop of blood being spilt. This would completely mystify and worry the young Amy until he magicked the thumb back whole again, to her relief. Then she would ask to see his index finger, which did have a missing tip due to an accident at work. Sadly no amount of magic would make that whole again.

Inspecting the car with them was their older daughter, Beryl. She was married to Tom, and they had recently moved into a house at the other end of the Crescent with their young family.

Amy couldn't help envying their old banger. Despite her dislike of car journeys because she suffered from motion sickness, she still wished her dad had a car. It was far more civilised than sitting astride a makeshift motorbike pillion.

Indoors, Mrs Williams from across the green was gossiping with Mum. She seemed to take great pleasure in deriding Amy. She told herself it was only jealousy because she had succeeded in passing her thirteen-plus, and Mrs Williams' darling Lucy had failed.

Dad spent a considerable time that evening giving Amy directions and mapping out routes so that she and Jean could travel to Wembley on Sunday without getting lost.

Before going to bed, Amy picked up her new music book for a quick browse in readiness for her first lesson the following evening. She recalled Mrs Falco telling her: "Just memorise that every good boy deserves fun." But now she couldn't remember, for the life of her, what it meant.

Pam's chair remained vacant during morning registration. Amy assumed she fancied taking the day off as it was the end of the week.

The gym was packed for the Friday lunch hour jive session where the girls could let their hair down and enjoy themselves. Yvonne and Amy chatted to Fat Frudge and her pretty friend Lally. Frudge was another happy-go-lucky individual like Yvonne. Round in face and body, she was always bubbling with laughter and good company. Whereas petite Lally was very demure and well aware that one glance from her big brown baby eyes or a sexy pout from her lips could reduce any red-blooded male into a quivering heap. Her stunning natural beauty was the envy of almost every other girl in the school.

"We're going to the Bull out at Swanley village tonight," Frudge informed Yvonne and Amy. "Why don't you two come and meet us there?"

"I've heard of the place but never been there. Is it any good?" Yvonne asked.

"It's really great. Me and Lally often go on Friday or Sunday nights because there's usually a live group playing. But I don't know the group playing there tonight, so I can't say whether they'll be any good. Have you heard of them, Lally?"

"No, I haven't, but who cares when there's plenty of good-looking blokes hanging around in the bars." Lally swept her hair back from her face in one smooth movement and smiled innocently. Amy thought her mannerisms were vaguely reminiscent of Marilyn Monroe.

"Sounds like it could be worth trying," Yvonne said, so they arranged to meet them at the Bull Hotel that evening.

After school, Amy went to her first piano lesson with Mrs Falco. They spent most of the time chatting and getting to know each other. However, at the end of the lesson, Mrs Falco gave her a load of scales to practise at home. The thought of tedious practise sessions, going up and down the scales gave Amy misgivings about whether she wanted to learn to play the piano after all.

Yvonne arrived at Amy's house at 8.30 pm. The bus stop for Swanley village was a good half-mile away. They reached it, not knowing when the next bus would show up. As they waited, shivering in the cold night air, a sleek red sports car drew up alongside them, and a smart-looking boy stuck his head out of the window, grinning at them.

"Where would two lovely girls be off to at this time of night?" he asked cheekily.

Amy nudged Yvonne and whispered out of the corner of her mouth: "Ignore him."

"We're going to the Bull at Swanley," Yvonne replied with a smile, batting her long dark lashes.

"How about we give you a lift since we're heading in that direction," he suggested. Without waiting for an answer, he opened the door, hopped out and pulled his seat forward. "It's a bit cramped in the back, but it's better than waiting in the cold for a bus."

Yvonne, rash as ever, didn't hesitate. She jumped into the car dragging a reluctant Amy behind her. "Don't worry, we'll be OK," she murmured as they huddled together with their knees almost touching their chins. "There's supposed to be safety in numbers, and this car is far too cramped for any hanky panky."

Amy tried to relax, but she could hear her mother's familiar words ringing in her ears: "Never accept lifts from strangers." Now she was bowling along a quiet country lane with two total strangers. The dark lanes wound for miles with no signposts or street lights. Eventually, they spotted a signpost and discovered they were heading in the wrong direction. Amy was sure the boys only feigned surprise when she pointed this out to them.

"Look, it's getting late, so why don't we just go for a drink at the first pub we come to?" the driver proposed.

"As much as we'd like to, we can't because we've arranged to meet our friends at the Bull," Yvonne explained. She used all her Scottish charm to convince the boys that they must turn the car around and get back on the right road. They arrived in the Bull's car park at 10 o'clock with the two boys still trying to persuade them to change their minds and go to a different pub with them. They finally accepted defeat and reluctantly allowed the two girls to clamber out of their uncomfortable car. Pleased to be able to stretch out straight again, the girls thanked the boys for the lift and hurried off in the direction of the loud music.

"Those two were dead narked because we wouldn't go for a drink with them," Amy remarked between gulps of fresh air. She was relieved she hadn't caused an embarrassing scene by being carsick.

The group playing at the Bull were pretty lousy. Amy and Yvonne soon realised they hadn't missed out on much as they looked around at the bored faces sitting in the bar. They ordered a couple of rum and blacks to warm themselves up and then searched for Lally and Frudge. They eventually found them in the dance hall and told them about their lengthy lift. Then it was time to leave and catch the last bus home.

Waiting at the bus stop, Yvonne was taken short and had to dive up an alleyway for an emergency pee. She was still there when the bus arrived, so Amy smiled sweetly at the impatient conductor standing on the platform.

"Er, can you hang on for my friend – she'll be joining us any minute now," she said, hoping he wouldn't ask what was keeping her. Amy received inquisitive looks from the other passengers as they craned their necks in her direction.

"I've got a very tight schedule to keep to," he muttered irritably, none too pleased to be kept waiting. Just then, Yvonne rushed out of the alleyway and leapt onto the bus, still adjusting her skirt. He glared at her, but she soon had him eating out of her hand – literally.

"Would you like some jelly babies?" she asked when he came to collect their fares. She rummaged around in the bottom of her handbag and found a few lying loose. She pushed them into his hand before he had time to refuse. He looked a little taken aback but seemed to cheer up when Yvonne gave him a warm smile.

"Those jelly babies were pretty old, but I don't think he noticed the fluff sticking to them," Yvonne whispered as the conductor vanished upstairs in search of more fares.

Amy walked to Coral's house Saturday morning to watch the boat race. She had always supported Cambridge for some unfathomable reason, perhaps because her parents were Cambridge supporters. She proudly wore a pale blue ribbon pinned to her jumper. Coral, sporting a navy blue ribbon, backed the Oxford team, who were the favourites, and of course, they won as usual.

Sunday was Mother's Day, so after the boat race finished, they walked into town to buy some presents. Amy selected a card and bought a bunch of daffodils, a box of chocolates and a can of hair lacquer. Coral also bought her mum some daffodils and opted for a practical pair of support stockings as her mum suffered from very painful varicose veins.

That night Amy fell asleep dreaming of Cliff in anticipation of the following day.

She arrived at the station early in the morning. To her surprise, Jean actually turned up - and on time! She was as excited as Amy at the prospect, of finally seeing Cliff in the flesh. They succeeded in finding Wembley Stadium without getting lost, thanks to Dad's diagram. They bought fags and a program before climbing into the gods to reach their seats. They were so thrilled to be watching such a vast number of stars performing live that it didn't matter to them that they were so high up.

David Jacobs acted as the compère. He came onto the stage looking dapper in a sharp suit and bow tie to make a devastating announcement.

"Ladies and gentlemen, I'm sorry to be the bearer of bad news, but I have to tell you that Cliff is suffering from laryngitis, and he has had to pull out. However, we are lucky to be able to offer you instead the fabulous Adam Faith, who has stepped in at the eleventh hour."

Not being an Adam Faith fan, Amy suffered great pangs of disappointment. She was determined to enjoy the show regardless. As each star was introduced, they only had time to sing one of their hits. The scene unfolding below had a surreal quality as the myriad of famous names paraded onto the stage. They included Marty Wilde, Helen Shapiro, Mike Sarne, Carol Dean, The Brook Brothers, Mark Wynter and Kenny Ball's Jazz Band. Alma Cogan even appeared wearing one of her renowned dresses.

"Oh, Jean, she was one of my favourite female singers in the fifties. I remember being totally in awe of her beautiful ostrich feather dresses when she appeared on the telly," Amy whispered excitedly.

Adam Faith, the new star of the show, was allowed to sing several songs. Amy could only think that it should have been Cliff down there. She found Adam's painfully skinny physique shocking as she watched him almost vanish when he turned sideways.

The seats were hard and uncomfortable, but the girls barely noticed, being so enthralled by the spectacle. The show was over before they knew it, and they were heading home on the train, exhausted but exhilarated.

Monday morning marked the start of a new week at school, but Jean and Yvonne failed to arrive, so Amy sat next to Pam during lessons.

They walked along the gravel driveway of the Grange on their way to the Manor for their next lesson, their satchels weighing them down with books. "I expect Jean's still recovering from all the excitement yesterday," Amy remarked. "And where did you get to on Friday?"

"As it was Friday, I chose to have a lazy day at home. But how amazing that Jean actually turned up for once," Pam said, sounding astonished.

"Well, she had paid for her ticket, so I suppose she didn't want to waste the money," Amy said with a hint of cynicism as they paused to cross the road. "By the way, do you know where Yvonne has got to today?"

"She had to make an appearance in court this morning to act as a character witness for Alex but doesn't want the school to know where she is. Clara would probably object to her going to court."

"Yeah, I'm sure she would," Amy agreed. She knew only too well Miss Hardacre's prejudices regarding courts. "But maybe Yvonne won't feel like singing his praises in court after their argument when they fell out," she added.

They climbed the stairs to Miss Catting's classroom, sat down and dug out the relevant books from their satchels. In addition to being their sports teacher, Miss Catting diversified by teaching history and religious knowledge.

"There's been no reaction from her as yet to the letter Yvonne left on her desk," Pam whispered, "she obviously can't have a clue who sent it."

"Just as well because it could get Yvonne expelled if she ever found out...." Amy tailed off as Miss Catting strutted past, giving her shoulder a sharp tap with her bony finger.

"No talking during lessons," she snapped. She was still in a bad mood, so Amy and Pam put their heads down to work.

Vie accompanied Amy home from school. Her romance with Steve was still going well, so they made a detour, on their way home, to where Steve and the lovely Bob worked. They couldn't see any sign of them but spotted their motorbikes parked outside some sheds. Vie fixed a note to the seat of Steve's bike telling him when and where to meet her that evening, and then they walked on into town and headed for Woolies.

"What do you think of this?" Vie asked, brandishing a false ponytail as they stood at the cosmetics counter. "Steve thinks they look great, so I'll surprise him tonight by wearing one."

Amy looked at Vie's unruly flyaway hair and had some misgivings. "Er, sounds like a good idea," she said and rummaged amongst the heap of hairpieces. "This one looks like a good match with your hair." She held one up. Vie beamed with delight and then dug into her satchel, searching for her purse to pay for it.

Yvonne bounced into class the next day, full of the joys of spring, having patched up her differences with Alex. "I had to stand in the witness box and take the oath, just like you see in films," she told the others breathlessly. "Then I explained to the judge how Alex was such a peaceful and responsible member of society. I smiled at the judge a lot in the hope that it might make him look more favourably on Alex's misdemeanour. I'm not sure whether it worked, but Alex did get off lightly – he was bound over to keep the peace, so now he can put it all behind him." She looked at Amy's glum face. "What's up, Bat? You seem to be a bit fed up today."

Amy sighed. "I don't suppose you remembered to bring back my records?" she asked with a heavy heart, knowing only too well what the answer would be.

"Oh, I'm sorry. Is that what's bothering you? With all the excitement, I forgot to pack them. I promise you'll have them tomorrow." Amy tried to hide the wave of irritation engulfing her. Yvonne didn't appreciate how much she missed playing her favourite records.

5G2 were told they didn't need to change into their P.E. kits as they were having a dancing lesson in the gym. The P.E. student from the physical education college down the road tried, without much success, to teach them the Madison. They all thought this was a pretty dull sort of dance, so instead, they taught her how to do the Twist and the Locomotion. After half an hour of energetic dancing, the student eventually agreed that these new dances were far more fun.

Amy, Pam, Fluff and Vie walked into town after school to save on their bus fares. On the way, they had to take an emergency detour through a hedge into an onion field to avoid being seen by Miss Hardacre when they spotted her Ford Anglia car. They would have been in deep trouble as none of them were wearing berets. They snagged and laddered their stockings as they pushed through the hedge and then had to force their way out again once the coast was clear.

They eventually reached town feeling dishevelled and hungry, so they promptly blew all their carefully saved bus fares on an enormous cream doughnut each. They strolled along the High Street laughing, joking and tucking into their doughnuts. Suddenly the ominous hulk of Mrs Snake loomed into view, heading their way. Newly appointed as deputy head to Miss Hardacre, she revelled in the powers this position gave her. The girls reacted quickly and dived up a nearby alleyway to avoid bumping into her.

"We'd have well and truly copped it if she had caught us looking like this," a worried Fluff said, pointing at their ragged stockings. She had always managed to keep out of trouble and was a stranger to detentions.

"Maybe she didn't notice us, or if she did, she was too far away to recognise us," Pam whispered, trying to reassure Fluff as they crouched down behind some smelly dustbins.

"She'd go potty if she saw us eating in the street. That school rule is like the eleventh commandment," Amy said bitterly. She and Mrs Snake were old adversaries from Amy's infant school. Mrs Snake had taught the five and six-year-olds, terrifying them into obedience with her dark, flashing eyes and fierce voice.

During the morning assembly, Mrs Snake stood up and read a report to Miss Hardacre. "Yesterday, I was in town and saw a group of girls looking an absolute disgrace to this school!" She paused and scanned the assembly, her face black as thunder. It became clear that she had recognised them as her steely glare came to rest in their direction. They were ordered to stand up as their names were read out. A stern lecture followed from Miss Hardacre in front of the whole school. The inevitable detentions were then handed out. Not to be outdone by her mates, Yvonne also collected a detention for losing her hymn book.

Yvonne remembered to bring four of the five records that Amy had lent her the previous week. To Amy's dismay and annoyance, her favourite Beatles record was still missing.

There followed a gruelling double games lesson with Miss Catting when she made the class run from one end of the hockey pitch to the other and back again. The girls were convinced that Catty had sadistic tendencies. She also had an odd, and no doubt, very uncomfortable habit of sitting on the straight end of her hockey stick as she lectured them on the finer points, of the game.

Back in the changing rooms, while they were dressing after their showers, Lally showed off her new fifteen denier tights in the latest dark brown shade of 'Fern'. She liked the way they highlighted the curves of her shapely calves. Everyone admired them and agreed that tights looked far more comfortable than stockings and suspenders. They even appeared to stay up without any sagging at the knees.

"They're bound to catch on," Pam said, gazing at their silky sheen wistfully, "but they're a bit too expensive compared to stockings, so I know I won't be getting any for a while yet."

Yvonne appeared briefly the next day at registration to tell Mrs Butler she had a hospital appointment, then left to spend the day at Alex's house. Amy sat at her desk and fumed because Yvonne still hadn't returned her Beatles record.

That evening, Amy puffed on a fag in the toilet but didn't risk standing on the seat, in case she slipped again. She forgot to open the window to clear the air, so her mum's nose soon detected the telltale smoke.

"What have I told you time and again, my girl," she said crossly, "cigarettes are for fools. They are bad for you – you've only got to hear your dad's cough to realise that. You must stop while you can before it's too late!"

Amy didn't care because she was feeling too sick and tired. The sick feeling developed into a stomach ache, so she went to bed early, nursing a hot water bottle. She sat huddled on the toilet at 4.30 in the morning, feeling like death warmed up. It occurred to her that she spent a disproportionate amount of her time in toilets for one reason or another. She had lain awake in pain for most of the night, so she looked pale and drawn at breakfast.

Mum quickly switched into her nurse Brown mode and took her temperature. "You're not well enough for school today. You must go back to bed and get some sleep."

"I'll be OK once I get out in the fresh air," Amy said, against all her better instincts. Her mother must not find out about the detention, or her sympathy would soon evaporate. She must force herself to go to school and get her detention over with, or she would only have to take it the following week. At least today, she would be sharing her detention with her mates making it less daunting.

Her stomach ache returned at intervals during the day. She wouldn't lie down in the medical room in case Miss Hardacre decided to send her home. Waves of dizziness and nausea swept over her throughout the detention, making it difficult for her to concentrate on the essay she was writing. Having struggled through the day, she refused to submit to the pains racking her body. With the detention completed, she staggered off to her piano lesson with an air of martyrdom. Today Mrs Falco allowed her to play using both her hands. After reaching such heights of excitement, she dragged herself home feeling drained and collapsed into the comforting dent of her little bed.

Twice in the night, she dashed across the landing to be sick in the toilet. This helped to cure her stomach ache, but in the morning, Mum insisted on sending for the doctor. After examining her, he diagnosed gastric flu, prescribing some disgusting medicine for her to take four times a day, to Amy's utter horror. She abhorred medicines and tablets, avoiding them like the plague unless it was a matter of life or death.

Coral popped in after lunch, so Amy tottered downstairs wearing her dressing gown and chatted for a while. She soon developed a headache and sore throat, so Mum swiftly packed her off, back to bed.

Amy was thankful for small mercies when the clocks went forward an hour that night. It gave her the mistaken belief that she would spend a bit less time lying in bed, bored witless and feeling sorry for herself. Her glands were swollen. She had hardly eaten a morsel since Thursday. 'I'm wasting away,' she thought despondently. If she had been feeling well, she would have been pleased about losing weight.

Amy was still running a temperature on Sunday, so she stayed in bed all day listening to her crystal radio set through the headphones. Before Christmas, she had mentioned that she wanted a small transistor radio. On Christmas morning, she had awoken delighted to discover a small white radio set in her stocking. Her enthusiasm soon subsided when she realised it wasn't a transistor but a crystal set. Dad had eagerly connected it up in her bedroom, with wires running out of the air vent in the wall to an aerial that looked like an umbrella skeleton hanging from the gutter.

He cheerfully explained how it needed no electricity or batteries. "It just uses what's called a cat's whisker," he said to a dubious Amy, "and doesn't cost anything to run, so it's the ideal radio!"

Amy was unimpressed. It sounded far more like Dad's ideal radio with no running costs. She discovered that if the wind was in the wrong direction, the reception could be almost non-existent.

She fell asleep that evening, still wearing the headphones after listening to Radio Luxemburg. She was jolted awake in the night, convinced that someone was trying to strangle her, and then realised the wires had become entwined around her neck. As she struggled to sit up, she hit her head on the glass shade of the lamp above her bed. She groaned, rubbed her head and tugged at the wires gripping her neck.

As she lay down again, she wondered whether she could be arrested for cruelty to animals. The guinea pigs' cages hadn't been cleaned out for two weeks. Would Bobby and Patsy ever forgive her?

Amy had inherited Bobby from the school's collection of pets. They were kept in the animal shed in the grounds of the Grange. She had been allowed to keep him because he was older and needed a quieter life. Each week girls could book a pet to take home for the weekend or the holidays. Golden hamsters were always the most popular pets, whereas the large black bad-tempered rabbit no-one was keen to take home, perhaps because it belonged to Mrs Snake.

One weekend, being the last pet to be booked, Amy had taken pity on the rabbit and decided to take it home. Accompanied by Coral, she carefully carried it in a box across the heath to the bus stop. Suddenly the rabbit thumped hard on the bottom of the box, causing it to burst open, and the rabbit fell out. Before the girls could catch him, he had scampered under a large thicket of prickly gorse. In a panic, fearing the wrath of Mrs Snake if they lost him, they had spent an hour scrabbling around and getting scratched before he could be coaxed out and recaptured.

Chapter Five

April
Clipped and Burnt Ears

Amy couldn't think of a worse way to spend her sixteenth birthday. "It's bad enough being born on April Fools Day. Now I've got the added misery of being cooped up in bed feeling grotty," she moaned as Mum dropped a pile of cards on the bed, newly arrived in the morning post.

"Well, look on the bright side. At least you don't have to go to school on your birthday," Mum said, picking up the breakfast tray. She left Amy to open her cards.

She had never really forgiven her mother for giving birth to her on the first day of April. 'If she had been the slightest bit considerate, she would have hung on for just one more day to save me from a heap of jokes!' Amy thought, not for the first time, as she tore open the envelopes.

Aunt Ruth called round after breakfast with her present of an umbrella in various shades of pink and two shillings to spend on sweets.

"Wow! What a gorgeous brolly – I love its pagoda shape," Amy said, starting to open it.

"Don't you go putting it up indoors. It's bad luck, and you know how superstitious your mum is," her aunt warned her.

"Yeah, you're right. I definitely don't need any more bad luck at the moment," Amy said, putting the brolly to one side.

Great Auntie Gertie had sent her a four-shilling postal order, and Ray gave her a comb, a bangle and a bag of boiled sweets.

Coral came round after school with another bracelet for her – gold plated with foreign coins hanging from it. Coral was looking whiter than usual and complained of feeling a bit unwell.

Mum looked at her suspiciously. "You've probably caught Amy's gastric flu," she pronounced, which didn't make Coral feel any better.

Amy got up for a while as Coral had brought some music for a duet. They started playing, but it sounded awful as they both felt under the weather, compounded by some of the keys sticking down. Desperate for some peace, Mum quickly dispatched her daughter back to bed, so Coral went home.

The following morning, Amy received a few belated birthday cards and a Get Well card from Aunt Ruth. Jean sent her a five-shilling postal order. Amy considered this so uncharacteristically thoughtful that she immediately sat up in bed and wrote a fourteen-page letter thanking her. She enjoyed composing it so much that she followed it with another one of similar length to Great Auntie

Gertie and a slightly shorter letter to Kathleen. Having spent most of the day scribbling frantically, the pain in Amy's hand indicated how it probably felt to suffer from writer's cramp.

Mum visited the hairdresser after lunch to have a perm and arrived home with her heavily lacquered hair resembling a rigid, tight curly wig. Wind and rain had failed to move a single hair out of place. Her bright red face, fresh from the hot dryer, beamed happily for a change. She was the only one who thought her hair looked good, though Dad loyally gave his approval.

Bad news arrived for Ray in the morning post. He had failed his eleven-plus. He was so devastated that Mum took pity on him and let him stay at home for the morning. Amy suspected he was lamenting the loss of the promised racing bike if he had passed. He only returned to school in the afternoon because Dad was there to make him go. Like Ray, Amy had also missed out on a brand new bike when she failed her eleven-plus. Her mum's old sit-up-and-beg Raleigh made a poor consolation prize.

Feeling much better now that the awful medicine was finished, Amy finally left her sick bed. That afternoon the two guinea pigs, Bobby and Patsy, found an opportunity to rebel against their squalid living conditions and made a bid for freedom. Mum spotted them running across the back lawn and called Amy to go and catch them.

"I bet those young Parks kids sneaked over the fence and undid their cage doors," Amy grumbled as she dashed out of the back door and attempted to round them up. She eventually recaptured them in a corner of the coal shed and had to sponge their coats to remove all the coal dust. Her conscience was pricking her, so she cleaned out the cages, including Snowy's. Bobby and Patsy squeaked their gratitude as they burrowed into the fresh hay.

Amy offered to make macaroni cheese for tea but used far too much macaroni and made the cheese sauce too thick, so instead of serving it with a spoon, she had to slice it up.

"This looks just the right size for wedging under the wobbly chair in my bedroom," Ray grumbled as the unappetising lump bounced onto his plate.

Amy glared at him. "At least I tried, which is more than you ever do," she retorted, "it's just a case of practise makes perfect."

"I refuse to be a guinea pig for any more of my sister's culinary disasters," Ray protested with a theatrical flourish of his knife and fork.

"Be quiet and eat your tea," Mum said sternly, for once not siding with him.

Dad leaned across the table to Amy. "Do you remember I promised you could have your ears pierced for your birthday?" Amy nodded, a mouthful of chewy macaroni preventing speech at that moment. Dad continued: "You were so keen at the time that I thought you would have booked up to have them done."

She gave her dad an apologetic look as she swallowed with some difficulty. "I've had second thoughts - I can't face being tortured for my birthday. Thanks all the same, Dad," she said, ignoring the chicken noises coming from Ray's direction. "But I might just risk having a perm instead." The chicken noises turned to derogatory snorts of laughter. Her hair had been so flat and lank as she languished in her sick bed that she was desperate to change it but was none too sure that this was a wise choice after seeing the state of her mother's hair. Ever optimistic, she kept telling herself that her hair would turn out totally different and heaps better.

Coral arrived after tea cheerfully flourishing their school reports. She was relieved not to have come down with Amy's gastric flu. Needless to say, Coral had done well in all subjects – she even achieved an A for religious knowledge. 'What a creep,' Amy thought as she studied her own marks. The best she could muster was a B+(+) for Art. She thought this was pretty good, but it didn't impress her parents.

"You must put a lot more effort into your English and Maths because these are the subjects that matter the most," Mum remonstrated. Dad threatened to go to the school and ask Mrs Slater to give her extra English homework.

"If he dares to do that, I shall definitely leave home," Amy muttered to Coral. "The very thought is enough to bring on a relapse of my rotten gastric flu."

Coral tried to cheer her up by producing a note from Yvonne asking how she was feeling. Amy jotted down a brief reply for Coral to take back in the morning. She wrote that she felt a lot better, but Mum had decided it wasn't worth her while to return to school until after the Easter holidays.

The holidays finally arrived to lift Amy out of the doldrums. She and Coral sheltered from a heavy snow shower as they walked into town under her new umbrella. Amy cashed in her postal orders totalling nine shillings and bought six jumbo hair rollers and some face cream. They stopped off at Dimashio's Ice Cream parlour for a chocolate sundae to give them the energy needed for the uphill climb home. At the top of the hill, encouraged by Coral, Amy called in at Thelma's Hair Salon and made an appointment for a perm the following Tuesday.

Amy's piano lesson that afternoon was at a slightly earlier time. Mrs Falco spent most of the lesson recalling fond memories of Italy, where she lived during her childhood. She didn't need much encouragement from Amy, who preferred listening to her reminiscences to playing tedious scales. As she was about to leave, Mrs Falco gave her another music book to practise from. On the way home, Amy stopped at the pet shop to buy a bag of pellets to keep the guinea pigs happy.

The sun melted the last of the snow the following morning, so Amy gave the guinea pigs' cages another clean to make up for neglecting them while she was ill.

Her dad strolled down the garden path wearing his greasy overalls as he had been busy servicing his motorbike. "Here's some birthday money towards your perm," he said, thrusting a ten-shilling note into her hand. Amy thanked him and stuffed the money into the pocket of her jeans.

"Can you hold Bobby while I put fresh hay in his bed?" She shoved the Abyssinian guinea pig into Dad's arms before he could escape back to tweaking the engine on his bike.

He leaned against the old chicken shed that housed the cages and stroked Bobby. "I've been thinking that you need a better piano now you're taking lessons. Some of the keys still stick on that one. Mind you, I'll have to tread carefully so as not to offend Ruth when I tell her the piano she gave you is a load of old rubbish."

"I suppose it goes without saying that you'll be on the lookout for a second-hand bargain then," Amy said with a resigned sigh. She took Bobby and settled him into his fresh bedding. "By the way, I've made a start, knitting you that green cardigan with cabling up the front, so I'm hoping to get it finished in time for your birthday as it's not 'til November. I'm pretty expert at cabling since that cable pattern on my yellow jumper turned out so well."

"I'll look forward to wearing it," Dad declared with a smile as he walked away. Mum had always knitted Dad's cardigans. However, Amy had persuaded Mum to let her knit the cardigan using the cable pattern now that she had proved her competence.

With the guinea pigs happily munching on pellets and a carrot in their clean cages, Amy went indoors and dug out her knitting. She needed a pair of size seven needles after completing the ribbing, with number nines. Mum was using her number sevens, so she suggested Amy pop across the green to borrow a pair from Mrs Boddington, who lived next door to the Williams. She, too, hailed from Wales. Amy was often tempted to compare their corner of the Crescent to a mini Rhondda Valley, especially on a warm summer's evening when the neighbours occasionally gathered on the green for a chat. The unmistakable singsong lilt of Welsh accents would drift across the green and through the open windows. Lucy Williams was very proud that she could say several words and phrases in Welsh. She would find any excuse to slip them into a conversation.

"I must pay a visit to my barber today," Dad announced, inspecting his thinning hair in the kitchen mirror after breakfast on Sunday morning. He visited Gordon Williams once a month for his short back and sides. The Williams' kitchen became an improvised barber's shop. Gordon owned a pair of clippers, though he had never trained as a barber, but then he didn't charge for his services which suited Dad just fine. He returned home with his hair shorn several inches above his ears – just how he liked it. Ray no longer accompanied Dad for a free haircut since the occasion when Mr Williams, engrossed in discussing with Dad the pitfalls of various pesticides used on vegetables, accidentally clipped Ray's ear lobe. Ray yelled and bled like a stuck pig. Nowadays, he insisted on going to a bona fide barber, much to Dad's dismay at the unnecessary expense.

This was Gordon's contribution to the community, mainly around the green, while Dad's contribution was a set of sweep's brushes. He didn't believe in paying someone to sweep the chimney when he could do the job just as well himself. Gordon got his chimney swept in return for the haircuts, and the brushes were available to anyone else who wanted to clean their own chimney. Word quickly spread when a chimney was being swept. The children would rush outside, necks craning upwards, staring expectantly at the chimney pot, waiting for the telltale puff of soot that proclaimed the imminent arrival of the brush. When the brush shot out of the chimney pot, a loud cheer would accompany it, and someone was promptly dispatched to tell Dad or whoever was on the other end that they could stop shoving rods up the chimney. Dad kept an old pair of overalls and a beret for the dirty job and carefully sealed the fireplace with old sheets to prevent any soot from seeping into the lounge. He knew that if one speck of soot ended up on the carpet or chairs, he would have Mum's wrath descending on him.

Amy got up early Tuesday morning to wash and set her hair ready for her intrepid visit to Thelma's for a perm. The following hours turned into a nightmare as her worst fears were realised. The hairdresser began by cutting her hair far too short and then used too strong a perm, which left her hair with one mass of frizz. To add injury, to insult, bright red blisters developed on her ear lobes, where they were exposed to the hottest heat from the hair dryer. The stupid hairdresser had turned the heat setting to high and left the control switch hanging out of reach down the back of the chair. The dryers were in a separate room, and Amy, unaccustomed to the contraption, found herself trapped and alone, suffering slow torture and unable to attract the attention of the hairdresser. She had always distrusted hairdressers, and now she positively loathed them.

She stopped off at Aunt Ruth's on her way home, hoping for some sympathy over a cup of tea, but her aunt didn't help much. "I don't know what you're worried about, dear, I think your hair looks perfectly lovely," she said as she offered Amy a biscuit, "though it's a shame you got your ears burnt in the process."

'There's no accounting for taste,' Amy thought as she continued on her way home, 'maybe she was just trying to cheer me up.'

She arrived home in a foul mood, slammed the back door and stomped through the house and into the lounge. "I'll never go near another hairdresser as long as I live!" she snarled, glaring at one and all. Even Ray felt sufficiently intimidated not to risk a snigger. She spent the rest of the day with a scarf tied tightly around her head.

In the morning, Amy washed and reset her hair behind her ears, but it emphasised her glowing ear lobes, so she had to comb it forward. No matter how she tried to adjust the style, she still disliked it intensely. Ray could see how fed up she was, so for once, he showed a little brotherly love by buying her a sixpenny chocolate crème egg to cheer her up as he knew how much she liked them.

Meanwhile, Dad found a piano advertised in the paper, so the next day he took Amy on his motorbike for a ride out to a small rural village to look at it. Amy assumed that the owners of the big posh house were wealthy, as they kept a huge, ferocious-looking Alsatian dog to guard their property. Fortunately, the dog was safely chained to his kennel when they arrived at the front door.

The piano looked well cared for, and when the lady offered to deliver it, Dad said he'd have it straight away and didn't even bother to haggle over the price.

The skies opened just as they were about to leave, and a heavy shower quickly soaked everything. The lady insisted Amy borrow her daughter's mac. Amy thanked her but was horrified to see the lady bring out a dreaded green Grammar School mac.

"I'll never live this down if anyone I know sees me in Grammar togs," she whispered to Dad through clenched teeth.

She was relieved to reach home unseen. They entered an empty house to discover that Mum had gone shopping. She had thoughtfully left a note suggesting Amy start on some housework.

"I'm supposed to be on holiday," she moaned. "What a life! This is no better than slave labour." She reluctantly dragged the vacuum out of the kitchen cupboard while Dad, ignoring her complaints, set about preparing the vegetables for dinner.

"What other mother has her family running around doing all her work for her?" Amy grumbled as she manhandled the vacuum towards the lounge.

"It's not often your mother asks for help around the house," Dad called after her, "she'll appreciate coming home to a clean lounge."

"She just better, had!" Amy retorted, kicking the vacuum.

In the morning post, Amy received ten shillings for her birthday from Aunt Nora and an extra large Easter egg to share with Ray. Aunt Nora was her mum's eldest sister and a bit of a dragon. She would sweep majestically into a room with her hair meticulously coiffed and her grand stature emphasised by her sumptuous furs. Amy was forcefully reminded of Lady Bracknell in the play 'The Importance of Being Earnest'. She wouldn't have been surprised if her aunt had fallen into character and boomed out those immortal words: "A handbag?" Amy was confident her aunt could give the Queen an inferiority complex. Her visits were infrequent affairs guaranteed to send Mum into a flurry of activity, frantically polishing the silver and digging out the best linen tablecloths and napkins. The house had to be even more spotless than usual, ready for any stringent scrutinising by her ultra-fussy sister.

Being Good Friday, they had hot cross buns for tea, and as Amy buttered her bun, she glanced out of the dining room window to discover the guinea pigs had escaped again.

"I think they have learnt how to undo the cage doors on their own without the help of the Parks kids," Amy declared as she jumped up and hurried outside. Bobby and Patsy were happily nibbling grass on the back lawn and were quite amenable to being recaptured for once.

After lunch on Saturday, Amy walked to Aunt Ruth's. On the way, she met Dennis the Menace meandering home from the pub, slightly the worse for drink, and he persuaded her to part with her last fag.

Aunt Ruth presented her with a freshly minted silver half-crown plus one for Ray because she hadn't bought any Easter eggs.

Amy arrived home to find her new piano had been safely delivered and the Grammar School mac returned. Aunt Ruth's old piano was now relegated to the back garden.

"I'll chop it up for firewood," Dad said cheerfully.

"That's her darling Alwyn's piano, and if Aunt Ruth finds out, she'll have your guts for garters!" Amy told him, but he remained unconcerned.

The rain was a permanent fixture for the whole of Easter Day. Amy ate her Easter egg from Mum and Dad and then made a start on the large one from Aunt Nora, which she was meant to share with her brother. Aunt Nora sent her nephew and niece an elaborately decorated Easter egg every year, beautifully arranged in its box, with the chocolate assortment displayed separately, not squashed inside the egg like lesser Easter eggs.

Amy let Ruby out of her cage for a run in the lounge while she listened to her records. She watched Ruby scaling the front of the armchair, pleased to see how well her broken leg had healed, leaving her foot splayed out a little to the side, but it didn't appear to cause her any problems. Ruby found a large piece of Ray's Easter egg lying on the arm of the chair, so she promptly stuffed it into her pouch and ran off looking distinctly lopsided. Ray came in and was far from amused when Amy told him what Ruby had done.

"Don't worry, I'll get it back for you from Ruby's larder once she's disgorged it," she said, laughing.

"You needn't bother!" Ray retorted, pulling a face.

For a while, Dad had been hinting at an outing to the zoo on Easter Monday. Now that day had arrived, he let everyone down by deciding his allotment needed urgent attention. Amy was bored out of her skin, so she spent an hour in the kitchen making an apple sponge for dessert. Then, still desperate to do something to pass the time, she washed the dishes, dusted the lounge and finally brought the washing in from off the line. Mum's Monday washday routine was immovable. It had been drummed into her by her mother. Her own rustic routines, deep in the heart of rural Suffolk, bereft of modern labour-saving appliances and hot and cold running water, had been equally rigid.

Mum never allowed Christmas, birthdays or bank holidays to interfere with her weekly wash every Monday morning, come hell or high water.

The next evening Amy dutifully sat down and wrote a thank you note to Aunt Nora for the money and Easter egg. Then she and Ray set about finishing the egg, with the usual quibbling over the assorted chocolates. Amy spotted Yvonne coming down the front garden path, so feeling generous, she left Ray the last few chocolates and went to open the door.

"Guess what!" Yvonne was bursting to tell her some news.

"Hang on a minute," Amy said and took her down the hall into the relative privacy of the kitchen. "So, what's up?"

"I'm going on holiday to Bognor Regis with my parents this summer, and they suggested you come along too! Won't that be great?"

Amy gave a whoop. "We'll have a smashing time. Just think – sunbathing on the beach all day and finding a good disco or club to go to in the evening," she said, her eyes sparkling. She was imagining a fun-packed holiday with Yvonne until it sank in just what Yvonne had said. "Your parents are coming? Won't they want to keep close tabs on us most of the time?"

"Oh, they won't be a problem," Yvonne said airily, "we'll easily give them the slip."

Amy made two cups of coffee while Yvonne fished around in her skirt pocket and produced a small package wrapped in wallpaper. "I nearly forgot, Bat, happy birthday!" she said, thrusting the present into Amy's hand. "Sorry about the wrapping." Amy undid it to find a small tartan purse shaped like a tam-o'-shanter, complete with a black bobble.

"Er, thanks, Yvonne," Amy said dubiously, suspicious that it was an unwanted present Yvonne had received from some Scottish relative.

Yvonne sipped her coffee and then remembered another piece of news. "By the way, Alex has packed me up – well, actually, it was mutual. We've been doing nothing but argue lately, so I suppose it was inevitable." Amy could tell she didn't appear to be too bothered by the breakup.

They listened to the radio and discussed ways of giving Yvonne's parents the slip at Bognor. They didn't realise how late it was until Yvonne glanced at her watch and saw that she had missed her last bus home.

Amy persuaded her dad to give Yvonne a lift on his bike. He didn't mind getting togged up in his biking clothes as he was in a good mood. Unlike Amy, Yvonne didn't find the whole scenario acutely embarrassing. She giggled as she struggled to cock her leg over the small pillion and then clung onto Dad's belt to stop herself from falling off.

In the morning, Amy went to the phone box and rang Jean to see if there was the remotest chance of paying her a brief visit.

Jean's voice betrayed a hint of panic. "Sorry, but I'm about to remove some facial hair, and then I'm visiting an invalid aunt for the rest of the day."

Amy walked home, chuckling to herself. 'What a ridiculous story,' she thought, 'I hadn't noticed that Jean was growing a beard when I last saw her at school!'

Yvonne came over after lunch and remembered to bring the Beatles record that she had kept for nearly a month. Amy was extremely relieved to finally get it back. They danced to records for a while, but Yvonne soon got out of breath and slumped into an armchair.

"Let's have a rest," she gasped, fanning herself with a copy of the Radio Times that Mum kept in a stiffened, intricately embroidered cover. "You'll be pleased to know that I've arranged a date for us on Saturday night with a couple of boys from my local youth club. They're nice lads and it should be a bit of a laugh."

"I'm not keen for you to make arrangements on my behalf without consulting me first," Amy said disdainfully.

"Oh, come off it, Bat, don't be such a killjoy. You can't let me down, and I guarantee we'll have a great time."

Amy thought for a moment, somewhat dubious about this blind date. "Well, I suppose I could go," she said, "even if it's only to satisfy my curiosity."

Yvonne stayed for tea, and afterwards, they sneaked into the toilet for a quick fag before she caught her bus home. There was just room for them to stand with a foot each on either side of the toilet seat and take turns puffing smoke out of the little window. Miraculously the toilet seat took the extra strain without breaking. While enjoying their illicit smoke, they arranged an outing to London the following day.

"We'll have a terrific day, Bat, just wait and see," Yvonne promised as she left to catch her bus.

Mum did a Miss Marple impersonation when she discovered a fag end floating in the loo. Dad rolled his own, and a shrewd piece of detective work revealed that this was a cork tip, so she confronted Amy with the evidence. Being an abject coward, Amy put the blame squarely on Yvonne because she knew Mum would never rebuke her.

Amy hauled herself out of bed the following morning at an unearthly hour to catch the bus to Yvonne's. She found her ready and waiting so they were soon travelling on the train to London Bridge. From there, they walked to the Tower of London with Yvonne needing the sustenance of coffee and rum babas from three Wimpy Bars en route.

At the tower, they wandered around inspecting the various places people had been incarcerated or beheaded. There was a long queue to see the crown jewels, so they didn't bother to wait. Instead, they headed off to the Kenya Coffee House at Bayswater, where Alex's sister, Fiona, worked as a waitress. They had lunch there, and Fiona brought them an enormous knickerbocker glory each.

She chatted with them between serving other customers. "I wish you and Alex would get back together again," she said wistfully, "I'm fed up seeing him moping around the house."

"Och, Fee, he didna seem that bothered when we broke up. He'll soon find someone else," Yvonne said and glanced around the dimly lit restaurant with its jungle of realistic-looking plastic plants sprouting everywhere. "How about trying to get us Saturday jobs here? I'm sure we could do waitressing dead easy." Amy wasn't keen on travelling all the way to London to work for one day a week. Neither did she like the prospect of waiting on people, but she refrained from saying as much. Fiona promised to put in a good word for them.

They spent the afternoon browsing around the shops before visiting a different Kenya Coffee

House, this time in Chelsea, for a bite to eat. An hour later, Yvonne dragged a protesting Amy into another Wimpy Bar for coffee and chips. Amy struggled to keep up with Yvonne's healthy appetite. As they made their way back to the station, a couple of sailors fell into step, beside them and started chatting them up.

"Ignore them," Amy whispered, ever wary of talking to strangers, but Yvonne had no reservations. The one who introduced himself as Bob held a bloodstained handkerchief against his nose.

"That looks like a bad nosebleed you've got there," Yvonne remarked and pulled the handkerchief away to get a better look. "It's still bleeding quite a lot – I think you ought to get it seen to. Come on – there's a small hospital not far from here."

She grabbed his arm and led him back the way they had come. Amy followed behind and asked his friend if he had been in a fight, but he strenuously denied it. At the hospital, a nurse successfully staunched the flow. As a token of his gratitude, Bob insisted on taking the girls into a nearby pub for a quick drink before they caught their train home.

The sailors were pleasant enough and keen to meet them the following night at Charing Cross to take them for a meal or a show.

"Och, that sounds great," Yvonne said without hesitating. She gave Bob her phone number. "Give me a ring tomorrow to arrange a time."

Mrs Falco was pleased with Amy's progress at her piano lesson on Friday, even though she had done virtually no practising. On her way home, she tried to phone Yvonne, but the first two phone boxes were out of order. Finally, at the box outside Coral's house, she got through to her.

"Sorry, but I've got some bad news," Yvonne said. "Those two sailors we met in London last night rang to apologise because they've got to leave a day early. They'll be setting sail tonight, so they can't meet us after all."

"Oh well, not to worry," Amy said, cheerfully. "There's still that date you arranged for us for tomorrow night."

"Er, there's been a slight hitch with that plan too."

"How do you mean?"

"Well, they've had to cancel their date too. Would you believe it – one of them has developed mumps!"

"We're not having much luck with boys, are we?" Amy said with a sigh.

"Oh, don't let it get you down," Yvonne said blithely. "Who needs boys? Tell you what – I'll come over after tea, and you can have another go at teaching me the new dance that you and Tibs concocted. I'll even bring some fags with me." The pips went before Amy could warn Yvonne about dropping fag ends down the loo.

Saturday morning, Amy awoke to the sound of rain pattering against her bedroom window. She still felt tired after an exhausting evening spent cavorting around the lounge, trying to avoid having her toes trodden on by Yvonne. After breakfast, feeling bored, she huddled under her pagoda brolly as she hurried round to Coral's to see if she fancied playing cards.

She had barely arrived on the doorstep when Coral flung open the door and dragged her inside. "Come and see what I've got," she said excitedly, taking Amy into the lounge to show off her brand new red and cream Dansette record player. Amy couldn't help being just a little envious as she had wanted one for years. From the age of ten, she had carefully saved up her weekly pocket money, becoming almost scrooge-like in the process. Her determination had never wavered: no treats and no ice creams. Two shillings a week, then two shillings and sixpence until she reached the grand total of thirteen pounds she had saved, but Dansette record players cost fifteen pounds. Mr Hamilton heard of her epic three-year battle and took pity on her. He promised he could get her a similar one at trade price and save her another four months of hard saving. He turned up one day with a Regentone which Amy had never heard of. Its boxy shape lacked the classy look of the Dansette. Despite being a little disappointed, Amy was thrilled to be able to play records at long last.

That afternoon, Mr and Mrs Hamilton and Kathleen arrived unannounced for an impromptu visit, so Mum invited them to stay for tea. Kathleen and Amy played a game of rummy while Ruby, freed from her cage to exercise, explored the skirting boards around the lounge.

Kathleen suddenly let out a scream. Ruby, fancying a bit of mountaineering, was ambitiously scaling the north face of Kathleen's chunky legs by hooking her claws into her stockings. Hamsters can move very quickly when frightened. Kathleen's scream sent Ruby scurrying upwards to seek sanctuary under the folds of her skirt, which only served to heighten her panic. Amy swiftly remedied the situation by grabbing Ruby before she attempted to climb any higher. Only after Ruby had been safely secured in her cage, out of harm's way, could Kathleen relax again.

The Browns were invited to make a return visit to the Hamiltons the following afternoon for Sunday tea. Mr Hamilton collected them as usual. After a formal meal around the dining room table, they retired to the lounge to play their favourite game of Newmarket using buttons for stakes. Dad's good behaviour throughout the meal petered out once the cards were dealt. As previously, he somehow managed to have the key card that everyone else needed. While they frantically searched through their own cards, he would beam innocently with the crucial card clamped triumphantly to his bald patch for all to see..... eventually. Amy had never known anyone so lucky at cards. Once he had won most of the buttons, everyone else conceded defeat.

Then Mrs Hamilton ruined the evening by suggesting that Amy and Kathleen entertain everyone on the piano. Amy felt nervous at the prospect, of attempting a duet on their posh modern piano. Kathleen, being the more accomplished player, confidently took the lead. Somehow even Amy's wrong notes sounded acceptable on their upright with its mellow tone.

As they were preparing to be chauffeured home by Mr Hamilton, Mum turned to Kathleen.

"If it's all right with your mother, why don't you come over for tea on Tuesday afternoon, as it's the last day of the holidays?" Kathleen accepted straight away, sure that her mother wouldn't mind.

Amy rang Yvonne in the morning and arranged to meet her that evening at the station. Her dad had relented on his ban of the Railway Tavern, with a little persuasion from the gingerbread finger biscuits. She waited impatiently on the platform for over half an hour until Yvonne eventually arrived by a later train. She jumped out of the carriage breathless and dishevelled as though she had just run all the way. Her ebullience soon restored Amy's good humour as they crossed the road to the Railway Tavern, intent on enjoying themselves. They shoved their way through the crowd heading for the dance room, then spotted Lynn and Vie perched on stools, drinking at the bar.

Yvonne waved to them. "Hi, Vie," she yelled, "are you and Lynn coming through to the back room for a dance?"

"We might come later," Vie said, "only I'm waiting for Steve."

As Yvonne and Amy entered the dance room, the heat and noise hit them like a wall. Yvonne wandered off and started flirting outrageously with a group of boys she didn't know. A Ringo lookalike in a leather Beatle jacket asked Amy for a dance. As they smooched around the floor, he told her his name was Tony and described his zany life in a London flat shared with a crowd of high-spirited mates.

"Why don't you and some of your mates come to a party at the weekend up at our flat?" he suggested. "Our parties can get a bit wild, but I promise you'll have a terrific time."

Amy knew it was useless to even consider it. "Sounds great, but my mother would have a blue fit if I asked to go to a party in London," she said.

"You ought to cut the apron strings and do your own thing," he urged, "you haven't lived 'til you discover the fun and freedom of living in your own pad."

"I'm sure you're right," Amy agreed. "One day I would love to have my own flat in London. It'd be great to have no parents breathing down my neck and be able to do whatever I like with my mates. I think it would be utter bliss!"

She noticed Yvonne's flirting getting out of hand. Her behaviour began to irritate Amy, so she excused herself from Tony's embrace and went over to remonstrate with her. En route, she sidestepped around a large group chatting together and unintentionally walked through an open doorway. To her intense embarrassment, she found herself in the gents' loo. She re-emerged into the dance room red-faced, and Yvonne made matters worse by pointing and shrieking with laughter. Amy feared she would end up rolling on the floor and peeing her breeks at any moment, but for once, she managed to control herself.

On Tuesday morning, Amy rang Kathleen and arranged to meet her at the local museum in the afternoon as she would be in town shopping.

Mum and Amy caught the bus into town and went to the small department store that stocked her school uniform so that Mum could buy her a new knife-pleated winter skirt for school. While Mum finished her shopping, Amy went to meet Kathleen, and they wandered around the museum gazing at the relics and artefacts. Kathleen was in her element, so Amy tried to show a vestige of interest.

A whole room had been devoted to a reconstruction of the payment system of the haberdashery and clothing shop that had recently closed in the High Street. The shop had enthralled Amy for as long as she could remember. Any excuse to go in and buy something or pretend to browse. Then she could watch the spectacle of wooden pots containing customers' payments, suspended on complex tram lines, whizzing overhead to the cashier. She sat high up in a small booth at the rear of the shop. The pots with their screw-top lids were fired off on their journeys by the shop assistant tugging on a wooden handle that looked like a loo chain. They hurtled across the ceiling at high speed to the cashier, who would secure the change and receipts into the pots and then send them, flying back, to the correct counter. Saturdays were the best time to visit the shop when all the counters were working flat out and the air buzzed with the little wooden pots criss-crossing above customers' heads. Amy had always marvelled at the way they inevitably found their correct destination. She found it immensely sad to see this once industrious and fascinating device now reduced to an immobile exhibit in a dusty museum. She consoled herself with the thought that, at least, it had been preserved for posterity.

Afterwards, they met Amy's mum and caught the bus home for tea. Coral emerged from the porch as they approached the front gate. She had been knocking fruitlessly on the front door, so Mum, being in a good mood, invited her to stay for tea.

Ray came in just as they were sitting down to eat. He squeezed in at the corner of the table next to the breadboard and betrayed his lack of breeding by shamelessly raising one cheek and letting rip with a loud fart. Mum immediately went into a hot fluster, firing off inane questions at Kathleen about the museum in a vain attempt to distract her. The girls played rummy after tea until the time came for Kathleen to leave, so Coral and Amy walked with her to the bus stop.

"Come over to tea on Saturday, Amy," Kathleen invited as she jumped onto the bus. "I've got some terrific pics of Cliff for you."

"Great! See you Saturday." Amy found the promise of dishy pictures of Cliff irresistible.

At the start of the summer term, Amy and Coral walked the three miles to school to save on their bus fares. They had agreed to wear their blue summer uniforms as this was the only term they were permitted. They discovered that they stuck out like a pair of blue twits in a sea of burgundy when they arrived at school because everyone else was still in winter togs.

During registration, Mrs Butler informed the class that she intended to leave at the end of term because she was expecting a baby. The girls had developed a genuine affection for their easygoing form mistress. They congratulated her and told her how much they would miss her.

Now that the summer term had arrived, tennis replaced hockey during double games, which pleased most of 5G2. Yvonne tried an overhead lob as the girls practised on the asphalt courts. She smashed the ball out of bounds, over the high fence and into the thick bushes on the heath. Amy and Yvonne spent over half the lesson searching for it. Yvonne eventually spotted the ball under a holly bush and tore her P.E. blouse as she tried to retrieve it.

"Oh, bugger it! Mum will be furious when she sees that," Yvonne said crossly.

Amy examined the ripped sleeve. "I think it can be mended so that it'll hardly show," she declared, "I'll take it home tonight and ask Mum to have a go if you like. She's great at invisible mending."

"Oh, would you, Bat?" Yvonne brightened up. "You're a real lifesaver! I'd have been in deep trouble at home."

Next to the holly bush, they discovered a wild cherry tree. Yvonne's eyes lit up. "Ooh, look at all that blossom, we must come back later when the cherries are ripe."

After their lunch, as the girls headed for the lower lawn in the Manor grounds, Amy handed over her final payment to Jean for the brown suede jerkin. She could call it her own at last. She stared at Jean's left cheek. "What's that on your face?"

Jean felt a bit self-conscious about a scabby lump. It had developed on her cheek towards the end of the holidays. "I think it might be impetigo," she said.

"And what's that when it's at home?" Amy demanded, suspicious that it was something she had invented.

"Mum told me it's a skin complaint which can be contagious," Jean said apologetically. Amy quickly took a step away from her upon hearing this worrying news. The last thing she wanted was sores erupting all over her face.

"What were you thinking, coming back to school with a contagious disease?" she yelled. "How stupid can you get?"

An embarrassed Jean tried to calm Amy. "It's alright – I've got a doctor's appointment later today, to get it diagnosed properly, so perhaps you and Yvonne could come with me to the bus stop?" Amy was only too happy to oblige to get her removed as far away as possible.

That evening, Mum commandeered the television to watch the highlights of the sumptuous wedding of Princess Alexandra, hailed as the wedding of the year. Mum, being an ardent royalist, was glued to every moment.

Amy took advantage of her good mood from enjoying the lavish spectacle to show her the ripped blouse. "I told Yvonne what a marvellous invisible mender you are," Amy said, hoping a bit of flattery would work wonders. Mum was only too happy to prove her right. She rummaged around in her needlework drawer at the bottom of the sideboard. She found needle and thread and set to work.

After school the next day, Amy and Coral stopped off in town on their way home so that Amy could buy some navy material and a pattern as she wanted to make a straight skirt.

At home after tea, Dad and Mum walked over to Ray's school to discuss with his teachers which secondary school he would be attending the following term. Their absence gave Amy a rare opportunity to play her records at full volume. In her opinion, this was the only way to fully appreciate them.

In the cloakroom the following morning, Pam, being the artistic one, drew a map for Amy so that she could complete her geography homework. She also gave Amy three shillings for her birthday. Yvonne spotted the money changing hands and promptly borrowed a shilling, which peeved Amy.

"That's the last time I help her out of a jam. She can darn her own flippin' clothes in future," she muttered crossly to Pam.

Amy had walked three miles to school and the same going home, followed by a further mile there and back to her piano lesson. That evening her legs ached from all the unaccustomed exercise. She found herself with no option but to drag her aching legs over to Ray's school with Mum and Dad for the open day. They insisted on her accompanying them to look at his work because Mrs Denton had complained about the noise she made with her record player the previous evening.

Ray's school had been her junior school too, and Amy felt awkward meeting her old teachers again. These days Midi Middleton limped and had to walk with the aid of a stick, but he still cut a formidable figure. Amy was intrigued to see 'Whiskers', his pet paintbrush, protruding from his jacket pocket, as usual, handy for striking some poor unsuspecting miscreant.

The boys always fared better than the girls when it came to punishment. Amy was sure, from her experience of a year spent in his class, that he didn't like girls very much. When the boys misbehaved, they had to stand up and bend over to be whacked across the buttocks by Whiskers. Some of the more saucy boys, mimicking their comic book heroes, would discreetly slip an exercise book into the seat of their pants without Midi noticing. No doubt he would have had irate parents beating a path to his door if the girls were meted out, the same punishment. They received their chastisement with a sharp rap across bare knuckles, which was far more painful.

Despite his foibles with 'Whiskers', Midi was extremely popular at the Christmas party every year when he performed clever magic tricks with playing cards and objects. He made them disappear and then reappear in a different place entirely. The children were entranced and mystified as to how he did it.

Ray's class had each written an essay in their neatest handwriting entitled 'A noise in the night', and the best were displayed on the wall. Ray's was among them. He described how he awoke one night to the sound of running water. Then it stopped, and just as he began to doze off, he was reawakened by a plopping noise. Still puzzled at breakfast the following morning, he asked Dad what it could have been.

"Don't be daft," Dad told him, "it was only your mother in the toilet!"

Ray obviously had no hang-ups writing about bodily functions. Needless to say, Mum was mortified that he had written such a thing about her. Worse still, it was exhibited on the classroom wall for all and sundry to read. Dad roared with laughter, but Mum failed to see anything remotely funny. Amy chuckled to herself. This confirmed what she had long suspected: Ray had inherited his dad's toilet humour.

Amy caught the bus over to Kathleen's on Saturday afternoon. They played rummy and Black Maria with Rosamund and Annette until teatime. Kathleen gave her the promised pictures of Cliff. She spread them out on the dining room table so they could drool over them. "They're great – I shall stick them on my bedroom wall with all the others," Amy said.

Then Kathleen dropped a bombshell. "I think you know a friend of mine from church. Her name is Maud Catting, and she mentioned the other day that she teaches at the Technical High School that you attend, Amy."

Amy was gobsmacked that Kathleen could be friends with Catty Catting. "You mean you actually like her?" she asked in disbelief.

Kathleen smiled. "She's very nice when you get to know her socially."

Rosamund came in with cutlery and place-mats to lay the table ready for tea. "We're off to Norfolk with Mummy in the morning," she informed Amy, "we'll be staying with our aunt." Amy couldn't help envying the extra-long holidays they enjoyed at their private school.

After tea, Mr Hamilton gave her a lift home. She fervently hoped her mum wouldn't find out that he would be fending for himself for a whole week again. Amy knew she'd invite him over to stay with them as before and make Amy once more forfeit her bed. Fortunately, he didn't mention it.

Amy set to work Sunday afternoon, cutting out her skirt from the navy material she had bought. Cliff appeared in his own show on television that evening so Amy was glued to the screen, lapping up every minute. Afterwards, she tried adjusting the pattern so that the skirt would fit tightly.

Monday morning dawned with pouring rain. Being Pam's birthday, Amy gave her two shillings towards her birthday money in the cloakroom. "We'll celebrate tonight at the Railway Tavern," Amy promised her.

Vie overheard the arrangement as she took off her wet coat in the next row and jumped onto the low bench to peer over the coats. "Me and Lynn will be going too, so we'll meet you there. It should be a good night."

Just as Vie predicted, the Railway Tavern was good but, as usual, packed out and far too hot. Vie and Lynn left early. Amy thought Vie looked a little fed up because she wasn't seeing Steve anymore.

"I don't know what went wrong between them," she said to Pam as they ordered ice-cold orange drinks at the bar, "she's very reluctant to talk about it."

Pam just shrugged. "By the way, I rang Yvonne to see what time she would be arriving at the station tonight, but she's had a row with her father, and he won't allow her out." Then Pam spotted Yvonne's new boyfriend, John, chatting to someone nearby, so she pushed her way through the crowd to pass on Yvonne's message that she wouldn't be able to meet him there.

Later, while Pam was in the loo, Amy asked the group on stage to play 'Happy Birthday' for her, which they were very pleased to do. As she emerged from the ladies toilet, a bright spotlight picked her out while she was still adjusting her skirt. She flushed with embarrassment as everyone sang 'Happy Birthday' to her but thoroughly enjoyed all the attention until someone yelled: "Give her the bumps!" She immediately dived into the loo and refused to venture out again until she felt it was safe.

After the rain of the previous day, Tuesday, by contrast, was hot and sunny all day.

Yvonne stomped into the form room for registration, looking fed up. "Would you believe it," she fumed, "my parents are packing me off to my gran's in Dundee for most of the summer holiday. I suppose they think it'll keep me out of mischief!" Yvonne was far from pleased with these new arrangements, which had been the cause of the friction yesterday with her stepfather.

"That means there'll be no holiday in Bognor now!" Amy said in dismay, "and I was so looking forward to it."

Yvonne thought of something that might cheer her up. She dug around in her satchel and produced a record of 'Cupboard Love' by John Leyton. "You can borrow this, providing you lend me 'Running Scared' by Roy Orbison," Amy agreed to bring it to school for her in the morning.

Chapter Six

May
The Scala Opens

Amy slung her satchel across Coral's bedroom and flopped down on her bed. She was feeling disheartened. Coral had been off school with a bilious attack and was looking as white as her pillow, curled up in bed studying a book on shorthand because she had an exam coming up.

"You look as fed up as I feel," Coral observed, putting her book aside. "What's the matter?"

Amy sighed. "Oh, you don't want to hear about my troubles. Besides, I popped in to see if you're feeling any better, but by the look of you, I'd say you'll still be in bed tomorrow."

"Thanks. You really know how to cheer me up," Coral said with a weak smile. "Take my mind off my nausea, and tell me what you've been up to."

"Well, needless to say, I've endured horrendously boring lessons all day and been given loads of homework. Then to top it all, me and Vie had a wasted trip into town after school to ask about Saturday jobs. We tried International and the Co-op, but neither had any vacancies."

"That's a bit of a coincidence – you want a job at the International, and my mum has just started there part-time." Coral pulled herself up onto one elbow. "Since they bought out David Greig, International has expanded and modernised the shop. They advertised for part-time help, so Mum ignored Dad ranting on with a hundred and one reasons why she should stay at home and decided it was time to do her own thing. She applied and got a job working on the cheese section of the new deli counter."

"That's interesting," Amy said, brightening up, "perhaps she could put in a word for me if a vacancy for a Saturday job crops up."

Coral promised to ask her. Amy stood up and heaved her bulging satchel onto her shoulder. "I'll call in to see how you're getting on tomorrow," she said, leaving Coral to her shorthand swotting.

Yvonne accompanied Amy home after school the next day. Fortunately, Mum was happy to lay an extra place for tea. If anyone else had turned up, unannounced, it would have thrown her into a bad mood.

"John's taking me ice skating this evening," Yvonne said as she and Amy climbed the stairs to Amy's bedroom after tea. "I'm hoping you'll be able to help me out because I don't have any suitable clothes to wear."

"I suppose you'd better look through my wardrobe," Amy said, suspecting that this had been Yvonne's real motive all along in wanting to accompany her home. Yvonne found a pair of jeans and a jumper that fitted her, so she quickly changed before rushing off to meet John, leaving Amy late for her piano lesson.

Mrs Falco felt Amy had progressed sufficiently to warrant moving on to a new book. Amy had profound misgivings when she saw the complicated music it contained.

On her way home, she called in to see Coral and found her lounging on the settee, looking much healthier. She assured Amy she'd be back at school on Monday.

Saturday morning, with the weekend chore of cleaning out the guinea pigs' cages and Ruby's cage done, Amy tackled the challenge of making a meat pie for dinner. Coral and her friend, Janet, arrived to borrow some records just as she was rolling out the pastry.

After they had left, Yvonne turned up briefly to collect her school clothes, but she had forgotten to return Amy's jeans and jumper. "We had a great time last night at Streatham Ice Rink – you should come sometime, Bat," Yvonne said, stuffing her clothes into the saddlebag on the back of her bike. "I can't stop because I'm meeting John up in London – he's taking me for a meal followed by a posh dance."

"Well, enjoy yourself, and I'll see you at school on Monday," Amy said. She watched her friend cycle off up the road, wondering if she would ever see her clothes again.

At dinnertime, the whole family agreed the meat pie tasted delicious – even Ray was complimentary. Amy glowed in their praise which made a pleasant change from cringing at the usual grumbles to her culinary disasters.

In the afternoon, Ray went to the swimming baths with his mates as the weather had turned warm. The sun's heat was essential to compensate for the freezing water in the unheated outdoor pool. The town desperately needed an indoor pool, but so far, only empty promises had been forthcoming from the council.

Sunday morning, Amy got up, still feeling unhappy with her hair. She tugged it into various styles, then rolled it into a French pleat. She liked this more sophisticated style because it made her look slightly older.

Coral arrived to return the records she had borrowed and stayed to help Amy finish her homework. It included a challenging domestic science project on eggs that Amy had no idea how to tackle. "By the way, I like your new hairdo," Coral said as she was leaving. Knowing Coral's dubious taste, Amy wondered whether she should keep it.

Dad had taken himself off to bed, convinced he was coming down with the 'flu. Mum laid down her knitting as Amy came back into the lounge.

"It's always the same with your father," she grumbled, "to listen to him, you'd think that no-one else ever suffers from a cold as badly as he does. He'll have me running up and down those stairs at his beck and call, just you wait and see."

Amy had a foreboding that the next few days would be hell with Mum taking out her bad temper on her and even her darling Ray. She made a mental note to keep a low profile.

Monday morning, Jean was back at school minus her contagious scabby lump. Her doctor had confirmed it was impetigo.

Pam and Amy wandered down to the large gloomy oval pond that lurked deep in the Manor grounds during the lunch hour and sat on the stone edge, trying to fish for newts with their hands. They eventually caught two and then returned them to their watery home.

"I'm fed up, Bat. Let's go to the Railway Tavern tonight," Pam suggested, drying her hands on her skirt. "It ought to be good."

"D'you know who's on, Tibs?"

"No, but the groups that play there are usually quite good."

They discussed what they would wear as they strolled across the road to the Grange for English with Mrs Slater.

The last lesson of the day was music with the Snake. She was in a formidable mood that worsened by the minute as she tried to coax a reasonable rendition of 'Nymphs and Shepherds' out of the class. Only Yvonne showed any enthusiasm. She gave it her best shot, decibels above everyone else, which evolved into a solo act when the others tried and failed to reach the higher notes.

Mrs Snake thumped the piano keys, her fat arms wobbling in time to the music. Her face was flushed with anger, and sparks seemed to fly from her dark eyes. "No! No! No!" she bawled, "I want it sung with feeling! You can all reach the top notes if you try harder. We will stay here until you get it right."

They started again for the fourth time, by now heartily sick of the song:

"Nymphs and shepherds, come away, come away...."

The bell sounded for the end of school, but Mrs Snake ignored it, as she yelled encouragement to the class and continued to pound on the keys, her feet stamping on the pedals.

".......come, come, come, come away!" But the only feeling Amy could muster, along with the rest of the class, was of being thoroughly fed up, except for Yvonne. She was still enjoying herself, singing fit to burst.

Girls were pouring out of the other classrooms in the Manor on their way home. They walked past the French windows of the music room and, behind Mrs Snake's back, pulled faces at 5G2 as they struggled to keep in tune for the fifth time. Mrs Snake finally had to admit defeat and allow the girls to escape home.

Coral had waited for Amy, and they walked home with Vie because, thanks to Mrs Snake, they had missed their bus.

"Will you be at the Railway Tavern this evening?" Amy asked Vie, "only I've arranged to meet Pam there."

"No, not tonight 'cause I'll be staying in to experiment with something," she said mysteriously. "Just wait 'til you see me arrive at school in the morning. If all goes well, I'll be the envy of every girl." Vie refused to say any more about what she intended to do.

Coral, bored with Vie's secret, changed the subject. "I found a hedgehog under my front garden hedge this morning. He might have been hit by a car because he seems rather sickly." Coral invited Amy home to look at him as they said goodbye to Vie at the top of the hill. "I've called him Herbert,"

Coral told her, “and I’m nursing him back to health in a box.”

Amy didn’t have the heart to refuse though she had little interest in a sick hedgehog. Coral lifted the box down from the top of the tall cupboard in her kitchen and opened the lid. Amy ventured the opinion that he didn’t seem too bad, not that she had much experience with hedgehogs. She left Coral, trying to coax him to eat a biscuit. Amy hurried home, wondering if hedgehogs were partial to biscuits.

She wore a black velvet bow in her hair when she met Pam at the Railway Tavern that evening. A new group called ‘Sounds 63’ were playing a lousy version of ‘Poison Ivy’. They succeeded in emptying the dance room as everyone headed for the bar. Pam and Amy invented another new dance to relieve the boredom. After over an hour spent vigorously cavorting around the dance floor, they left to walk to the chip shop in town, as the dancing had made them hungry. They met Lynn and her new boyfriend, Skid, waiting at the bus stop. Amy recognised him as the eldest son of Mr and Mrs Boddington. She had rarely spoken to Skid because he looked such a drip. With his receding hairline, he was turning into a younger version of his bald dad.

“I can’t help wondering what on earth Lynn sees in a boring twit like that,” Amy remarked to Pam as they joined the queue at the chip shop. “He’ll be as bald as his dad before he’s left his teens behind.”

“Looks aren’t everything - maybe she’s discovered an unknown quality that he possesses,” Pam said with a grin.

Vie arrived at school in the morning doing a brilliant impression of a very miserable Red Indian squaw. She had reddish brown streaks all over her face, arms and legs, and the palms of her hands had turned bright orange.

"Did your experiment go wrong then?" Amy asked somewhat superfluously, trying to smother a giggle.

Vie forced a sheepish grin. "I was trying out a new brand of instant suntan cream that's invisible when you apply it," she explained to her astonished mates. They were finding it difficult not to laugh. "You rub it on before going to bed, and the idea is that you wake up in the morning with a marvellous tan which develops as you sleep. The only trouble is, you can't see where you've smeared it on or how evenly it is spread, so if you're not very careful, you end up with missed areas of skin that stay white."

"Och, but surely it'll wash off fairly quickly," Yvonne said, grabbing hold of Vie's hand and rubbing a red streak vigorously with her finger, to no avail.

Vie shook her head. "It's no use," she wailed. "Once the tan has developed, it's completely impervious to any amount of washing and worse still, it's guaranteed to glow for at least six weeks!" Vie was inconsolable.

Miss Catting pounced on her after assembly and gave her a long lecture about her appearance letting down the whole school. She relented from giving her a detention when she saw how wretched she was. "Have you tried bleach diluted with milk?" she suggested as a parting shot. Poor Vie promised to try it. She was so desperate she'd have tried cats' pee if she thought it might work.

Yvonne and Amy wanted to play tennis at lunchtime but found the balls were locked away in a cupboard in the staff changing room. They wandered into the gym instead, where they got out a couple of hoops and did some energetic hula hooping. They soon tired of that, and then Yvonne found some chalk.

"How about we write some poetry on the walls?" she suggested with a wicked gleam in her eyes. They were still feeling a bit peeved at not being able to play tennis, so Amy readily agreed. Their combined talents were pretty limited. Yvonne's masterpiece amounted to:

'Oh dear, Oh dear, I do feel queer,
As if I had a spasm – I very often has 'em.
I must go down to the corner shop
And buy myself some peppermint drops.'

Amy racked her brains for something poetic to write, but all she could come up with was:

'The lessons you can keep
'Cos they send me to sleep.
The dinners are chronic,
And the teachers moronic.
So down with schools
'Cos they're only for fools!'

That evening, Dad heroically dragged himself down from his sick bed after tea and flopped into his armchair. He called Amy. "Be a pet, and pop along to the phone box and ring my work to let them know I'll be back in the morning."

Amy sighed, fed up with his histrionics. "Oh, all right, but I've never known anyone else to make such a fuss over a common cold."

"Nonsense. I've had a bad bout of 'flu at the very least," he asserted. He felt slightly hurt that his daughter was unsympathetic to his illness. He expected and got, indifference from his wife after several days of waiting on him hand and foot when he banged on the floor with the walking stick that he kept handy by the bed.

Mum heard what he said as she came into the lounge. "If you had 'flu, you'd have been running a temperature. Your temperature was normal when I took it, so you've only had a cold," she countered firmly. Her husband's constant demands for attention over the past few days had put her in the predicted foul mood. She had been taking it out on her children, snapping their heads off if they spoke out of turn.

Amy called for Coral the following morning on the way to school. She saw Coral's next-door neighbour coming out of his front door, whistling. He had his black leather jacket slung over his shoulder. He smiled and winked at Coral, making her blush.

Amy nudged Coral. "He's a right dish," she whispered, "how come you've never mentioned living next door to such a gorgeous-looking boy before? I think you should introduce me."

"Bernie Dodman is *my* neighbour, so I'm not going to spoil my chances with him by introducing you to him, am I?" she retorted. This was a side of Coral Amy hadn't come across before. She consoled herself with the thought that if he fancied Coral, he must have poor taste.

After a double games lesson spent running around the hot tennis courts, 5G2 dashed into the changing room to take a quick shower. Amy discovered she had forgotten to bring her towel, so Miss Catting fined her tuppence and gave her a roller towel. To her dismay, she found it impossible to hide her modesty behind a towel with a gaping hole at its centre.

While they dressed, Miss Catting stomped up and down the aisles, ranting about the mindless vandals who had chalked on the gym walls. "Be in no doubt," she shouted, "I'm on the warpath and intend to track down the culprits responsible."

Yvonne glanced furtively along the bench to where Amy struggled to get her damp legs into her stockings. "Hey, Bat," she whispered, grinning, "doesn't sound like she appreciates poetry!"

After school, a worried Coral asked Amy indoors to look at Herbert, the hedgehog. She climbed up on a chair and lifted the straw-lined box down from the top of the kitchen cupboard, where it stood next to Henry the hamster's cage. "Mum doesn't know I've got a hedgehog hidden up there. She'd go mad if she found out."

They peered in at Herbert for several minutes as he lay motionless, and then Amy plucked up the courage to gently prod him. He moved slightly but didn't attempt to roll up into a ball.

"He refuses to eat everything I try to give him," Coral said sadly. "I think he'll probably die." Amy was forced to agree with her as she studied the lacklustre look in his eye.

Jean arrived at school in the pouring rain the following morning looking fed up because the threatened three-day rail strike had been called off. Being one of the few girls who came to school by train, this would have given her the perfect excuse for a three-day holiday. Pam and Vie were both absent, but Yvonne, Jean, Fluff and Amy found themselves roped into serving dinner to the mistresses at lunchtime. They sat at three large tables across the top end of the dining hall. Amy felt demeaned by being forced to act as a waitress – especially when she received a lambasting for accidentally dripping gravy into Miss Hudson's lap.

"Look what you're doing, girl!" snapped Mrs Snake.

"Don't worry, it's only a spot – it'll wipe off," Miss Hudson said with a smile, trying to reassure Amy.

"Hurry up and get these dirty plates stacked and take them back to the kitchen," Mrs Snake barked, glaring angrily at her. She made Amy feel so nervous that she dropped a knife on the floor. She could sense Mrs Snake's eyes boring into her back as she bent down to pick it up. She hurried off to avoid being yelled at again.

The remainder of the lunch hour was spent in the science lab doing homework corrections because Miss Stevens had been furious with the shoddy standard of class 5G2's homework.

Coral had an appointment with the dentist at 4 o'clock. After such a grotty day, Amy was pleased to escape from school to accompany her, even if it did involve sitting in a dreaded dentist's waiting room. At least for once, it wasn't her that had to sit in the formidable chair. Visiting the dentist didn't appear to hold the same terror for Coral as it did for Amy. She happily made another appointment to come back for a filling.

They stopped at the pet shop on their way home so that Amy could buy two pounds of oats for the guinea pigs. Next door at the butchers, she scrounged a free bag of sawdust for the animal's cages since they stocked plenty for sprinkling on the floor to soak up the blood. On reaching Coral's house, they made the sad discovery of Herbert the hedgehog, dead in his box. Coral insisted that Amy attend his funeral the following day as it was Saturday.

Despite the relentless rain, which hadn't stopped all day, Mum paid a visit to Mrs Hamilton that evening as Mr Hamilton was away on business. Ray was having a meal at his friend's house. This left Amy and her dad to get their own tea. Amy arrived home from her piano lesson to find Dad in the kitchen, busy baking a batch of fruit buns. He liked to keep his hand in, doing yeast cookery. He had once been an apprentice working at his older brother's bakery in his youth.

"I think you missed out on your true vocation, Dad," Amy declared after eating a delicious hot bun oozing with melted butter.

"Aye, you're right there," Dad said with a sigh. "Unfortunately, I developed an allergy to the flour, so I had no choice but to leave the bakery."

Mum went upstairs to have a bath when she returned home, so Amy had no alternative but to wash in the kitchen sink, which didn't please her. It brought back uncomfortable memories of childhood evenings spent sitting on the wooden draining board with her feet in the washing-up bowl. She had worn only a vest and knickers as she cleaned her grubby hands and knees. Beside her on the draining board had stood a large jar of washing powder and a spoon, used for washing up before the convenience of washing up liquid arrived. She remembered trying to clean a graze on her knee by rubbing it with some of the washing powder. The agonising pain she unwittingly inflicted on herself had burned indelibly into her memory.

Amy hurried to Coral's house the following morning to attend Herbert's funeral. Coral, having strong religious convictions, performed the ceremony with due reverence. She said a prayer before solemnly laying him to rest in the flower bed under a rose bush. He had a shoe box for a coffin, and Amy created a wooden cross from a couple of lollipop sticks.

Feeling in need of some lighter diversion to cheer themselves up, they walked into town, and Coral helped Amy choose a new pair of shoes for best. She finally opted for a beautiful pair of blue patent leather sling-backs. Back home, she dashed upstairs and hid them in her wardrobe to avoid the inevitable row with her father. He insisted on soling and heeling all new shoes to make them last longer. His shed became a temporary cobblers where he hammered away on his last with its array of various-sized iron feet. Any dainty, fashionable footwear was quickly converted into practical, clumsy-looking shoes as Dad worked, shaping new leather soles and thick rubber heels. He even added metal studs sometimes for good measure. Amy was determined this wasn't going to happen to her new shoes.

After lunch, she returned to Coral's house with a pile of records. Coral had pleaded with her to come and help entertain her seventeen-year-old cousin, Roger, who was paying her a visit that afternoon.

“How come, after years of calling at your house, I’ve not met him, before?” Amy asked as they sorted through the records.

“That’s because he’s only recently moved to this area from up north,” Coral explained. Coral had never mentioned her cousin before. Amy was pleasantly surprised when he arrived, and Coral introduced him. He bore no family resemblance to Coral. In fact, Amy thought he wasn’t too bad in the looks department with his dark hair and deep blue eyes. They chatted and played records on the Dansette until teatime when Amy had to leave to get ready for an evening out at the town hall in Pam’s home town.

This was her first dance at the town hall, and she was filled with anticipation, when she met up with Pam, Yvonne and John because the Searchers were topping the bill. A large glass ball revolved slowly, suspended from the centre of the ceiling, dappling the walls and floor with swirling coloured lights, creating a surreal atmosphere in the dimly lit hall.

Halfway through the evening, the Searchers finally arrived on stage to a deafening welcome of screams and whistles from the packed dance floor. The noise continued through most of their first song – their hit single: ‘When You Walk in the Room’. Amy and Pam stood close to the stage, completely starstruck. Then the group launched into an ear-splitting version of Little Richard’s ‘Good Golly Miss Molly’. Unable to keep still, they broke into frenzied dancing, and Yvonne joined in while John fought his way to the bar for a drink. They found it difficult not to jab elbows into each other as they danced because the crowd was jostling to get closer to the stage. The enormous loudspeakers loomed over them from the edge of the stage, blasting out sound waves so strong that the vibrations almost knocked them off balance. Finally, at the end of the evening, they said their goodbyes outside and agreed it had been a great night.

Amy hobbled home from the bus stop with difficulty because of the painful blisters on her heels caused by her new shoes. She stopped to buy a bag of chips and met up with Coral's sprightly gran, who had been to her regular bingo session. She lived at Coral's house, so Amy accompanied her home, sharing her chips.

Monday morning, during registration, Mrs Butler announced that they were to wait on table for the mistresses all week.

"It wouldn't be so bad if we were being paid as part-time waitresses," Amy grumbled.

"No such luck," Yvonne said, adding, with a twinkle in her eye, "but it has got its compensations if you think about it – we'll have the first pick of any decent leftovers."

"I'm not sure I want to eat leftovers. Nevertheless, I intend to get through today without dropping anything," Amy said, determined not to repeat Friday's fiasco.

That evening, after a day free from disasters, Amy met up with Pam and Yvonne at the newly opened Scala dance hall in the town centre.

"Where's John tonight?" Amy asked Yvonne as they queued to get in.

"Oh, didn't I tell you? After the dance on Saturday night, he took me home as usual. Then, as we said goodnight, he told me he intended to start dating his previous girlfriend again. What a cheek!" Yvonne feigned indignation and then laughed.

"At least you don't seem too upset about it," Pam remarked, but Yvonne wasn't listening. She had spotted a boy she knew standing on the opposite side of the foyer and was waving and yelling at him.

"I thought he intended to finish with her on Saturday by the way he kept ignoring her," Amy whispered to Pam.

"Well, she hasn't wasted any time bouncing back to her normal scatty self," Pam said as they followed the crowd through the glass doors into the gloom of the dance hall. They had to negotiate a tricky spiral staircase to reach the cloakroom where they deposited their coats. Next to the cloakroom was a large balcony with a bar and seats overlooking the dance floor and stage below. The girls returned downstairs to the dance floor, where tables lined the sides. They found one unoccupied and sat down.

"I think this place is great!" Yvonne exclaimed, gazing around at the coloured lights flashing in time to the music. "It's a shame there's no live band on stage, but at least the music is loud, and the place has a good atmosphere."

The girls enjoyed an evening of energetic dancing in the hot, crowded hall. Then they headed for the ladies to adjust their hairdos and make-up before leaving. Yvonne shouted: "It's this way," and charged off down some steps. Pam and Amy followed but soon wished they hadn't when they discovered she had led them into the gents' toilets by mistake. A chorus of wolf whistles and lewd invitations greeted them. Amy felt herself blushing to the roots of her hair. They turned and ran out, aware that the disturbance was attracting attention on the dance floor. With heads bowed, they dashed across the floor and down the opposite steps into the ladies.

"We shan't make that mistake again!" Yvonne said, giggling. Unlike Pam and Amy, she thought the whole incident had been hilarious.

Back home, in the kitchen, Amy gathered her ingredients, ready for a gruelling domestic science practical exam in the morning. Overhead, on top of the cupboard, Ruby raced along in her exercise wheel, getting nowhere fast. The constant squeak from her wheel had kept Amy awake for the last few nights, so she found a can of oil and clambered onto the worktop. 'At least tonight I should get a better night's sleep,' she told herself, dripping oil onto the wheel. As she refastened Ruby's cage, her elbow caught the can. "Bugger!" she yelled, trying to grab the can as it fell into the middle of her ingredients. Then her foot slipped; she lost her balance and toppled off the worktop.

Ray came into the kitchen to find his sister sprawled on the floor. "What are you doing down there?"

Amy glared at him. "Just give me a hand up," she said, rubbing her tender posterior.

Ray grinned. "I see you had a soft landing."

"It's a good job I removed my shoes, or else I might have sprained an ankle. Now I've got to find fresh ingredients." Ray left her rummaging in the pantry and muttering to herself.

Everyone dreaded the ordeal of the cooking exam in the morning. The menus were varied – Amy had to make a chocolate pudding, queens cakes, cheese and potato pie and boiled spring greens, then wash up the dishes – all in less than two hours. She found it hectic trying to complete everything in the limited time. She was pleased her dishes turned out quite well, barring the spring greens, which looked none too appetising as they lay in a soggy heap on the plate. Amy didn't manage to drain them properly because Miss Snodgrass had ordered everyone to stop whatever they were doing as the time was up.

"I think you should consider taking domestic science next year for GCE," she said to Amy after awarding her a B grade for her efforts.

But Amy hadn't enjoyed the experience of cooking food under such pressure. "Perhaps I'll give it some thought," she said and then realised she wouldn't be taking domestic science anyway if Miss Hardacre had a say in her choices.

After the break, the six girls took advantage of the fact that the P.E. students didn't know the number of girls they should be teaching in class 5G2. They hid in the toilets during P.E., and Jean opted to join them instead of watching the others doing energetic exercises.

"There'll soon be more of us in the bogs than taking P.E. at this rate," Amy said, settling down on a loo seat with the cubicle door open. Yvonne sat on the window sill, lit a cigarette and passed it around.

"That neighbour of yours, Bat, the one who came to the club – what's his name?" Jean asked from the adjoining cubicle.

"D'you mean Dennis the Menace?"

"Yeah, that's him. I've seen him walking past my house in the mornings on his way to work. If he sees me, he always says hello. D'you think you could put in a good word for me if you happen to be talking to him?"

"You don't mean to say you actually fancy him, do you?" Amy could barely conceal the derision in her voice.

"Well, he's not bad looking, and I like the Rocker type."

"I'll try, but don't hold your breath," Amy said. She was convinced Dennis wouldn't be interested in a lump of lard like Jean.

"A circus has arrived at Danson Park," Pam announced. "I fancy having a day off tomorrow to go there. Does anyone else want to come along?"

"I'll come with you, Tibs," Fluff piped up quickly, "I need a rest after that horrible D.S. exam today."

Yvonne groaned. "I'm broke."

"Me too," chimed in Vie.

"I've got the rotten dentist tomorrow, else I'd have skived off too," Amy said gloomily.

A message arrived on Mrs Butler's desk at morning registration. Jean's mum had rung the school to explain that Jean was absent because she had sprained her wrist. Pam and Fluff were also absent, enjoying themselves at the circus.

Yvonne had brought her new transistor radio to school so the girls could listen to it during the break. She had to keep it hidden from the teachers, or it undoubtedly would have been confiscated.

The teachers were huddled in a staff meeting for most of the afternoon, so there were no lessons, and everyone was allowed to leave school early. Amy met up with her mum and Ray at the station.

They caught the train for the half-hour journey to the dentist. Amy's teeth were OK though he reaffirmed his previous decision that she would have to wait another year before he could crown her front tooth.

Amy felt totally frustrated. How could he possibly appreciate the utter urgency of her situation? She tried pleading with him but to no avail – the dentist was adamant. "I know you're disappointed," he said, "but another year is imperative to ensure the tooth has time to finish growing." She would have to accept that boys would find her unattractive for the coming year.

Amy cheered up a little when she learned that Ray had two small cavities that needed filling. After losing so many teeth the last time he visited the dentist, this time, he put up a fight. Two nurses pinned him down in the chair until Ray bit one and kicked the other. The dentist gave up and stipulated that he would have to be given sedatives before his next appointment.

Vie arrived at school the following morning, looking slightly green about the gills. This was no improvement on the bright orange streaks, which had now faded to a grubby yellow.

"I went on a bit of a drinking binge last night with Steve and his mates," she said sheepishly, "we were celebrating getting back together again." She sat down and held her head in her hands as though it might fall off if she moved too quickly. "He had too much to drink and got into an argument which turned into a fight. He was arrested for pub brawling, so I kept him company at the cop shop while he waited to be charged."

"Sounds like he's not a very good influence on you, Vie," Jean commented snootily. She had arrived back at school that morning with a bandaged wrist. No-one had bothered to ask how she had hurt it.

"I'm quite capable of looking after myself, thank you, Jean," Vie retorted, giving a wince as her head pounded from her hangover.

"Why don't you tell Mrs Butler that you're not feeling well and ask if you can go and lie down in the medical room?" Amy suggested.

"I do feel a bit sick," Vie admitted, "perhaps I will 'cos I don't think I can face any lessons today."

Vie spent the day lazing in the medical room. Meanwhile, the others tried to be on their best behaviour during the lunch hour as they waited on table for the teachers and their important guests – the stuffy school governors.

Fortunately, there were no mishaps. Afterwards, Yvonne's transistor cheered them up as they relaxed in the gloom of the Manor stables for the remainder of the lunch hour.

Amy craved some pancakes at teatime, but she compromised and made a batch of banana fritters instead. She appeared to be the only person who suffered all evening with chronic indigestion but then she did eat most of the banana fritters.

To the girls' relief, Friday was their last day serving the teachers at lunchtime. They hovered in a corner, waiting for the teachers to finish their dinners.

"I'm bored," Yvonne said, "I think I'll go and get some tuck as I'm still hungry – you ones will cover for me, won't you?" She dashed off before anyone had time to protest.

Amy scowled after her. "I'm getting very irritated with her slapdash ways," she said, "she still hasn't returned my records or my clothes!"

"I know what you mean," Pam said with a sigh, "she has got some of my clothes and records that she borrowed from me ages ago."

"I think I shall tackle her about returning some of the money she owes when she comes back," Amy said. But Yvonne didn't bother to return to wait on the teachers. Amy didn't get an opportunity to speak to her until the end of English Literature.

When Amy did finally ask her, Yvonne promptly pleaded poverty. "But I don't even have the bus fare home, Yvonne. If you don't cough up, I shall have to walk." Yvonne's conscience appeared to have pricked her because she went to Mrs Slater, who was busy tidying her desk.

"Och, Mrs Slater, could you help me out, please. I've lost my bus fare home." Her large brown eyes became dark liquid pools of innocence as she gazed at her short-sighted English teacher and batted her eyelashes. Amy could hardly believe her audacity as she wheedled sixpence out of Mrs Slater to give to Amy.

Amy spent her piano lesson slogging away at the Barcarole for the third week without making much progress. She arrived at Coral's to find her attacking the front privet hedge with a pair of shears.

"I'll give you a hand if you like?" Amy offered, feeling in a generous mood. Coral quickly found another pair of shears in the shed, and together they set about pruning the ragged hedge. Mr Whippy's ice cream van pulled up on the other side of the hedge playing a deafening jingle on its chimes. They persuaded the driver, Robin, to cut the top of the hedge from his vantage point at the van's serving hatch. Then Dennis strolled around the corner and found himself roped in, too, despite protesting loudly. With the extra help, the hedge was soon trimmed back into shape.

That night a disgruntled Amy was again washing in the kitchen sink as the bathroom was occupied. "I shall have to draw up a rota for the time we spend in the bathroom. It'll be the only way I get my fair share," she muttered to herself and then yelped in pain as she burnt her elbow on the hot tap.

Coral arrived at Amy's house Saturday morning, still smitten by the gardening bug. Amy suggested they walk down to Dad's allotment and give him a hand. Dad wasn't there, but they started weeding between the rows of vegetables. After half an hour of grubbing around, Amy had had enough, so she persuaded Coral to walk into town with her.

They washed back at Amy's house before heading into town for a browse in Robby's record shop, where Amy bought a copy of the Beatles record, 'From Me to You'.

After lunch, Amy was hanging a tea towel on the line when Dennis waylaid her looking for a chat. They often chatted over the fence, sometimes for an hour or more, usually arguing over who was best – Elvis or Cliff. Today, while Dennis still argued for Elvis, Amy had switched camp to the Beatles, which naturally led to a heated debate between the clean-cut Mods and the greasy Rockers.

"I've no time for wimpish Mods who pootle around on poncy scooters covered in mirrors," Dennis asserted with contempt.

"At least Mods take pride in their appearance," Amy said defensively. "They're far more peace-loving than you Neanderthal Rockers who are always spoiling for a fight."

"Well, I do enjoy a good fight," he admitted. "I dish out me best punches with me right hand," he bragged, giving his knuckles an affectionate stroke where the word HATE was plainly tattooed.

Amy feigned a yawn of boredom. "By the way, my mate Jean says she sees you walking past her house on your way to work each morning."

Dennis gave a puzzled frown. "I don't know how she does 'cos I bus all the way to work. P'raps she's confusing me with someone else."

"Yes, I suppose she must be," Amy agreed absently while thinking, 'yet another whopper, Jean!'

Sunday morning, after breakfast, Amy began cleaning out her guinea pigs. She hurled a shovelful of muck onto the manure heap, lost her balance and slipped headlong into it. She swore as she picked straw and other smelly bits out of her hair and clothes before stomping indoors to take a bath. Coral arrived later and kept Ruby occupied while Amy cleaned out her cage.

"D'you know, I really think your Ruby is a Rubinstein," Coral declared after studying the hamster as it climbed up her arm.

"Come off it. How can you possibly know about such things?" Amy scoffed.

"Well, I've had male and female hamsters, and Ruby's rear end has got a definite extra bulge to it, the same as Henry's," she said.

"Oh!" Amy said, surprised by Coral's knowledge of distinguishing the sex of a hamster. "In that case, I'd better start calling him Rubinstein before he gets a complex," she said.

After Coral had gone home, Amy spent the afternoon putting the finishing touches to her navy skirt. She made it tighter and shorter than the pattern and felt pleased with how it turned out.

Dad came in looking chuffed with himself. He rubbed his hands and beamed. "I've been to look at another motorbike," he announced, "and I've arranged to collect it Tuesday evening."

"If it looks and goes better than your old pop-pop, then it's got to be an improvement," Amy said.

"Just wait and see – I think you'll like it," Dad said confidently.

Monday morning, Amy sat in the New Building toilets scribbling like mad. Yvonne and Fluff were in adjoining cubicles doing likewise throughout assembly and their first lesson of Religious Knowledge, where they hoped they wouldn't be missed. They hadn't done the previous week's homework or the current week's homework or copied up their science notes.

Miss Hardacre spotted Amy walking past her study at break time and called her in. She looked cross, and Amy wondered what trouble she was in now. Had Catty Catting noticed her absence during R.K. and reported it to Clara?

"Amy Brown, if you insist on wearing fifteen denier stockings instead of the regulation thirty denier, then you must wear socks over the top of them," she said imperiously.

"Yes, Miss Hardacre." Amy hung her head in acquiescence while inside, she fumed over why it should be her who got singled out when the others all wore fifteen denier with impunity.

Vie belatedly gave Amy two shillings of birthday money, and Yvonne lost no time dragging her off to the village shop during the lunch break to spend it on a large bag of sweets.

Jean's birthday arrived, and Amy forgot to take her birthday money to school. Jean looked fed up during registration, so Amy tried to cheer her up. "I'll take you for a birthday drink this evening if you like," she offered, wondering why she was suggesting this when in all probability, Jean wouldn't turn up. "Meet you at the station at seven-thirty – and don't be late!"

Jean perked up and grinned. "Don't worry, I'll be there, and we'll have a great time," she promised.

Amy, Vie and Fluff took advantage of the P.E. lesson being held by a student to hide in the New Building toilets while Yvonne and Pam did the same in the Manor toilets. They managed to get some more of their homework and copying up done, and Vie borrowed Amy's geography book so she could catch up with her homework.

The bell eventually rang, telling them it was time to head for their domestic science class, where they learnt how to make brandy snaps. Amy didn't like them much, so she took them home and fed them to Rubinstein, who seemed to enjoy them. What he didn't want straight away he stored in his larder.

Ray brought a schoolfriend home for tea, so Mum produced a large pile of delicious cream cakes she had bought earlier at the bakers. Amy couldn't resist them and ended up feeling decidedly sick. Going drinking with Jean was out of the question, so for once, she turned the tables on Jean and let her down.

Dad arrived home after collecting his new motorbike, and Amy felt well enough to accept the offer of a trial ride to his allotment. Unfortunately, the bike came with teething troubles. When he kick-started it, the engine just spluttered and conked out. Amy thought it looked far more respectable than the ex-GPO bike. At least this bike had the luxury of a proper pillion and footrests so she wouldn't keep burning her ankle on the exhaust.

When it finally started up, it roared louder because it was a bit more powerful than his previous bike. Because it looked less of an eyesore, Amy didn't feel as embarrassed to be seen on it. Though Dad still showed her up wearing his cranky motorbike garb.

At the allotment, she helped him plant some vegetables while he enlightened her on the finer points of his new bike's vital parts.

Jean's absence from school the next day indicated to Amy that she also hadn't turned up the previous evening and obviously thought she had let Amy down.

Yvonne was absent too. The girls knew she had a job interview at a local bank. Nobody mentioned this to Mrs Butler when Yvonne's name was called out during registration, so she was marked absent. At the end of the first lesson, as the girls crossed the road from the Manor, Yvonne arrived looking smug.

"I'm sure I made a good impression on the bank manager because he kept smiling at me," she said to Amy as they walked up the drive to the Grange. "Anyway, I reckon he'll offer me the job once he's interviewed the other applicants. I'll tell Clara at lunchtime that I intend to leave school at the end of term."

"I bet you were fluttering your eyelashes at him," Amy said with a grin.

"Shouldn't you wait until you are actually offered the Job?" Pam asked, "you might be stirring up unnecessary trouble."

"My mind is made up," Yvonne declared as they entered the classroom for their French lesson.

After lunch, the girls sprawled on the lower lawn in the Manor grounds trying to do some revision for a science test the following day. Ten minutes later, Yvonne galloped down the steps and flung herself on the grass beside them. "I've told Clara I'm leaving, but she refuses to believe me," she panted, sounding indignant. "She told me to go and discuss it with my parents – what a cheek!" She glanced at the books spread out on the grass and laughed. "I don't know why you're all bothering to study for that science exam. Fanny Stevens is away today, so she'll probably be away tomorrow too."

"Knowing my luck, she won't be," Amy muttered. "I'll revise anyway."

Vie went off to the doctor for a vaccination jab after lunch. Too late, Amy realised Vie had her geography book in her bag, and the geography lesson was next. After receiving a severe reprimand from Miss Finley, she was given a piece of paper for drawing a map of the British Isles.

Miss Catting was absent when they arrived for their games lesson. Somehow a replacement teacher to supervise their lesson had been overlooked, not that anyone would complain. They had great fun playing tennis with a lot of larking about and no teacher to spoil it.

Amy arrived home from school to find her mother in another bad mood.

"This afternoon, while me and Mrs Boddington were enjoying a quiet cup of tea and a chat in the lounge, two of those American Elders arrived unannounced. In no time, they had persuaded us to join them in a prayer. We felt like a right pair of twits when they insisted on us kneeling in the bay window. I just prayed that we wouldn't be seen by any other neighbours! And it's all your fault," she ranted. "If you didn't associate with those morons, me and poor Mrs Boddington wouldn't have ended up in such an embarrassing predicament."

"They're Mormons, not morons," Amy pointed out.

"That's a matter of opinion," Mum snapped. "It doesn't alter the fact that you shouldn't associate with religious fanatics."

"Now you're exaggerating. They're really nice people if you take the trouble to get to know them."

"Unfortunately, we probably will get to know them better because we have been invited to tour their church in London. We felt obliged to agree to go because they would probably have been offended if we'd refused."

"Oh, you'll have a great time," Amy assured her, "it's a lovely building." But Mum just grimaced, looking unconvinced.

Dad was in his chair with his head buried in the paper. Now he looked up and changed the subject, trying to calm them down.

"I think I might get one of those newfangled transistor radios," he said, closing his paper. "It would be handy to carry around so that I could listen to the news or music whenever I liked. I could even listen to it while I work on my allotment." Amy's jaw dropped in amazement. Her father spending money on something so frivolous was unheard of.

Early the following morning in the Manor cloakroom, Amy found it impossible to concentrate on completing her geography homework with Yvonne driving her potty, practising her scales yet again in readiness for a singing competition on Saturday evening. She had practised at every opportunity despite repeated assurances that she had reached perfection. She went on to give a moving rendition of 'Danny Boy' until it was time for registration.

As Yvonne had predicted, Miss Stevens was absent, so there was no horrid science test, which relieved everyone.

Coral and Amy were lounging at the bus stop after school when Coral's piano teacher pulled up in his old banger and offered them a lift into town. Amy thought the old fuddy-duddy looked very short-sighted, judging by how he hugged the steering wheel and peered closely through the windscreen. She wondered whether he could manage to read music, though Coral's progress in learning new chords and tunes meant he couldn't be that bad.

In town, they thanked him as he dropped them off at Pott's, the small department store that stocked their school uniform. Mum had decided Amy needed a new jumper for school. She hadn't got time to knit one, so for once, she had given Amy the money to buy one. Coral helped Amy choose a fine burgundy jumper that could not be mistaken for a thicker home-knitted one.

After her dad's unexpected interest in transistor radios the previous evening, Amy called at the television and radio shop across the road to enquire about the prices of various transistors. The smallest and cheapest started at £3. 19s. 11d.

"I definitely can't see Dad forking out all that money on a tranny," she remarked as they left the shop.

After her piano lesson, Amy changed into her newly finished blue skirt. She returned to town to meet Vie as they had arranged an evening at the flicks to watch the 'X' rated 'Day of the Triffids'. She found walking difficult and realised she had made the skirt too tight. Her knees felt as if they were tied together, so she could barely hobble along. In the cinema, they spotted Jean and her friend Sheila a few rows in front of them, so they moved down to join them as there were several empty seats. An irritating boy sitting in front of them kept turning around to offer his grubby bag of sticky sweets to Vie, who he obviously fancied. Vie didn't appreciate his attention and eventually retaliated by poking her ice cream up his nose. His mates hooted with laughter, but he was far from amused.

By the time Amy arrived home, having missed the bus because she couldn't run for it, her knees felt badly bruised from knocking together.

Saturday morning, she rummaged through her mother's needlework drawer for needles, pins and thread so she could stitch the sleeves into the overblouse she was making in her needlework class at school. It had already taken her months to get this far. With much cursing and pricking of her fingers, she finally set the sleeves to her satisfaction. Then she turned her attention to her overly tight skirt and added some much-needed slits up the sides.

Yvonne wasn't the only one entering a singing competition. Ray had been monopolising the bathroom to exercise his vocal cords as the acoustics sounded best there. If the noises emanating from there were anything to go by, he needed every scrap of help he could muster.

Mum persuaded Amy to go with her to the Girls' Grammar School, where the singing competition was taking place for all the surrounding junior schools. Ray had been chosen to sing in his school choir. This decision baffled Amy because, in her opinion, his singing was more off-key than a crowing cockerel with croup. As she expected, Ray's school choir proved useless and didn't come anywhere.

They stopped at Aunt Ruth's on their way home for a cup of tea as the hot weather had made them thirsty. Mum bragged to Aunt Ruth about the contest contriving to make it sound as if Ray's choir had fared much better than they actually did.

That evening, Amy went over to Yvonne's as she was going to accompany her to the talent spot contest, which was being held at her local youth club. Yvonne took Amy into the kitchen and made her feel ill when she gargled with beaten raw eggs.

"Yuk, Yvonne – how could you?" Amy said, pulling a face.

"They do wonders for my vocal cords," Yvonne assured her.

On the stage at the youth club, she sang her rendition of 'Danny Boy', beautifully and with such feeling that it almost brought tears to Amy's eyes. She didn't appear nervous, and when she finished singing, she revelled in the appreciative standing ovation from the audience. Amy felt sure she would win, but in the end, she was pipped at the post by an excellent violinist and had to be content with second place. Nevertheless, she was jubilant with the result, spending the rest of the evening basking in the congratulations she received and loving every minute of it.

The warm weather brought out the dreaded May bugs the following evening. Their fat pale brown bodies made them look like cumbersome flying Murray mints. Amy loathed and feared them due to the rumour that if they flew into your hair, the only way to get them out was to cut it off.

Dennis led a band of neighbours on the green in the annual game of batting the May bugs while Amy watched from the safety of her bedroom window. Cricket bats were the preferred weapons, but any plank could serve as a bat. Where the bugs came from nobody knew. They only lived for twenty-four hours, but Amy dreaded their appearance at the same time each year. Any girls brave enough to join in the game always took care to wear a scarf to protect their hair. The evening air resounded with satisfying cracks as the bats hit the hard outer case of the bugs. Despite the slaughter, some always managed to fly down the chimney and hide in the folds of the curtains. Amy couldn't relax until Dad had carefully shaken all the curtains each morning, to remove any unwanted lodgers.

Monday morning, she took a pair of lens-less sunglasses to school. As the girls headed to the geography classroom, Pam challenged Amy: "I dare you to wear them during Frog-eyed Freda's lesson," she said with a grin.

"You just watch me," Amy said. In the classroom, Amy sat down and put on the glasses, feeling rather conspicuous. Miss Finley kept giving her suspicious sidelong glances. At the end of the lesson, she scowled at Amy and Jean and summoned them to go and see her. Amy hid the glasses in her satchel, but Miss Finley didn't mention them. She had another matter on her mind.

"Can you two explain to me how your homework is worded exactly the same?" she demanded. Her eyes sparkled with anger as they flicked from one girl to the other. Amy feigned indignant shock at the allegation while Jean said nothing but blushed to the roots of her blonde hair. "I will give you the benefit of the doubt this time – but don't let it happen again."

As the girls left the classroom, Amy turned on Jean. "You idiot!" she stormed, "if you must copy my homework, at least try to paraphrase it instead of lifting it verbatim out of my book." Jean looked abashed and just mumbled an apology.

Yvonne was disappointed not to have been offered the job at the bank. She found her way back into Amy and Pam's good books by finally returning their records at long last, though not the clothes.

Vie and Amy walked home together after school instead of catching the bus with Coral because they wanted to save on their fares. As they strolled along, Amy asked after Steve.

Vie sighed. "He's still waiting to go to court for pub brawling," she said.

"I'm sure you'd stand by him even if he committed murder," Amy declared. "You're obviously very smitten with him."

"Yes, he means a lot to me – more than any other boyfriend I've ever had," Vie said fervently.

Amy felt a slight pang of jealousy. She knew she stood little chance of getting a boyfriend until her front tooth was fixed. "Well, I just hope he appreciates you," she said.

Amy spent a tedious domestic science lesson stuffing tomatoes. Afterwards, she stayed in the toilets with Pam during P.E. so they could write out their domestic science homework.

Pam lit up a fag, took a long drag and passed it to Amy. "I've brought something to show you," she said, rummaging through her satchel. Finally, with a flourish, she produced a book. "It's a bestseller called the Kama Sutra," she explained. "It belongs to my dad, but he doesn't know I've borrowed it."

Amy glanced through it but couldn't make much sense of it. "Huh – it's just pictures of people in odd postures and a lot of Indian words that need translating," she said, unimpressed.

"It's a famous Indian book all about different ways couples can couple," Pam said, giving Amy a knowing nudge.

"Oh, I see." Amy giggled. "But what's your dad doing with a book like this?"

"He keeps a lot of books hidden under his bed. He doesn't know I've discovered his hiding place, so I'll have to return it before he realises it's missing."

After school, Amy bussed home with Coral for a change. Coral couldn't wait to tell her all about her new boyfriend. "His name's Mick, and I met him on a church outing," she said proudly. "He's a bit of a Mod, and he's even got a 'tache'," she added, knowing this would impress Amy. "He took me to the pictures last night."

"Well, he sounds a lot better than the boys you normally meet at church," Amy conceded, but she wondered what he saw in prim and proper Coral.

The rain overnight had softened the ground by the morning, so Dad cajoled Ray and Amy into helping him do some weeding on his allotment that evening. Every year he had an unacknowledged competition with Gordon to see who could grow the best vegetables.

"This year I'm determined that, for once, my vegetables will be bigger and better than Gordon's," he said as he set them to work between the rows of onions. "I'm fed up with him waving his huge sprouts under my nose and bragging about the size of his cabbages." Amy camouflaged a laugh with a cough as she tugged at a dandelion.

Class 5G2 played rounders during their double games lesson on Wednesday morning, which made a pleasant change. Amy got stumped out at first the base, so she went off, searching for Yvonne to keep her company. She found her hiding in the toilets because she had forgotten to bring her maroon knickers to school to change into.

"Those nylon see-through panties you like to wear are always getting you into trouble," Amy said, taking the offered half-smoked cigarette from Yvonne.

"Och, Bat, I just hate those awful sugar bags that masquerade as school knickers."

"Well, at least they keep you warm in winter," Amy pointed out.

"I'd rather stay cold!" Yvonne retorted.

That evening, after tea, the Elders in their minibus collected a pair of reluctant passengers – namely Mrs Brown and Mrs Boddington – for a visit to their main Mormon church in London. Their ardent praying in the bay window the previous week had obviously fooled the Elders into believing they had a couple of potential converts on their hands. They were given a guided tour of the church, including the baptising pool in the basement where Yvonne had enjoyed her swim. Poor Mrs Boddington wasn't so lucky. She didn't look where she was walking and lost her footing. With a loud yell and a splash, she suddenly found herself floundering in their font. Two Elders quickly fished her out and found some towels and dry clothes. She arrived home, looking fed up with her hair hanging in limp rats' tails.

"I hope those Elders realise they have lost their would-be converts," Mum declared, collapsing into an armchair.

"Amy grinned. "They're not known to give up that easily."

During morning assembly, Miss Hardacre announced that no girls would be allowed to enter school until after 8.30 each morning.

Amy leaned towards Pam. "That doesn't give us much time for doing our homework," she whispered.

"I expect that's why she made this new rule," Pam whispered back, "perhaps someone's been telling tales."

The following morning, Amy and her mates congregated on the lower lawn of the Manor grounds at 8.00 am to do their homework since they couldn't get into the cloakroom.

"Are you all looking forward to the outdoor rave-up this evening?" Vie asked.

"Och, it's going to be fantastic," Yvonne declared, "it's a huge park, and there should be crowds going to see the groups playing live. It's a pity you're not coming with us."

"I'll be at the flicks with Steve instead," Vie said. "You'll have to tell me all about it."

Being half-term, they were let out of school early. Amy and Coral rushed across the heath to a different bus stop where an earlier bus would take them directly home for a change.

They had almost reached the bus stop when Amy stopped dead and pointed. "Look, Coral, there's Mrs Jagger over there." Across the road, a woman laden with shopping bags was walking along very slowly.

"Are you sure that's her?" Coral asked dubiously.

"'Course I am! You wait. When the Stones have made a few more hit records, Mick should be able to treat his mum to a chauffeur-driven car."

"If you go and ask her, she might get Mick's autograph for you," Coral suggested.

"Of course, she wouldn't," Amy scoffed, "anyway, collecting autographs is so naff."

"OK, so go and offer to carry her shopping home for her," Coral said with a hint of cynicism, "you never know – Mick might be at home and answer the door when you get there."

Amy's eyes lit up. "That's a great idea, but you must come with me – I daren't go on my own."

Amy was about to dash across the road when Coral called out: "Here comes our bus, and I'm not going to miss it." Amy groaned as the bus drew up beside them, and Coral jumped onto the platform. Amy reluctantly followed, cursing Coral under her breath.

"That was a great opportunity we've let slip by," Amy said, flopping down next to Coral on the top deck and craning her neck to see if she could still see Mrs Jagger out of the window.

"I don't know what you see in him anyway with his long scruffy hair and big rubber lips," Coral said dismissively.

"I wouldn't expect you to understand – it's not about looks - it's about sex appeal, and Mick's definitely got it." Coral just looked pityingly at her friend and shook her head.

On the way to her piano lesson, Amy met Dennis the Menace ambling along.

"I've bin thinking about what you were tellin' me the other day about your friend, Jean," he said. "If she's bin tellin' you that she sees me each morning, it sounds as if she might fancy me. What d'you reckon?" he asked hopefully.

"Jean is definitely not your type. She's a podgy dollop who lives in a fantasy world," Amy said bluntly, "I'd advise you to forget about her."

Dennis grinned. "I'm no good at takin' advice," he said, "anyway, I like my women on the big side, so I think you should introduce 'er to me, someday soon."

Amy walked on to Mrs Falco's, wondering whether she should play Cupid or not get involved and finally decided on the latter option.

She dashed home after a gruelling piano lesson, changed out of her school uniform and dashed out again to meet Pam's cousin Colin. Pam had arranged for Colin to pick up Amy in his van at the top of the Crescent to avoid any awkward questions from her parents. He had already collected Yvonne, and she was yelling and waving excitedly out of the van window as it drew up. Colin reminded Amy of Buddy Holly with his black-rimmed glasses and mop of curly dark hair. He drove to Pam's to collect her and Fluff before heading to the Railway Tavern, where he had agreed to meet his mates for a drink.

Colin looked uncomfortable sitting in a pub with four girls and felt relieved when his mates finally arrived. They all left for the park in the next town and found it packed out. They pushed through the crowds to reach the stage. It was erected at the top of an incline where several groups each had about an hour on stage. The music sounded fantastic but deafening to anyone within twenty yards of the loudspeakers. The drinks were expensive, so after a while, one of Colin's mates invited everyone back to the Railway for some liquid refreshments. The girls gladly accepted but then found eight people trying to cram into one car. Yvonne, squashed on some bearded chap's lap, got the giggles when her foot became wedged in the glove compartment. Amy glanced anxiously across at her. Fortunately for the bearded young man, Yvonne managed to control her bladder. They piled out of the car and into the

Railway Tavern for a round of drinks. Then they had to squeeze back into the car once more for the uncomfortable return journey to the rave-up.

Yvonne and Amy wandered off on their own, and Yvonne was soon chatting with a couple of nice-looking boys lounging by a burger stall. Just then, who should walk by but the lovely Ken. Amy drooled discreetly and refrained from mentioning Ken to Yvonne for fear she would charge straight over to him and try to arrange a date for her. Yvonne suddenly spotted someone she knew and, grabbing Amy by the arm, dragged her off to meet Ivor, the Queer. 'Where does she find them?' Amy wondered as Yvonne introduced him to her. He was a pleasant young man, despite being a bit limp-wristed, and wearing foundation cream and mascara.

The rave ended just before midnight when Colin brought the girls home safely in his van.

As he pulled up to drop off Amy, he announced: "Everyone's off to a barbecue at the coast over the weekend. Do any of you girls fancy coming?"

"You can count me in," Yvonne said, without hesitation, "I'm sure I can persuade my parents to let me go."

"There's no way mine will agree to me going," Amy said glumly, "not for a whole weekend."

Pam and Fluff shook their heads. They had the same problem.

Chapter Seven

June
Great Auntie Gertie Pays a Visit

Amy called for Coral on Saturday morning as she wanted help choosing a new swimsuit, but only for sunbathing as she was a non-swimmer. In town, they hunted around the clothes shops until Amy saw a Mod bikini in a shop window, which stopped her in her tracks. "Wow! Look at this!" She pressed her excited face against the glass, gazing at the red top with wide shoulder straps and blue hipster shorts with a white belt.

"Um – I think it'll suit you, but it's rather patriotic," Coral surmised. Mum had given Amy two pounds towards it, so she added the other seven shillings and sixpence.

Back home, she showed it to Mum, and for once, she approved. "At least it's not too skimpy – but whatever you do, don't tell your father how much it really cost because he'll go bonkers," Mum warned her.

After lunch, Amy walked to Coral's house. Her cousin Roger was there again so they all played a game of Monopoly at the dining room table. Roger's manners proved impeccable, as he held Amy's chair for her when she sat down. He politely offered her Mayfair and Park Lane when he landed on them instead of trying to grab them for himself. They played all afternoon until Coral had to get changed for her date at the flicks with Mick.

As Amy got up to leave, Roger showed her to the door. "Er, I don't suppose you'd like to come back after tea and finish that game of Monopoly?"

Coral's mum overheard him and yelled from the lounge: "Sounds like a good idea. Why not come and keep Roger company while Coral's out?" Amy couldn't think of a reason for not returning, so she agreed and came back after tea to beat him easily in one hour flat. Amy suspected that he had diplomatically allowed her to win. Mrs Manser smiled as she brought them mugs of coffee, then discreetly withdrew. Amy sensed she was trying to nurture their friendship. She quickly drank her coffee and then made an excuse to leave. Roger summoned the courage to ask her for a date the following Saturday, so they arranged to meet outside the flicks. Amy noticed Coral's parents smiling at each other as she passed through the lounge, on her way to the front door. They obviously approved of the assignation.

Back home, Amy switched on the radio in the kitchen and made herself a bacon butty for supper. She listened to Radio Luxemburg while slicing and buttering the bread. Billy J. Kramer had reached number one with the Beatles' song 'Do you want to know a secret'. In the States, the Four Seasons with 'Big girls don't cry' filled the number one slot. She liked both songs and sang along to them absently as she grilled the bacon. Her thoughts were occupied trying to decide whether she really fancied Roger. She concluded that she didn't know and would have to wait until the following weekend to make up her mind.

Amy enjoyed a cooked Sunday breakfast in bed with the sun streaming in through the window. Mum had got up in a good mood and decided to give her daughter a treat. The sunshine didn't entice Amy out of bed until gone noon.

She listened to records in the lounge while making essential alterations to her new bikini shorts. They needed elastic around the hemline to stop the legs from flapping about.

Yvonne arrived and bounced into the room with her swimsuit wrapped in a towel under her arm just as Amy finished the second leg. "Hey, Bat, it's a lovely day, and your bikini looks great. How about we go to the baths, and I'll teach you to swim?" she suggested eagerly, "after all, it's about time you learnt."

Amy replaced the unused elastic, needle and thread in the drawer and shook her head. "I don't know," she said, carefully examining her handiwork. "Every time someone attempts to teach me to swim, I end up underwater doing a brilliant impression of someone drowning."

"You just lack confidence," Yvonne said. "Besides, it would be a shame not to show off your new bikini."

"But I don't seem to have the same degree of buoyancy as everyone else," she protested.

"Nonsense, Bat. If anyone can get you swimming, I can – and what's more, we'll have a great time in the process." Amy reluctantly agreed to try her luck at learning to swim once again.

As they walked to the baths, Yvonne told Amy about her ill-fated trip to the beach barbecue on Saturday. "Honestly, you didn't miss a thing yesterday. It was pretty boring, and as for the idiots that passed for girls at that barbecue! They irritated me so much with their silly giggling. I couldn't take any more of it so I hitch-hiked for sixty miles and eventually arrived home safely, despite fending off some unwanted canoodling from a car full of boys."

"Well, what d'you expect if you accept a lift from a load of boys," Amy said, exasperated by her friend's naïve behaviour.

"Oh, they were harmless enough," Yvonne reassured her, "just over-amorous knights of the road."

A group of rowdy yobs on motorbikes passed by, whistling and waving. Yvonne waved back and fluttered her long lashes at them.

"No wonder you had problems yesterday if this was how you thumbed lifts!" Amy said scornfully.

At the baths, they changed in one of the wooden huts that lined the poolside and put their clothes in a locker. Once in the chilly water, Yvonne supported Amy horizontally and promised faithfully not to let her go. "Now, move your arms and legs in a synchronised movement," she said, but Amy couldn't get the hang of it. Her limbs thrashed around in uncoordinated panic, so Yvonne let go, hoping against all the odds, that she would somehow swim.

After three near drownings, Amy had had enough. “Never again will I be persuaded to learn the joys of the breaststroke,” she spluttered, as she bobbed up for the third time.

Yvonne refused to accept defeat so readily. “How about next week, I bring along my cousin?” she offered. “She can help to hold you afloat.”

“I’m going to get my feet back on solid ground, and that is where I intend to keep them,” Amy said through gritted teeth as she hauled herself up the steps out of the water.

Back at Amy’s house over tea, Yvonne had some good news. “I still keep in touch with Alex and his sister, and she told me about a job at the Kenya coffee bar in Chelsea. They need an extra waitress for Sundays, so she pulled a few strings and now I’ve got the job – isn’t that great? It’s good money, with plenty of tips as well. And what’s more,” she added, “they need more staff. Why don’t you come and work there too?”

“I don’t know if I fancy slogging away all day on a Sunday,” Amy said dubiously.

“Well, why not just work for one day next Sunday and see if you like it?” Yvonne suggested.

Amy sighed. “I suppose – I could do with the money, so maybe I’ll give it a try.”

“That’s terrific! We’ll make a great team, just you see,” Yvonne was thrilled at the prospect of them working together. “Me and Alex have been getting on a lot better lately, too, and have started seeing each other again occasionally.”

“That’s great, Yvonne. You were always very keen on him.”

After tea, Amy accompanied Yvonne to the bus stop. As the bus drew up, Yvonne reminded Amy that she was meeting her and Pam at the Scala the following evening.

Amy grinned. "Yeah, I'll be there – it should be a good night."

On arriving home, Amy discovered Yvonne had left her gabardine hanging over the banisters in the hall.

At breakfast, Dad was scowling into his teacup. Mum had accidentally left the receipt for the bikini lying on the sideboard, and he had found it.

"All that money for a couple of scraps of material," he grumbled, "Mum could have made you something suitable out of the oddments I use for my rag rugs!"

Irritated by her father's tight-fisted attitude, Amy stomped out of the house, and walked round to Coral's, only to find she had gone to the seaside for the day with Roger and his friend. Amy felt peeved. 'She might at least have invited me along!' she thought bitterly. Not wanting to return home just yet, she walked into town and bought some more blue material to make another skirt.

She cheered up that evening when she met Pam and Yvonne at the Scala. Yvonne was in her usual buoyant mood, flirting outrageously with every boy in sight. She bragged for most of the evening about her terrific job at Chelsea. After a long dancing session, they found a table to sit at for a rest and flopped into the chairs.

"Just think, Bat, all those dishy blokes we'll meet when they come in for coffee or a meal," Yvonne continued, "you're going to love working there."

Amy smiled, trying to look keen at the prospect.

"It sounds almost too good to be true," Pam commented. "D'you think Alex's sister can get me a job there too?"

"I'll ask her, Tibs. Wouldn't it be great if all three of us had jobs there!"

They walked to the Railway Tavern for a quick drink before hurrying to catch their last buses home. Amy sat on the bus rummaging through her handbag for the fare when she discovered Yvonne's sunglasses. She couldn't fathom how they had got there. 'That girl would lose her head if it wasn't screwed on!' she thought wryly.

Everyone seemed to be in the doldrums on their first day back at school. Vie was absent, and nobody was on speaking terms with Yvonne because she had a bad case of the sulks, but no-one could work out why.

"What we need is a bit of fun to cheer us up," Amy proposed to Pam, Fluff and Jean as they sat on a bench in the Manor grounds sharing a bag of crisps during their break.

"Sounds like a good idea to me," Pam mumbled through a mouthful of crisps. "How about we all go to the coast Sunday week?"

"Yeah, let's, only we won't tell Yvonne about it," Fluff said. "I don't see why we should invite her if she can't be bothered to talk to us."

"I vote we go to the Kursaal at Southend for the day," Amy declared, "and maybe by then, Vie will be able to come with us." The others all agreed it would make a great day out.

The sun beat down relentlessly from a clear blue sky the next day, so Amy didn't bother wearing her blazer or cardigan to school. She and the other girls spent the lunch hour sunbathing on the Manor lawn while Yvonne wandered off alone. There was no improvement in her demeanour so nobody bothered trying to speak to her.

After school, Amy walked into town with Pam and Fluff. They had sensibly worn their gabardines, so it didn't matter to them when the heavens opened, and the rain came down in torrents. Amy, on the other hand, wearing just her skirt and blouse, got soaked.

She arrived home bedraggled and miserable and had to quickly change into some dry clothes. She glanced out of her bedroom window and noticed Dennis bringing a new girlfriend home. Dennis looked up, spotted her and stuck out his tongue. Irritated by his behaviour, Amy promptly retaliated by putting her thumb on the end of her nose, wiggling her fingers at him and pulling a face.

Friday was also hot and sunny, so during the lunch hour, Amy returned to the lower lawn in the Manor for further sunbathing instead of going to the jive session with the others.

Jean kept her company, sitting in the shade of a tree. "This heat makes me swell up," she complained, fanning herself with an exercise book.

Amy glanced at Jean's corpulent figure but couldn't notice any difference.

"I think I'll pop over to see you Sunday evening, then you can tell me how your first day at the coffee bar went," Jean continued.

"Yeah, why not," Amy agreed half-heartedly, knowing only too well that pigs would fly long before Jean would ever turn up. "But if Yvonne's attitude doesn't improve, then I shan't bother going to work in London with her."

During the last lesson of the afternoon, the sky turned leaden and long streaks of lightning shot through the heavens accompanied by ear-splitting cracks of thunder. This was the prelude to an exceptionally heavy thunderstorm. The torrential rain formed large puddles in no time. The town centre became badly flooded since it lay in a dip, causing Amy's bus to take a long detour.

The flood even warranted a mention on the six o'clock news, according to Mrs Falco, when Amy arrived for her piano lesson. "They showed several rowing boats in the town centre, and the large fish that inhabit the ponds of Central Park had escaped and were seen swimming down the High Street."

"They'll have a job recapturing them," Amy said, with a giggle.

She was rudely awakened early in the morning by Coral banging on her front door in a panic.

Mum let her in and she dashed upstairs to Amy's bedroom. "Get up, quick," she yelled, throwing her clothes at her.

"What on earth's the matter?" Amy asked groggily, reaching for her knickers.

"I want you to come with me – I have to take Henry to the vet – he's become all swollen and bloated," she explained, looking white with worry.

"Perhaps he's got Jean's trouble and been sitting in the sun for too long," Amy joked, trying to ease Coral's agitation, but she failed to be amused.

The vet examined Henry and seemed to be at a loss, so he prescribed the usual antibiotic pills. At Coral's, they had the same old problem trying to get Henry to swallow them. He happily pushed the pill into his cheek pouch and later spat it out in his pantry. Amy left Coral, trying to coax Henry into eating a bit of apple with a pill embedded in it.

"Oh, Roger asked me to remind you not to forget your date with him this evening," Coral called out just as Amy was about to close the front door behind her.

"As if I'd forget!" she retorted with a hollow laugh though she realised as she hurried home that she wasn't really looking forward to her date with Roger. She feared he would turn out deadly boring with his overly polite good manners.

She changed her clothes and dashed down to Central Park to meet Pam. The floodwaters in the town centre had subsided. She was surprised to see most of the fish were now recaptured and swimming happily in their ponds again. A travelling fair had arrived for its annual visit, and the caravans, rides and sideshows were set up on the higher ground in a large grass field near the bandstand. As they wandered around, they bumped into Yvonne and her cousin, Vanessa. Yvonne was back to her usual good-humoured self, so they thought it best not to ask why she had ignored them all week. Yvonne bought each of them an enormous cloud of pink candyfloss and then suggested they all have a ride on the octopus. That was a big mistake for Amy. She felt sure she was about to throw up. She managed to control herself until she got off the ride. Her legs had turned to jelly, and she felt awful. There was no way, she could spend the rest of the evening sitting in a stuffy cinema with Roger, so she chose to stay in the fresh air at the fair.

She eventually arrived home to be confronted by her mother, demanding to know why she hadn't turned up at the cinema. "I've had Coral's younger sister, Susan, round here asking for you. I told her you were out, but I didn't know where you had gone. You'll be in the dog house round at the Manser's house unless you can come up with a good excuse, my girl."

"I didn't feel well enough to go and meet Roger," Amy said crossly, "I think I'll go to bed – I'm tired."

"You might not get much sleep tonight because Jumbo Shepherd is holding his twenty-first birthday party next door to the Parks. Judging by the raucous noise, it's starting to get out of hand. Ray and two of his mates are camping out all night on the back lawn in his scout tent, so I don't suppose they'll get much sleep either."

"That tent leaks like a sieve," Amy said over her shoulder as she climbed the stairs to bed. 'I hope it rains and they all get soaked to the skin!' she thought, allowing her irritability to get the better of her.

Amy dragged herself out of bed at the crack of dawn Sunday morning to catch the train to Chelsea with Yvonne. The job in the coffee bar turned out to be nothing like she had been led to believe. Yvonne swanned around amongst the tables playing the part of a glamorous waitress flirting with the male customers and thoroughly enjoying herself. But Amy was relegated to the humid, stuffy basement kitchen where she slaved over a steaming sink of hot soapy water and a never-ending supply of dirty dishes. Just as she came to the end of one large load, another arrived via the dumb waiter in the wall. She was only allowed the briefest of breaks. At the end of a very long, hot and exhausting day, Amy's pay was twenty-five shillings and a pair of red prunes for hands to show for all her hard work. Yvonne got thirty-seven shillings and sixpence plus tips, for her, not such hard work.

Yvonne took Amy for a celebratory plate of chips and a rum baba at the Chelsea Wimpy Bar on their way home.

"I shan't be doing that again in a hurry," Amy said firmly, easing her aching legs under the table.

"Look, Bat, I promise I'll try and get you a job as a waitress so we can work together," Yvonne wheedled. "It's not much fun when we don't see each other all day."

"You needn't bother because I'm just not interested," Amy said adamantly. "I prefer my Sundays to be a bit more relaxing – in fact, a lot more relaxing!"

As expected, Jean didn't show up at Amy's that evening. Feeling drained of energy, she dragged herself upstairs for a long soak in the bath.

On her way to school, Amy heard from Coral just how unpopular she had become with her family after Saturday night.

"Roger intended to take you to the fair rather than the cinema as it was such a warm evening. When you didn't show up, he took Susan instead. Where, exactly, did you get to?" she demanded.

Amy confessed that she had also been at the fair. She was glad she hadn't bumped into the two of them there, as it would have been rather embarrassing. "If Roger did, but know it, he had a lucky escape from sitting next to me on the octopus after I'd eaten that candyfloss!" she said with a grimace.

Vie arrived at school looking down in the dumps. Steve had packed her up. “Bob persuaded him to do it because he wants Steve to go on holiday with him,” she said bitterly.

“What a sod!” Amy exclaimed. “I’ve gone right off him now.”

“Steve is as much to blame for allowing himself to be persuaded. It goes to show just how little he thinks of me.” Vie sniffed and put on a brave face. “I’m better off without him,” she declared stoutly.

The day worsened when Mrs Snake pounced on Amy’s gang during the lunch break and gave them a harsh telling-off for looking scruffy.

“Think yourselves lucky I don’t put you all in detention,” she snarled, flashing her dark eyes.

“I wonder who’s upset her,” Fluff said as they hurried into the Manor grounds.

Amy arrived home after school to find her mother in a grotty mood, elbow-deep in soapsuds. Her washing machine had conked out, and she was reduced to hand-washing everything. “It’s all your father’s fault!” she shouted angrily at her mystified daughter. Amy just shrugged and hurried out of earshot, aware that logic had once again deserted her mother. Whenever anything went wrong in the Brown household, the blame inevitably landed squarely on her father’s shoulders, regardless of whether he had anything to do with it.

During tea, Dad, fed up with Mum’s constant moans about the washing machine, steered the conversation to Amy’s search for a Saturday job. “How about I phone the surrounding hospitals tomorrow at work if I get some spare time. I can ask about a suitable Saturday job for you,” he said, having heard about her traumatic ordeal at the coffee house. "And besides, I'm none too keen on you travelling all the way to Chelsea to work with Yvonne."

"Sounds like a good idea," she agreed, "since I've no intention of returning to that steamy, hot kitchen. Talk about slave labour! I'm sure it was far more humid than the thickest Borneo jungle!"

At that moment, Toots ran indoors with a starling in his mouth and let it go. The petrified bird managed to flutter away and take refuge behind the copper in the corner of the kitchen, which was still warm from Mum boiling her whites earlier in the day. Lying flat on the floor, Amy needed a lot of patience before she could coax it out with the copper stick. She examined the terrified bird. It looked unhurt, so she went outside and gently released it onto the shed roof, much to Toot's disgust. He obviously thought it a waste of a tasty meal.

A sixth-form prefect tapped Amy on the shoulder as she strolled along the lane from the bus stop to the gates of the Grange with Coral the following morning. "Put your beret on immediately, or I'll report you to Miss Hardacre," she ordered. "You know they must be worn at all times to and from school." Amy scowled, pulled out the beret from her satchel, and defiantly tugged it down over her ears. The prefect, looking satisfied, walked on. When she was out of earshot, Amy whispered to Coral: "What a creep! She's one of Clara's darlings."

Clara Hardacre glared at Amy and her five friends during assembly. She announced that she wanted to see them before lessons. They stood huddled outside her study, waiting to be summoned.

"That'll be old Snake-in-the-grass," Vie whispered to the others. "I bet she went slithering to Clara telling tales."

"I think we all look smart enough in our uniforms," Amy declared, fastening a button on her blouse. "I really don't know what all the fuss is about."

Vie was right, and they all received another lecture on their untidy appearance with another threat of detentions if they didn't make more effort. Amy and Pam hovered behind the others hoping Miss Hardacre wouldn't notice their laddered stockings.

The school held a rehearsal after lunch for a planned fashion parade, so 5G2 was let off from lessons to watch. The girls modelled the clothes they had made during needlework. Coral was in the show looking angular and awkward in a ghastly floral dress, which billowed out from the waist. Amy was relieved her overblouse was still unfinished.

They were allowed to leave school early, so Amy raced across the heath to catch a bus on the alternative route that would take her straight home to the Crescent. The same handsome conductor was on board as before. Amy felt mesmerised by his dark eyes. He gave her a lovely smile making her blush with confusion, then thrust tuppence into her hand, insisting she had overpaid. She was positive she had given him the correct fare.

Dad came home from work and stood in the middle of the kitchen, struggling to extricate himself from his voluminous mac. "I'm sorry, pet, but I've had no luck trying to track down a Saturday job for you," he confessed to Amy as he tugged his arm free. "I rang round all the local hospitals, but they don't have any vacancies at the moment."

"It doesn't matter, Dad, since I prefer the idea of shop work anyway," she said. "Besides, I don't want to work in a hospital kitchen – that would probably be worse than the coffee house."

The next day promised to be a scorcher. Yvonne wore her swimsuit under her school uniform, ready for some serious sunbathing during the lunch break. Amy accompanied her to a remote corner of the Manor grounds where the teachers rarely ventured. Yvonne would be in hot water if a teacher spotted her in a swimsuit. They lay beside a hedge with the heath on the other side. After ten minutes, they heard whispers and giggles from the far side of the hedge and realised a pair of peeping toms were spying on them. Yvonne quickly pulled on her clothes and hurled a rude remark over the hedge before they moved to a more secluded area behind the summerhouse.

"Perhaps we ought to report them," Amy said half-heartedly, "Clara is always on about reporting any strangers that we see on the heath lurking near the school."

"It's not worth it," Yvonne declared. "We'd have to explain what we were doing over by the hedge, which, strictly speaking, is out of bounds."

Coral was allowed home early, as she had to go back in the evening for the fashion show that was being put on for the parents. Amy walked all the way home with Vie instead. She was still upset over losing Steve.

"You probably can't see it now, but one day you'll realise you're much better off without him," Amy said, trying to cheer her up. "After all, you don't want to be lumbered with a convicted criminal if he's found guilty of pub brawling," she reasoned.

"I would have stuck by him through thick and thin," Vie admitted, "but I suppose it's all water under the bridge now."

"Never mind, Vie, we'll have such a great time at Southend that you'll forget all about Steve. I want to alter my jeans into bell-bottoms now that they're all the rage and wear them on Sunday, but I don't have any suitable material for the flares."

"I've got some brown corduroy you can have if you like," Vie offered.

"Thanks – that should look good with the denim. I'll pop round tomorrow evening."

Jean and Pam were both absent the next day. During the lunch break, Vie and Amy accompanied Fluff to the bus stop as she had a dental appointment. As they waited for the bus, Fluff checked her purse and discovered she didn't have enough bus fare, so they had no choice but to walk across the heath to another bus stop that would make the bus fare cheaper. On the way, they passed loads of cars parked in the bushes with their windows steamed up in the steady rain.

"We know what they're up to," Vie said, nudging Amy and grinning.

"They might just be having a picnic in their cars," Fluff said primly.

"Pull the other one!" Amy scoffed.

After seeing Fluff safely onto her bus, Vie and Amy returned to school just in time for the first lesson of the afternoon – geography. Amy wished she hadn't bothered to return when Miss Finley scolded her for not finishing her homework.

"That woman really gets on my nerves," she whispered to Vie, "I hate the old cow!"

Coral stayed late after school doing a mock typing exam, so Amy made her way home alone. She found her mum in a good mood because the engineer had been to fix her washing machine, so she didn't have to suffer washday-red hands anymore.

After tea, Amy walked around to Vie's to collect the brown corduroy material she had been promised for altering her jeans into bell-bottoms.

"In return for the material, will you come with me to the ice cream depot as I have to see a friend of my dad's?" Vie asked. Amy felt she had no choice but to agree.

"He promised us a second-hand television some weeks ago, so I've got to find out what has happened to it," Vie explained as they walked along. "We're so looking forward to getting a telly."

Vie found her dad's friend loading an ice cream van with boxes of cones. He was full of apologies for the delay, promising faithfully to deliver the television round to Vie's house at the weekend. As they left to walk back home, Vie almost jumped up and down with euphoria at the prospect. "Oh, it's so exciting. At last, we'll have our very first telly!"

As they passed Lynn's house, she appeared at the front door and invited them in for a coffee. They stayed chatting for a while and listening to records in her bedroom. She told them she wasn't seeing Skid anymore as she found him too boring. This came as no surprise to Amy.

In needlework the following morning, Amy was relieved to reach the final stage of her overblouse. She was thoroughly fed up with it by now. The press studs needed to be sewn on, and then she could forget about it because she knew she would never wear it.

Yvonne got the giggles during maths as she watched Tibby artistically change a rectangle in her geometry book into a lawn with flowerbeds. She drew amusing cartoon characters sunbathing on it. An exasperated Mrs Butler threw Yvonne out of the lesson when her giggles grew into loud cackles.

Vie started knitting a new school jumper during the lunch break, but not being very adept at it, she palmed off the various pieces onto each of her friends. Amy and Fluff found themselves allocated a sleeve each, while Yvonne volunteered to knit the front. Vie wrote down the knitting instructions for each of them on pages she had torn out from the back of an exercise book.

That evening, after her piano lesson, Amy slit the side seams of her jeans to the knee and inserted triangles of the brown corduroy to make them into bell-bottoms. She was so chuffed with the result that she used the remainder of the material to make a matching large saggy shoulder bag.

Dad came in, and surprised her by giving her five shillings spending money for the outing to Southend on Sunday. He assumed it would be a harmless day out for a bunch of schoolgirls.

Amy spent Saturday morning listening to Saturday Club on the radio while knitting some of Vie's sleeve. During a lull in the music, the sound of hammering drifted in from the shed. Dad was busy bashing away at a piece of metal. He was fashioning a heavy-duty rot-proof tray for the floor of Rubenstein's cage because the toilet corner in his cage had corroded into a hole.

After a while, Amy became aware of raised voices outside. She put her knitting down and went to the window to investigate. Skid's younger brother, Stephen Boddington, sought to brighten up a mundane Saturday. His mum was occupied buying her vegetables from Tom, the mobile greengrocer, parked across the green. Meanwhile, Stephen, naked as the day he was born, was proudly displaying his own meat and two veg at his bedroom window. Someone in the greengrocer's queue spotted him and gasped, pointing up at the window, causing everyone else to turn and look. Mrs Boddington's mouth dropped open in horror when she saw her youngest son with hands and feet stretched to the four corners of the window in a perfect 'X' shape. She rushed indoors, waving and yelling at him to get down immediately. The ladies in the queue found the spectacle highly amusing, as did Stephen. Amy felt sure he must have done it for a dare because he certainly had nothing to brag about.

Early Sunday morning, Amy leapt out of bed, anticipating a great day ahead. She tied her hair into bunches and tugged on her bell-bottom jeans before dashing off to the station to meet Pam, Fluff and Vie. Needless to say, Jean failed to turn up but wasn't missed.

The dull, overcast sky sent them scurrying for the Kursaal the moment they arrived in Southend, and by 4 pm, they had spent all their money on rides and side shows.

They stood by the water chute, trying to decide what to do when a group of boys came along. They started chatting with them, but the girls soon discovered they were also broke, so they lost no time dumping them.

They wandered over to the dodgems, where another bunch of lads tagged on and offered to take them on a few rides. One, called Bill, invited Amy on a boat ride through some caves. She thought he was OK but nothing special. His mate, Pete, took Pam into the boat behind them. Taking advantage of the darkness, Bill grabbed hold of Amy and kissed her. At the end of the ride, he showed her a stall that sold large badges and bought her one which read: 'I feel fine'. Pete bought Pam a badge announcing: 'I am a Virgin islander'.

Fluff looked at the badges and giggled. "They're a bit risqué aren't they? You need a magnifying glass to read the last word."

Suddenly, Amy spotted Midi Middleton, her junior school teacher, strolling towards her using his walking stick. Whiskers, his faithful paintbrush, was sticking out of his jacket pocket. To avoid meeting him, she quickly dragged Bill into the haunted house. The lads accompanied them to the station in the evening and saw them off on the train home.

Amy collapsed on the long seat in the compartment and put her feet up on the seat opposite. "I'm glad we didn't bother making arrangements to see them again," she said, adjusting her bunches, "they were alright for a few hours of fun at the fair, but that was all."

Vie was hanging out of the window and started yelling and waving. She turned to the others with a grin. “Come here and see what I’ve found.” They rushed over and squeezed together to peer along the train. A few carriages further down, a group of boys were doing the same; and waving and yelling at them. The boys jumped out of their compartment at the next station and ran back to join the girls. The remainder of the journey flew by as they joked and giggled with the boys who teased them about their badges. The boys got off the train a few stops earlier than the girls. They tried persuading the girls to meet them again as they said goodbye. But the train pulled away from the platform, leaving the arrangements incomplete.

“Oh, it’s probably for the best,” Pam said as she removed her badge and tucked it away in her bag. “Mum will do her nut if she sees this.”

Amy saw the lovely Ken as she walked home up the hill from the station. He strutted along on the opposite side of the road, absorbed in stroking his neat Beatle haircut. ‘I ought not to fancy someone who loves himself as much as he obviously does,’ she thought. With great reluctance, she mentally struck him off her list of potential boyfriends.

She tuned in to Radio Luxemburg while making a cup of coffee. Billy J. Kramer’s ‘Do you want to know a secret’, had been knocked off the number one slot and replaced by Gerry and the Pacemakers ‘I like it’.

“Well, I don’t bloody well like it!” she said irritably. She switched off the wireless, drank her coffee and went to bed.

She found herself consoling a depressed Coral on the way to school. Henry hamster had died despite the antibiotic pills. “You haven’t had much luck with your hamsters this year.”

Coral pulled back her shoulders and put on a brave face. "I performed the burial service yesterday," she said. "He's now laid to rest, beside Fred and Herbert in the back garden." This news was a great relief to Amy as she didn't relish the prospect of attending another hamster's funeral.

At school, nobody was talking to Jean.

"I tell you, I got to the station yesterday morning just as your train was pulling out," she reiterated. Everyone knew this was a blatant lie because they had been hanging out of the window to check the platform until the train turned a bend further up the track. There had been no sign of her.

"I vote we have it out with Jean in the lunch hour about her lies," Pam said to Amy and Vie as they strolled along the Grange driveway to their first lesson.

Amy agreed. "I'm sick of her fabricated stories."

But when lunchtime arrived, and it came to the crunch, they chickened out. Big-hearted Vie couldn't help being compassionate. "I know she deserves it, but we'll only hurt her feelings, and she'll end up being totally ostracised, thanks to us." So they agreed to give her another chance.

That afternoon, they sat for the first part of their GCE art exam. Mrs Host, the art mistress, was confident they could take their GCE art a year ahead of their other subjects. The first of the three-part exam was entitled 'Imagination'. The painting had to contain active people, so Amy opted to paint a tennis match, as this had been her choice for the mock exam. She emerged from the classroom three hours later into the warm sunshine feeling reasonably pleased with the result.

After sitting still for so long, Amy and Vie felt they needed a little exercise, so they walked home. On the edge of town, they met Dennis leaving the Smoky Rock cafe, the local haunt of leather-clad bikers and greasers. He was looking fed up.

"Be a darlin' and lend us the dough to buy a bag of chips for me tea," he begged, "only I'm skint 'til payday." Feeling magnanimous, Amy took pity on him and gave him the shilling she had just saved from her bus fare.

The following morning, the class endured the second part of the GCE art exam – object drawing. Various objects were placed around the gym. Pam and Amy were allocated a doll in a pram, standing on a wooden box with a rug draped over a wheel. The whole morning they were engaged in drawing and painting, but at least they didn't have any other lessons.

Dad monopolised the television that evening. He was glued to the boxing because this was the much-hyped big fight between Cassius Clay and Henry Cooper. Big-headed Clay won in the fifth round just as he had predicted because Cooper had to retire with a cut eye.

Mum showed Amy a letter she had received from Great Auntie Gertie. She was coming to stay for her annual visit and would be arriving on Saturday.

Amy groaned. "I suppose that means I'll be kicked out of my bedroom again."

"You just be nice to her," Dad advocated. "She's a dear old soul, and I wouldn't be surprised if she's worth a bit."

'I might have guessed you'd have an ulterior motive in pandering to her,' Amy thought but didn't dare say as much.

Nobody appeared to be in Yvonne's good books. She hardly spoke to anyone the next day, preferring the company of the older girls in the upper-sixth during the break.

Amy was forced to risk the terrible wrath of Mrs Snake descending upon her. She had no alternative but to catch up with her geography homework during the music lesson. With Miss Finley's lesson next, she suddenly realised she had forgotten to do it. For once, luck was on her side. She escaped detection, as her desk was hidden around a corner, out of the Snake's sight.

Pam and Amy found themselves once again serving the mistresses lunch. Today there was nearly a whole tray of sponge left over and two large bowls of thick whipped cream. Not wanting to waste good food, they furtively piled it into bags when no-one was looking and sneaked it out of the kitchen window into the flower border below. One large dollop of cream missed the bag and splattered on the floor, sending them into convulsions of giggles. A large florid-faced dinner lady, laden with a tray of water jugs, headed in their direction. They quickly disowned the splodge of cream and moved away. The next moment, they heard a loud yell and a crash as the dinner lady found it with her foot. She skidded into a sitting position with the metal jugs scattered around her.

The girls bolted outside to retrieve the bags of mangled sponge and cream from the bushes. Then they scurried off into the depths of the Manor grounds, where they met up with Vie, Fluff and Jean for a victorious feast of sickly cream sponge. Yvonne missed out on the food as she was elsewhere, sucking up to her new mates in the top year.

"I shan't be in school tomorrow because I'm going to meet Daddy. He's coming home from a business trip to the Channel Isles," Jean bragged, wiping a lump of cream off her chin with her finger and licking it. The others grunted non-committally or ignored her, irritated with her habitual boasting.

After lunch, they knuckled down to the last part of their art exam – a plant drawing. Amy drew a sprig of mock orange blossom in such detail that she didn't finish it in time. She felt happy with what she had done but undecided whether she had passed or failed overall on the three exams. She suspected the latter.

Vie and Amy needed some fresh air as they still felt slightly sick after pigging out on the cream sponge, so they walked the three miles home again after school.

Jean turned up unexpectedly at school in the morning. "Daddy phoned to say he's been delayed and won't be coming home until this evening," she explained, ignoring the looks of disbelief and derisory snorts.

Pam was absent, so Vie waited on table with Amy serving the staff their lunch.

"What d'you think is up with Yvonne?" Vie asked as they staggered back to the kitchen, clutching a pile of dirty dishes each. "She doesn't seem to want to talk to any of us these days."

"Oh, I don't know, Vie." Amy paused to plonk down her load on the worktop. Vie did the same, and then they returned to the tables to collect the empty tureens. "I'm getting fed up with her attitude – only speaking when she feels like it!"

Back in the kitchen, Vie carefully checked the tureens. "Those greedy buggers!" she muttered, "they've only eaten all the fish and chips and haven't left us a single chip."

At least after the dessert, there were some biscuits over. They smuggled them out of the window in a bag. Being so small, Vie lost her balance as she leaned out the window and got her head stuck in a flowering shrub. She gave a yell that brought Amy dashing to her rescue. She grabbed Vie's thrashing legs and hauled her back inside. Her hair now stood on end, making them giggle helplessly until a stony glare from Mrs Snake sobered them up. The biscuits made a tasty snack during the afternoon break.

Pam turned up unexpectedly at Amy's that evening to do her geography homework as she didn't have the correct textbooks due to her skiving off school for the day. It took them until 10 pm to finish all their homework, by which time they were starving. Dad, taking pity on them, got out the chip pan and cooked them a large batch of chips. By the time they had finished eating, Pam had missed her bus home, so Dad donned his mac, beret and goggles to give her a lift on his motorbike. She looked decidedly nervous as she gingerly clambered onto the pillion and buried her face in his back as he drove off. Amy guessed she felt acutely embarrassed at being seen on such a frumpy machine.

During Friday's assembly, Miss Hardacre announced a clampdown on untidy uniforms. Amy flinched under her hard stare, convinced Clara was speaking directly to her. "From Monday," she boomed in her most imperious voice, "black laced shoes and sixty denier stockings will be compulsory. Anyone disobeying this rule will be given a detention."

"Bloody granny togs!" Amy whispered in Pam's ear. "She's doing this just to pick on us."

Amy brought Yvonne's gaberdine to school but didn't get so much as a 'thank you' out of her when she returned it. "Yvonne is really pissing me off!" she complained to the others during the break.

"Oh forget about her, Bat," Pam said. "We'll have a great time at the Scala tomorrow night without her."

Amy walked to Pam's house the following afternoon with a bagful of clothes ready for the evening. After tea, they changed and caught a bus to the Scala, where they met up with Lynn. They each paid five shillings to get in because Saturday, there was always a live group which upped the entrance fee. Tonight Bern Elliot and the Fenmen were appearing.

"A friend of mine is going out with Bern Elliot," Lynn said as they queued to put their coats in the cloakroom.

"Well, you might have persuaded her to get a few free tickets out of her boyfriend," Amy said reproachfully.

"I shouldn't think he's got much clout with the management here," Lynn said with a sniff, "after all, they're only a local group."

That evening, a rumour spread around the Scala like wildfire. Amy arrived on the dance floor from the ladies bursting with the news. "You'll never guess who's booked to appear here on August 7th," she gasped. "None other than the Beatles!"

"You're joking!" Lynn scoffed in disbelief. "They'd never come to a provincial dump like this."

"It's amazing!" Pam sighed. "Just think, I'll see George in the flesh at last - it'll be wonderful!"

"It'll be flippin' fantastic!" Amy squealed gleefully. "You can drool over George while I swoon over gorgeous Paul. Wild horses won't keep me away."

Towards the end of the evening, the girls took a break from dancing to get out in the refreshing, cool night air. They walked through the town to the Railway Tavern for a quick drink. Who should they bump into there but Yvonne with her new boyfriend, Alfie. Yvonne made an effort to be a bit friendlier. She introduced Alfie, who seemed very affable and was quite good-looking too.

"I don't know where she keeps finding them," Amy commented as they left the Railway.

"I don't fancy going back to the Scala. Let's have a coffee in the Wimpy instead," Lynn suggested.

The Wimpy Bar was crowded, but they managed to get a table by the window. Here they could watch who was out and about in town. Some Mod boys came over and asked if they could share their table. The girls squeezed up to make room for them as they seemed a pleasant bunch of lads. They introduced themselves and chatted for a while. One, in particular, was rather dishy and a dead ringer for John Lennon, only he had the unfortunate name of Fred Bloggs.

Amy got home to find her bedroom taken over by Great Auntie Gertie. She had arrived for her annual visit, so Amy had no choice but to sleep with her mother while Dad moved in with Ray again.

She took out her irritation on the bathroom door, kicking it shut. 'Why is it never Ray but always me who has to give up their room?' she thought. 'It wouldn't be so bad if I was at least asked if I minded.'

For Sunday lunch, there was roast chicken. Afterwards, Auntie Gertie insisted on helping Mum with the washing up despite Mum's protests. Auntie Gertie washed the dishes so fast that she didn't notice the food still sticking to them. She liked to think she could still make herself useful, but her eyesight was none too good these days. She mistook the chicken dripping, which Mum had carefully saved, for a bowl of dishwater and chucked it down the sink.

Dad had been anticipating his favourite supper snack of chicken dripping on toast. When Mum told him it had been accidentally poured down the plughole, he tried to be diplomatic and put on a brave face. "We must make allowances because she is a very old lady now."

Auntie Gertie called everyone 'dear', which inevitably started Mum off too. Amy found the conversation a tad monotonous at the tea table.

Using her posh telephone voice and playing the perfect hostess, Mum offered around a large plate piled with slices of bread and butter. "Bread and butter, dear?"

At the far end of the table, Auntie Gertie cupped her hand behind her ear. "What was that, dear? Oh, yes, please, dear. I couldn't see you behind the celery, dear."

And so the scintillating conversation dragged on.

After Auntie Gertie had gone to bed, Mum returned to the kitchen for the nightly ritual of discreetly rewashing the cutlery and crockery so as not to hurt her aunt's feelings.

In the lounge, Amy was sprawled on the sofa, idly flicking through a magazine, when she came across an advert that grabbed her attention.

Blazoned across the page were the words: 'Do you hate your freckles?' How she hated her freckles! They were the bane of her life, and now, here was this marvellous product, that claimed to get rid of freckles for good. She had always longed for a clear complexion, and now her prayers had been answered. According to the advert, her freckles would miraculously vanish by applying Lergyll's Birch Balsam daily. She resolved to somehow get hold of this wonder ointment.

During 5G2's art class the next day, Mrs Host made a worrying announcement. She informed the girls that those who had drawn in the wooden boxes on which the objects had stood for the object drawing in GCE, would automatically lose marks. Amy had included the box in graphic detail, so now she knew without a shadow of a doubt that she would fail.

"How stupid to put a box in full view and expect everyone to ignore it," she complained to the others at break time. Pam had been one of the few who hadn't included it. Art, being her best subject, she had no misgivings.

"If it's any consolation, you weren't alone. Nearly everyone drew in the box," she said.

That evening, after tea, Auntie Gertie started sneezing, and everyone automatically started counting. She insisted she always sneezed five times once she had started. Never three, four or six. It had become an obsession trying to catch her out, but so far, she had always reached five – no more and no less.

The long back gardens behind the Browns' and their neighbours' houses were about to be sacrificed to accommodate several blocks of garages. Mr Brown was offered a garage with a personal door leading directly into his smaller back garden as compensation, ready for the day when he might own a car. “I don’t need all that garden anyway because I’ve got the allotment for growing vegetables,” he reasoned, “and in the meantime, I can keep my motorbike in the garage.”

The bulldozers moved in that morning to clear and level the back gardens in readiness for laying the foundations of the garages.

At school the next day, Yvonne was pleasant to Amy for long enough to con a shilling out of her, to spend in the tuck shop. Amy was furious with herself for being such an easy pushover. “I must be mad lending her money after how she’s behaved towards us lately,” she told the others during their break. “I intend to get that money back by hook or by crook!”

Amy’s day went downhill when, in domestic science, they made tea cakes, but someone took hers and left her with a batch of rock-hard ones.

Then the day declined even further for Amy while serving the staff at lunchtime. She accidentally dropped a tureen of cabbage into Mrs Slater’s lap. She was unusually understanding, but Miss Stevens puffed herself up and gave Amy a sharp telling off.

She cheered up when she arrived home from school to find a bunch of burly sun-tanned lads, stripped to the waist, busy mixing and laying concrete in what was once the far end of her back garden. A chorus of wolf whistles shrilled when they spotted her, making her blush and hurry indoors.

After tea, everyone had settled down to watch television when Auntie Gertie suddenly got up.

"I'll just go and see if Toots wants to come in," she muttered, nearly tripping over the cat sprawled out on the rug in her haste to reach the door. Amy didn't think her aunt's eyesight was that bad.

"It's her way of excusing herself when she needs to leave the room to break wind, dear," Mum explained in a discreet whisper as a loud raspberry reverberated from the hall.

Amy accosted Yvonne in the cloakroom when she arrived at school in the morning and managed to retrieve nine pence of the shilling she had loaned her.

Miss Finley summoned Amy and Jean to see her at the end of the geography lesson and once again accused them of copying. Amy was furious with Jean because it had been her who had done the copying.

Jean quickly came up with a lie. "I'm sorry, but I had no other alternative than to copy from Amy because I've been absent and needed to catch up." Miss Finley reluctantly accepted her story and let them off with a warning not to do it again.

Amy met up with Vie at the end of her road that evening, and they headed off to the Veterans Club as it had reopened regardless of protests from nearby residents. Jean failed to show up despite promising faithfully to be there. Vie spotted Steve lounging in the corner, browsing through the record collection. "I'm going to ignore him," she said firmly, composing herself.

"Good for you, Vie. You show him you don't give a hoot that he's here." They went to the opposite end of the hall, where a group of girls were chatting.

One of them came over. "You don't happen to know who that gorgeous hunk is standing over by the records?" she asked, indicating Steve, "only we've been ogling him ever since he walked in the door."

Vie grabbed Amy's arm. "I can't take any more of this," she said. "Come on, let's go into town." Ignoring the girl, they turned and walked out.

Once in town, they went into Dimashio's and spent the rest of the evening drinking orange juice and playing the pinball machines.

As they strolled home up the hill with arms linked, Vie gave a long sigh. "Sorry I spoilt your evening at the Vets. I suppose someday I'll get over Steve."

"'Course, you will," Amy said encouragingly. "Before long, you'll meet some dishy bloke and wonder what you ever saw in Steve. Besides, we had some fun on the machines tonight, didn't we?" Vie nodded and managed a smile.

Amy arrived home from school the next day and walked in the back door to find Mum emptying the pantry. "There's an army of ants coming in through the air vent," she grumbled. Amy assumed her dad would somehow end up getting blamed for the invasion.

She pulled out a knitting pattern from her satchel. "Pam gave me this so I can knit a cardigan," she said, shoving it under her mum's nose.

Her mum glanced at it and shook her head. "You can't knit that," she said firmly. "It uses far too much wool."

Amy stomped outside in a huff. 'How bloody tight-fisted can you get?' she thought bitterly.

The workmen were busy building the garages. One of them, a muscular chap nicknamed Hercules, spotted her and called over. "Any chance of doing a spot of babysitting for me? I only live a few streets away, and I'll pay you well," he bribed.

Amy went indoors to ask her dad, but he quickly put his foot down. "You can't possibly do that – you don't even know him," he told her. She stomped off to Ray's bedroom, taking her record player and records to cheer herself up. She was feeling fed up with her miserable parents.

She glanced out of the window and spotted Auntie Gertie's underwear billowing in the wind. Two pairs of combinations and a treble-boned corset had been washed and hung out to dry on the line. Such antiquated underwear was a rarity these days. Then a devastating thought struck her: 'They must have been waving above my head when Hercules was talking to me!' She cringed with embarrassment and fervently hoped he hadn't noticed them. The cumbersome combinations flapped around as though taunting her. She studied them, trying to work out how her aunt managed to get in and out of them. There was no obvious way, apart from a flap in the seat of the pants. It looked like an emergency exit. She smiled, recalling her dad's comments that morning after Auntie Gertie had left the breakfast table. With a twinkle in his eye, he had insisted that each morning Auntie Gertie nailed her combinations to the bedroom door and then backed into them!

She remembered a previous visit when she had heard her aunt complaining to Mum about the difficulty she experienced replacing her corsets and combinations. Then Auntie Gertie had gone shopping in town. She was over the moon when she discovered a little old-fashioned shop in a side-street that still stocked her particular brand.

Whenever Amy had occasion to walk past the fusty old shop, she wondered how it kept going. She concluded that Auntie Gertie's annual visit to restock with several of these revered garments must give their turnover, a much-needed boost.

In the science laboratory Friday morning, class 5G2 endured the gruesome sight of a rabbit being dissected and then had to draw a detailed diagram of the rabbit's innards in a futile attempt to broaden the boundaries of their biology education. The rabbit stunk something awful, and Pam refused, point blank, to have anything to do with it. Miss Stevens lost her temper and sent her out of the lesson, which suited Pam. Amy wished she could join her because the smell made her feel queasy.

Fortunately, her appetite was unaffected at lunchtime as she tucked into her favourite meal of fish and chips. Amy and Pam even succeeded in waylaying some of the staff's chips while they served them.

After tea, Amy switched on the television to watch Ready Steady Go. The music caused Auntie Gertie to have a peculiar turn. She turned her chair around so that she sat with her back to the television, covered her face with her hanky and made little huffing puffing noises. This turned out to be her way of showing disapproval of any program on television that she didn't want to watch. Amy ignored her. She turned up the volume until Mum entered the room and ordered her to turn it down again.

Pam arrived, oblivious to the finer points of Auntie Gertie's idiosyncrasies. Auntie Gertie removed the hanky from her face and then went on her usual errand searching for the cat. She only reached the lounge door before letting rip, causing Pam to get a bad attack of the giggles. Auntie Gertie continued, unabashed, out to the front door. Amy quickly dragged Pam off to Vie's house as she needed to borrow Vie's geography books to do her homework. Once back at Amy's, they knuckled down to their homework at the dining room table.

After an hour of writing, Pam put down her pen and stretched. "That's me done, thank goodness. By the way, there's a new club opened up not far from me. How about we give it a try tomorrow night?"

"Yeah, we might as well, as there's not much else to do," Amy agreed as they packed away their books.

"Why don't you come over for tea, and then we can change and get ready for the Residents Club," Pam suggested.

Amy arrived late Saturday afternoon, just as Pam was clipping her younger brother's hair, giving him a Beatle haircut. He had a basin clamped on his head which Pam was using as a template. He squirmed and blushed with embarrassment when Amy walked in and burst out laughing.

Pam's mum was busy frying chips at the stove, a cigarette hanging from her bright-red lipstick-smudged mouth. "Hello, Amy dear," she said with a wink, then turned to Pam. "Hurry up with Ron's hair 'cos tea's almost ready." Mrs Tibton had a disconcerting habit of winking almost every time she spoke. Pam had reassured Amy on several occasions that it was only a nervous tic.

Tea consisted of fried egg and chips on a tray while sitting in the lounge watching television. Monty, the family pet, was a black and white mongrel who was always very happy to clean any scraps off the plates if they were within reach of his tongue. Amy sat on the settee and absently stood her mug of tea on the floor. Before she had a chance to retrieve it, Monty had lapped it dry.

Mrs Tibton came in and, seeing Amy's empty mug, thought she must be thirsty. "Of course, you must have some more," she insisted with a wink, ignoring Amy's protests. Amy reluctantly sipped her refilled mug of tea, trying to block out the smell of doggy-breath.

They danced to a live group at the Residents Club, who played for most of the evening. Fat Frudge was there with some of Yvonne's new friends from the upper-sixth.

During a break, when records were being played, Frudge came over. "Yvonne was supposed to be here tonight, but when I rang her, her mum told me she had gone to bed with tonsillitis."

"Maybe I'll ring tomorrow to see how she's feeling," Pam said. The group arrived back on the stage and started up, making further talk difficult, so Frudge waved goodbye and returned to her friends.

"Why not sleep over at my house tonight?" Pam suggested as she and Amy were leaving.

"It'll mean contacting Mum through Mrs Carter's phone to ask permission," Amy said dubiously.

"Then let's do it," Pam said, grabbing Amy's arm and dragging her into a nearby phone box. Amy dialled Mrs Carter's number with trepidation. She lived several blocks away, but hers was the only house in that part of the Crescent with its own private phone.

One of the Carter's many children was dispatched to fetch Mum, so it took a while before she arrived, out of breath, on the other end of the line. “What on earth is the emergency?” she demanded crossly. Amy had had it drummed into her often enough that this should be the only justification for bothering Mrs Carter. Amy contritely asked permission to sleep at Pam’s and then put Pam on the phone to talk her round as she knew Mum would be more likely to agree if Pam asked her.

“Oh, I suppose it’s alright,” she said grudgingly, “but tell her I want her home first thing in the morning – and she mustn’t go bothering Mrs Carter again!”

As they emerged from the phone box, two boys caught them up and accompanied them to Pam’s house. They had also been at the club and asked if they could meet them on Thursday. They looked like a pretty harmless pair, so Pam and Amy agreed.

Amy spent an uncomfortable night with Pam, crammed into her single bed, unable to move. The dog had taken an unaccountable liking to her and was pinning her legs down.

After a hard-boiled egg for Sunday breakfast, Pam and Amy felt they ought to show a little compassion for Yvonne, so they went to the phone box to ring her. Her mum answered and told them she had gone to work at the coffee bar. They concluded that she couldn’t be feeling too ill after all.

Amy caught the bus home and found a note from her parents saying they were taking Auntie Gertie back home.

With the house to herself, as Ray was out, she made the most of the occasion by playing her records very loud, while she washed and reset her hair in a

Mod style – flat at the front with a slight curl in front of her ears and backcombed at the back.

That night, she was relieved to be in her own little bed again. She had missed its comfortable dent, which fitted her like a glove.

Chapter Eight

July
Burning Berets

After school on Monday, Amy walked into town with Pam, Vie and Jean. At Sherry's fabric shop, Vie and Jean helped Pam choose some blue cotton material for a calf-length shift dress while Amy popped across the road to the chemist to buy some liquid eyeliner. As the shop was empty of other customers, she plucked up the courage to enquire about Lergyll's Birch Balsam. The assistant looked blank and then went to find the manager, who also hadn't heard of it.

"What's it for?" he asked.

Amy flushed and looked down. "Er, apparently, it removes freckles," she mumbled, aware of their eyes boring into her freckle-spattered face.

"Never heard of anything that can remove freckles," the manager declared flatly, "besides, what's wrong with a few freckles?"

'You wouldn't need to ask if you were plagued with them,' Amy thought as she hurried out of the gloomy shop into the dazzling, freckle-inducing sunshine.

Jean was conveniently absent the next day. Amy was convinced it was because she had arranged to come to her house that evening.

"There's no way she'll turn up tonight," Amy said as she and Vie went into domestic science. "I bet you anything you like, she'll be away tomorrow too, so she doesn't have to go to the Veterans Club tomorrow night either."

Class 5G2 donned their pinafores and knuckled down to making and baking Swiss rolls. Amy's looked alright until she tried to roll it up, then the sponge split, the jam oozed out, and made a sticky mess.

Most swiss rolls were eaten after lunch to fill the gap left by the cheese salad dished out in the canteen. Amy and her friends sat on the lower lawn in the Manor grounds, picking at the crumbly cakes in their tins.

"I really like the pattern I've got for a shift dress," Pam mumbled, then swallowed her mouthful of Swiss roll. "Why don't you get some blue material like mine, Bat, and make one too?"

"Yeah, I could, but we'd look the same going out in identical shifts."

"Well, I don't mind us dressing alike," Pam declared.

Amy gave it some thought. "Maybe I'll get a slightly different pattern."

"Oh, by the way, has Ray got a school cap?" Pam asked.

"Yeah, somewhere – he never wears it."

"D'you think I can borrow it tonight, to use as a pattern for a large floppy cap to match my shift?"

"Don't see why not, though we'd better be careful not to let him find out what you're doing with it."

After school, Amy stopped off in town on her way home to buy a pattern and some of the same blue material.

Pam arrived at Amy's house after tea, armed with her blue material cut out and ready for sewing. Amy set up her mum's heavy Singer sewing machine on the dining room table, so Pam could sew up her shift. She cursed as she broke two needles in swift succession.

"Don't worry, I'll hide them in the rubbish. What Mum doesn't know about, she can't moan about," Amy said as she finished cutting out her shift and scooped up the few remnants of leftover material. "I've managed to borrow Ray's school cap, unbeknown to him, of course, and unpicked the seams, so that you can use it as a rough pattern. If he knew what I've done to his cap, he'd kick up a right stink, and I mustn't let Mum see it either."

"I don't think she would appreciate our need for resourcefulness," Pam said as she pinned the well-spaced out cap pattern to some spare material.

Mum came in as Pam was trying on the finished cap. Amy quickly slid the pieces of Ray's cap, out of sight, under her shift.

"Oh, that looks so nice on you, dear," Mum declared. "If you would like a cap the same as Pam's, I'll buy you some material." Amy looked at her in amazement. "I think a corduroy cap would look nice," Mum added, and for once, Amy wholeheartedly agreed with her.

After tea the following evening, Amy changed and went to meet Pam and Vie on the way to the Veterans Club. Vie smuggled Pam and Amy in through the toilet window, as they were both broke after buying the material for their shifts. They found it a bit of a tight squeeze but managed to clamber in without tearing their clothes.

"What a cheek, increasing the entrance fee just because the Saracens are appearing," Amy said crossly. The girls walked into the hall to be greeted by a raucous din as the Saracens sang their hearts out on stage. They weren't making much of an impression on their audience, who stood around, looking bored.

"It was hardly worth the effort of climbing in for free," Pam yelled in Amy's ear. "It looks as though Jean hasn't appeared, as expected."

"She didn't turn up last night at my house either – I knew she wouldn't."

After a couple of hours spent dancing to the grotty Saracens' music, which showed little sign of improving as the evening wore on, the girls called it a night and headed home.

Lorna Potter had been bragging about having her two penfriends stay with her. She brought her handsome French penfriend to school the next day. Pierre had come over to stay with her family for a couple of weeks. She had proudly shown everyone the sexy letters he had written to her, saying he wanted to drink her bath water through a straw. Now she was revelling in the envious looks she received as she introduced him to the class.

"Perhaps now he's met her and seen the way she plasters pan-stick on her face to try and hide her acne, he'll have second thoughts about drinking her bath water," Amy commented.

"You can never be too sure about the strange things the French like to do," Pam said, with a giggle.

"Yes, but surely there are limits, and drinking Lorna's dirty bath water must be one of them." Amy pulled a face at the thought. "Yuk!"

Jean condescended to honour the class with her presence again. She didn't bother to offer any excuses for her non-appearances.

That evening, Amy and Pam waited in vain near Pam's house for the two boys to show up as arranged the previous Saturday.

"Those buggers have stood us up!" Amy snapped. "How dare they!"

"We've waited long enough. Let's walk to my gran's house and visit her instead," Pam suggested.

Her gran only lived a few streets away, and she was pleased to see them. They didn't have the heart to tell her she was their second choice of company for the evening. They stayed for tea, biscuits and a chat until Amy had to leave to catch her bus home.

As they waited at the bus stop, an enormous black beetle landed on Pam's back. They both screamed, and it took all of Amy's courage to swing at it from arm's length with her shoulder bag. She missed and clouted Pam round the head twice before her aim improved, and she finally dislodged it, by which time Pam was nigh hysterical. Fortunately, Amy's bus arrived at that moment, so she quickly jumped aboard with a brief wave and left Pam to calm down as she walked home.

Lorna brought her German penfriend, Hans, to school after lunch the next day. He was tall and a bit spotty and could hardly speak any English.

"She's only showing off because both her penfriends happen to be staying with her," Amy said to Vie as they busily tailor-tacked during needlework class. With the overblouse finally finished, Amy had started work on a flared skirt. She and Vie had shared a pattern, though Vie was making her skirt a bit straighter.

"I don't think he looks the type who'd want to drink her bath water," Vie said, giving him an appraising glance. He sat with arms and legs crossed and a bored expression, watching Lorna sew.

"Perhaps she stocked up with straws just in case," Amy said with a mischievous grin.

At home that evening, Amy finished sewing her shift. She had enough material left over to make a matching floppy cap, so once more, Ray's school cap came in useful as a basic pattern.

Saturday morning, Amy awoke to the sound of rain pattering hard against her bedroom window. By the afternoon, the rain still hadn't let up. She decided not to meet Pam in town as they had arranged because she felt sure Pam wouldn't turn up in the rain. Two hours later, an irate and bedraggled Pam arrived on Amy's doorstep looking extremely soggy, her hair hanging like dripping string. "Where the hell were you?" she shouted, taking off her coat and shaking it. "I waited for over an hour before I realised you weren't going to show up."

"Sorry, Pam, I didn't think you'd come out in all this rain," Amy said feebly and then dashed upstairs to fetch a towel for her. After a mug of hot coffee, Pam began to cheer up. They donned their new shifts and caps to wear to the Residents Club that evening.

"I think you both look very smart," Mum said as they were about to leave, to catch the bus.

"They look like a pair of terrible twins to me," Dad declared with a twinkle in his eye.

"At least the rain has stopped for you," Mum said, watching them walk down the front garden path.

"Perhaps these shifts weren't such a good idea after all if Mum approves of them," Amy said as they hurried to the bus stop.

"I think they look good, so stop worrying, Bat."

At the club, Yvonne came over briefly and admired their shifts which helped to put Amy's mind at rest.

"Isn't that your boyfriend, Alfie, over there?" Amy asked, indicating a boy drinking alone at the bar.

"More like an ex-boyfriend," Yvonne said with a dismissive shrug. Then she caught sight of her new friend Susan from the upper-sixth, chatting to Frudge, so she dashed off to talk to them instead.

"I get the feeling we're no longer good enough for her," Pam said disdainfully, watching Yvonne fawning up to Susan.

One of the two boys from the previous Saturday came over, hesitantly at first and then plucked up the courage to apologise for not turning up on Thursday. His name was Alan Starling, and he introduced them to another friend of his called Graham.

After giving Alan the cold shoulder, Pam eventually thawed and condescended to dance with him, so Amy danced with Graham. The dance hall was hot and stuffy, so when the number ended, the boys suggested a short walk outside to get some fresh air.

Pam walked along with Alan while Graham followed, chatting with Amy. She noticed that he, too, had a chipped front tooth which helped her to feel more at ease with him. He was tall and gawky, wearing Hank Marvin-type glasses with thick rims. He had a mad streak in him that made her laugh. The boys hung around all evening, and when the time came to leave, they walked the girls home to Pam's house and arranged to meet up with them at the flicks on Sunday afternoon.

Amy stayed at Pam's overnight again as her mother had given her permission. She spent another uncomfortable night with the dog lying across her legs once more after he failed in his bid to squeeze into bed with them.

Pam accompanied Amy home on the bus in the morning, so they could do their homework together in the hope that it would get done that much quicker.

After lunch, they caught the bus to the next town to meet Graham and Alan outside the cinema. The boys wasted no time in leading them straight to the back row, so they didn't get to see much of Ben Hur.

During the second half, Graham nuzzled into Amy's neck and whispered how much he loved her. Amy was taken aback by this unexpected admission of his feelings for her. She knew she didn't like him that much, but not wanting to hurt his feelings, she lied and told him she loved him too.

When Graham brought her home, Amy was dismayed to see her mother spying on her through the lounge window without even bothering to be discreet about it.

'I'll give her an eyeful,' she thought crossly and grabbed a surprised Graham by the neck and pulled his face down to give him a long kiss. She glanced at the lounge window and was pleased to see that her mother had gone. After Graham got his breath back, he arranged a date with her for the following Friday evening.

Amy walked into town with Coral in the morning to catch their usual bus to school. Pam turned up unexpectedly at the bus stop. She usually caught a bus directly to school from near her house.

"Bat, it's such a nice day - too nice to be cooped up in school – let's play truant!" Coral, the straight-laced, goody-goody, clearly disapproved of the proposal, but Amy didn't need any persuading. A choice between school or a day spent enjoying themselves was an easy decision to make.

They caught a bus to Pam's and wandered around the shops until her parents had left for work. Once the coast was clear, they went into her house to change. Pam lent Amy a pair of bell-bottom jeans and a jacket. They walked into town to the Wimpy Bar, where they sat by the window drinking coffee and playing records on the jukebox. Fred Bloggs, the boy they had met the other evening with his mates, happened to wander past.

Amy nudged Pam excitedly. "Look who that is – I think he recognised us."

"I don't think so 'cos I'm sure he couldn't possibly resist coming in for a chat and a swoon," Pam joked.

Amy gulped down her last mouthful of coffee. "C'mon Tibs, if we hurry, we might be able to catch him up." She grabbed Pam and dragged her out of the Wimpy Bar. They hurried along the High Street but could see no sign of him.

"Perhaps it's just as well since it would look a bit odd – us dashing up to someone we hardly know," Pam said. Amy reluctantly agreed. "Mind you," Pam added, "he is rather dishy with his Beatle haircut and black leather Beatle jacket. He could almost be mistaken for John Lennon."

Amy's heart sank. She knew only too well that she wouldn't stand a chance if Pam decided she fancied him. 'Any bloke in his right mind would prefer Pam's model looks and clear complexion to my freckles and chipped tooth,' she thought ruefully.

They stopped to buy a bag of chips and some sweets before returning to Pam's house. On the way, they almost bumped into some of Mrs Tibton's friends, so they quickly turned down a convenient cul de sac to avoid them. Once safely back at Pam's, Amy changed into her school togs again and walked all the way home, strolling through the back door at the right time to avoid arousing suspicion.

"I want you to take your school shoes to the snobs," Mum said before Amy had time to put down her satchel. "They need repairing, and Dad says to make sure you check the cost first, and if it's too expensive, you'll have to bring them home, and he'll find time to repair them himself.

Amy's worst fears were confirmed: The shoe repair shop charged far too much for Dad's liking. With great trepidation, she had no choice but to let her father loose on them with leather, last and hammer down in the shed. The last pair he repaired for her, ended up with thick soles and metal studs on the toes and heels. He never allowed fashion to get in the way of a good solid repair that would easily outlast the life of the shoes. Amy looked glumly at the cumbersome, ungainly school shoes he proudly handed back to her. “That’s what I call an impressive repair,” he declared.

“I’m never *ever* going to let you near my best shoes,” she told him vehemently.

At school the following morning, Amy realised, somewhat guiltily, that today was Vie’s birthday. Even if she had remembered, she didn’t have any money to buy her a present. She couldn’t even afford to buy her mother a birthday present. Her birthday was only a few days away.

Pam and Amy handed in their carefully forged absence notes during registration but, to their consternation, Miss Hardacre made an announcement at the end of assembly. “I want to see every girl who was absent last week or yesterday, as there have been far too many absentees.”

She questioned everyone in her study and carefully checked their parents’ notes explaining the absences. Fortunately for Pam and Amy, she didn’t suspect their handiwork.

“Isn’t that typical of Clara to check up on every absent girl just when we decide to have one measly day off,” Amy grumbled to Pam. They were sneaking into the domestic science room with Vie, Fluff and Jean to make some coffee during the morning break. No teacher came to disturb them for a change. They toasted Vie’s birthday with basins of coffee before heading into the toilets because the next lesson was P.E. which none of them fancied.

They took a cubicle each and shut the doors in case a teacher should happen to pop her head around the door. Pam fished out a flattened fag from the bottom of her satchel. It was passed along the cubicles under the gap at the base of the dividing walls. Each occupant could enjoy a swift drag, except Fluff, as she was a bit wheezy and therefore didn't smoke.

As Amy bent down to pass on the fag, she felt a sudden sharp twang. "Oh, bugger it! My bra has just busted."

"Don't worry, it's your lucky day," Fluff said cheerily from the adjoining cubicle. "I always carry a safety pin around for such an emergency." A few minutes later, a hand waved at Amy from under the partition holding a safety pin.

"I wish I was as well organised as you," Amy called out as she struggled to fix her bra in the confined space of the cubicle.

"I'm just pleased I can help," Fluff replied modestly.

"Me and Vie are going to Woolies after school to take a maths test for Saturday work," Jean announced.

"How come you didn't tell me that Woolies is looking for Saturday staff?" Amy demanded, irritated by Jean's smug manner because she knew only too well that Amy had been looking for a Saturday job for ages.

"Don't worry, Bat, I'll ask if they need any more Saturday staff while I'm there," Vie said.

Mum bought Amy some maroon corduroy material in town that afternoon for another floppy cap, as she had promised. While Mum, Dad and Ray were attending a meeting at Ray's new school that evening, Amy searched everywhere for her brother's school cap but couldn't find it. "I bet he's deliberately hidden it because he's found out about it being unpicked for a pattern," she muttered irritably. As she rummaged through the chest of drawers in his bedroom, her search was interrupted by Mrs Boddington. She had come over to borrow some surgical spirit for her Alsatian dog. "Rocky's been and got one of those horrible ticks," she explained. Amy found the bottle in Mum's first aid box and gave it to her.

"Thanks, dear. Tell Mum I'll return it as soon as the tick's dropped off."

"Have you been officially baptised into the Mormon faith yet, or did your impromptu backstroke count as a baptism?" Amy asked with a grin as Mrs Boddington was leaving.

Mrs Boddington smiled too. Now, she could see the funny side of her dip in the font at the Mormon church. "I suppose I should blame you for getting me and your mum, involved with those flippin' American Elders. I make myself scarce if I see them coming down the road now."

Jean came into registration the next day, looking fed up. "Somehow, I managed to fail that rotten maths test at Woolies yesterday," she said, dropping her satchel onto her desk with a bang. Then Vie burst into the form room, and her beaming face spoke volumes.

"I take it you passed the test for Woolies," Amy said.

"I start work this Saturday," she said excitedly, "and what's more, I arranged for you to go for a test tomorrow evening after school."

"That's great! Thanks, Vie." She had made Amy's day. Jean rummaged around inside her desk, the lid hiding a scowl.

During double tennis, Amy took a wild swing at the ball. It sailed over the fence into the bushes on the heath. Pam and Amy were dispatched to search for it, but instead, they found the wild cherry tree that Amy and Yvonne had come across back in April. Now the branches were draped with delicious ripe fruit, so they gathered handfuls of cherries and sat on the grass beneath the tree to enjoy them, safely out of sight of the tennis courts.

After school, Amy walked all the way home to save her bus fare. Vie accompanied her part of the way but stopped at her friend, Rose's, as she had been invited for tea. Amy walked through the town and spotted Alan Starling wandering along, in a trance. Not surprisingly, he didn't notice her. 'He's probably daydreaming about Pam,' she concluded.

Class 5G2 started a collection for Mrs Butler's leaving present in the cloakroom before morning assembly. Lundy was considered more sensible than most of her classmates and therefore entrusted to look after the money.

During maths, Amy watched Mrs Butler scribbling sums on the blackboard. "From the size of her, I reckon it could be twins!" she observed in a whisper to Jean, who started giggling.

"Any bigger, and she won't fit through the doorway," Jean muttered. Mrs butler swung round and glared, not at Jean, but at Amy.

"Leave my lesson right now, as you obviously can't stop talking!"

Amy left the room simmering with outrage. 'Flippin' cheek!' she thought, positive it had been

Jean who Mrs Butler had heard, and then she worried whether Mrs Butler had overheard what they had said about her.

With school over, Amy walked into town with Vie and Jean. She went into Woolies to take the maths test and was put in a small bare room with just a desk and a chair. She was given two sheets of sums and problems to solve. She found them no worse than anything Mrs Butler had set for the class, so she passed the test with comparative ease. To her delight, she was told she could start on Saturday.

She rushed outside to tell the others the good news. They congratulated her, though Jean seemed a little peeved. A scruffy-looking boy with dark curly hair, came sauntering along with his hands in his pockets and wearing a broad grin.

"Oh, here's Ricky," Vie gasped excitedly. "He pestered me to go out with him when I was dating Steve."

"Well, you're a free agent now, Vie," Amy said.

"Yes I am, aren't I," Vie said with a smile and stepped across the pavement to say hello to him. The magnetism between them must have been mutually strong because no sooner had they spoken than they were snogging passionately in the middle of the High Street. Jean and Amy disowned them and went back into Woolies so that Amy could get her mother a card and a white nylon scarf for her birthday with the money she had managed to save from the bus fares.

Later that evening, as she knelt on the lounge floor wrapping up the scarf, it dawned on her that her mother already had a white nylon scarf. She sighed and finished wrapping it anyway. She glanced across the floor and noticed Ray's school cap half hidden under the settee. She started unpicking the seams once more to use it as a pattern for a second cap in the maroon corduroy material.

Mum's birthday arrived, so Amy gave her the card and present at breakfast. She seemed to be genuinely pleased with the scarf. 'Perhaps she's forgotten that she's already got an identical one,' Amy thought as she left for school.

A staff meeting was held after the morning break. Amy and Vie accompanied Jean to the bus stop as she was leaving early to go on holiday. She liked to brag about how well off her parents were.

"Just think, I'll be sunbathing on the French Riviera this time tomorrow," she boasted as the bus drew up. "We're going to a luxury villa with its own private swimming pool."

"She has nothing but holidays from school," Vie grumbled as they headed back.

"I bet you anything you like, she's going no further south than Bognor!" Amy said peevishly.

They arrived back at the Manor to find Yvonne and Frudge with the mob from the upper-sixth creating havoc. They were careering around the lower lawn on bikes they had borrowed from the bike rack in the large shed next to the stables. They laughed and shouted as they weaved at high speed in and out of the groups of girls lounging on the grass.

"Looks like the staff meeting still hasn't finished," Amy remarked, watching the ongoing mayhem. "Yvonne spends most of her time with that lot these days – and what's more," she added bitterly, "they're welcome to her!"

Frudge pedalled over and skidded to a halt in front of Amy, gasping to get her breath. "That chap you were with on Saturday night at the Residents Club. I'm sure I know him - his name's Graham, isn't it?"

"Yeah, I'm supposed to be meeting him tonight," Amy said offhandedly.

Frudge grinned. "You're so lucky to be going out with him. I think he's rather dishy," she said enviously.

Amy smiled back, thinking, 'there's no accounting for taste.'

"If you should get fed up with him, will you put in a good word for me?" Frudge pleaded.

"Gladly!" Amy said as she walked away.

After school, Amy took her birth certificate to the Employment Bureau to get her insurance card because she needed it to start work in the morning. She had to dash home, gulp down her tea and fly round to Mrs Falco's for her music lesson, before she returned home to change for her date with Graham.

She felt a little apprehensive. Last Sunday, at the pictures, she had been part of a foursome, but tonight would be her first date alone with a boy. She tugged on her flared jeans and then hurried to meet Graham at the top of her road, away from the prying eyes of her family and neighbours.

He was waiting patiently and presented her with a gift of nine Biros he had purloined from work. 'How romantic!' Amy thought sarcastically, bundling them into her shoulder bag.

They walked into town and strolled around Central Park, chatting until nine o'clock when Graham suggested a chip supper. He took her to a nearby chip shop for a bag of chips to eat on the way home. 'He really knows how to impress a girl,' Amy reflected, ironically, as she sucked on a soggy chip. Suddenly, he grabbed her and plonked her on top of a four-foot-high wall, totally mortifying her. She stood there trying to keep her balance and not drop her bag of chips.

Ignoring her pleas to be put back on solid ground, Graham began to serenade her at the top of his voice with Frank Ifield's hit: 'I'm confessing that I love you'. She didn't like the song when Frank Ifield sang it properly, and liked it even less when sung diabolically by Graham. 'Why do I attract nutters?' she wondered, ignoring the curious stares of passers-by. 'I'm sure Pam doesn't have these problems with Alan.'

That night, as she lay in bed mulling things over, she concluded that Frudge was welcome to mad Graham because that had been her last date with him.

An excited Amy was up bright and early in the morning for her first day working at Woolies. She met Vie at 8.20 am and had walked almost into town before she realised she had forgotten to bring her insurance card.

In a panic, she ran home and then caught the bus back into town. Fortunately, she wasn't too late, so didn't get into trouble on her very first morning.

She was disappointed to be assigned to work on the nappy and Fablon counter tucked away in the basement. A chatty, elderly lady called Joan, who had worked on the counter for years, showed Amy what to do. This included measuring out lengths of the large rolls of Fablon and oilcloth that hung on the rear wall at one end of the counter.

Amy quickly discovered that standing around all day made her feet ache badly. There was a stool under the counter, but she soon learnt it was put there purely to comply with the regulations. "Woe betide anyone the manageress catches sitting on it," Joan warned her.

Amy met Vie for lunch in the canteen. She was on the sweet counter and could chat with the kids hanging around the adjacent record counter. "I think I'll go mad if I hear Woolies lousy cover version of that rotten Frank Ifield record anymore today," she moaned. "I can't believe it's actually reached number one. I reckon it must be all the mums drooling over him who've rushed out and bought it."

"Yeah, even my mum thinks he's lovely," Amy said. "Still, at least you're working up where the action is. You can see everyone passing through while I'm stuck in the stuffy basement where I can't even see daylight."

Vie was still dating Ricky and was obviously very smitten with him because she spent the rest of the lunch hour raving about him.

They finished work at 6 pm and were handed their first pay packets – fifteen shillings and nine pence after three pence had been deducted for a stamp. They walked home feeling happy and wealthy but tired.

By the time Amy had eaten her tea, washed and changed, she was late leaving for Pam's, causing her to miss her bus. The rain pelted down relentlessly as she struggled to keep the umbrella over her. She splashed through the puddles on the long walk to Pam's house. As she turned into Pam's road, suddenly, the heel snapped off her shoe.

She limped through the front door feeling like a drowned rat. Mr Tibton helped her take off her wet coat. She liked Mr Tibton; he was quiet and unflappable, not brash like Mrs Tibton. Pam had inherited her dad's good looks – tall and slim with dark hair and the same brown eyes.

Mr Tibton gallantly offered to fix her shoe. Amy thanked him but had a few misgivings as she handed it over. Did he also have a last in his shed for doing heavy-duty shoe repairs, like her dad? He disappeared out of the room only to return a few minutes later with a tube of glue in his hand, which relieved Amy.

"I'm afraid you've missed Pam," he said apologetically. "Yvonne called round for her and dragged her off to the Residents Club. Pam said to tell you that they'd see you there." Feeling totally exhausted after her day's work and peeved that Pam hadn't waited for her, Amy opted to stay at Pam's house and watch 'That was the week that was' with her parents instead.

Mr Tibton glued the heel back on her shoe so she could wear it home while Mrs Tibton gathered up the mugs that had been licked dry by Monty and went to make a fresh pot of tea. Amy's first inclination was to politely refuse the tea when offered it. But Mrs Tibton thrust a steaming mug of doggy-breath tea into her hands regardless.

"I'm sure you must be thirsty after walking over here in all that rain," she said with a wink. "We'd much rather Pam spent her time with a nice sensible girl like you than that scatty Yvonne. I think she's a bad influence on Pam."

Amy sat there positively glowing from the praise being heaped on her, even though she realised it wasn't deserved.

Pam eventually arrived home and took Amy to her bedroom to tell her about her terrific evening at the Residents Club. She was full of excitement about the new boyfriend she had met there.

"But what about Alan Starling?" Amy asked, "I thought you were keen on him."

"Oh, he annoyed me yesterday evening when he turned up late and then had the cheek to get me to buy the drinks at the pub because he hadn't brought enough money. I don't go out with cheapskates," she said haughtily.

"I suppose Graham was at the club," Amy said. "That was one of the reasons I didn't fancy going tonight."

"No, neither he nor Alan showed their faces all evening. I spent most of the time dancing with Den. He's so lovely; I can't help swooning over him. I can hardly wait until I see him again next week," she said dreamily.

Pam persuaded Amy to stay overnight, so once again, they crammed into Pam's small bed along with the dog. Amy soon wished she was back home in her bed with its comfortable dent. She lay there in the dark, thinking, with Monty's cold, wet nose pressed against her neck and his hot breath wafting unpleasantly over her.

"Y'know, Tibs, I get the impression that Yvonne is trying to get back in with us again and using you to do it." The only response she got from Pam was a gentle snore.

The end-of-year tennis finals between the girls and the staff were held after the morning break on

Wednesday. Yvonne, Frudge and her gang skived off to have coffee in the sick room. Amy and the others hid in the Manor toilets. They held a long, in-depth discussion on the Mods and Rockers from their individual cubicles. Vie and Jean sided with the Rockers, while Amy and Pam stuck up for the Mods. Fluff held the middle ground as she wasn't all that interested in either. They got so embroiled in the discussion that they didn't notice the time and ended up late for lunch.

They hurried into the canteen to find their places had been taken, so they pinched some younger girls' seats instead. Miss Catting saw them creeping in late. As a punishment, she gave them the tedious job of clearing away the chairs after lunch.

As Amy struggled with a stack of chairs, Yvonne appeared and offered to help carry them. "How about me and you go over to the Residents Club tomorrow evening?" she suggested, smiling and blinking innocently as though no rift had sprung up between them. Amy was so surprised by her friendly attitude that she was momentarily lost for words. "I tell you what," Yvonne continued, "I'll come round for you at seven o'clock. There's a boy called Bill who'll be at the club - I'll fix you up with him if you like."

"Oh, I don't know about that," Amy said uneasily. She wasn't sure she wanted to be fixed up with someone Yvonne knew. "I don't like the idea of a blind date."

"Och, but you'll like Bill – he's a right laugh and quite good looking too – so I'll see you at seven," she said, assuming it was all settled, and hurried off, leaving Amy still clutching the stack of chairs.

She and the others finished clearing away the chairs and then headed for the Manor grounds, where they lounged on the lower lawn.

Frudge and the gang from the upper-sixth soon disrupted the peace by riding bikes around the lawn again. They quickly scooted off when they spotted Miss Hardacre heading in their direction.

"I'm bored," Amy declared, tugging a handful of grass out by the roots. Vie and Pam grunted in agreement.

"Let's go home," Pam suggested, "I'm sure no-one will miss us this afternoon."

Amy and Vie jumped up. They needed no second bidding. The girls got as far as the village when Miss Catting came along in her battered, rusty red Mini and drew up beside them.

She slid open the window and poked her head out. "Where do you think you girls are off to?" she demanded. They stood shuffling their feet and trying not to look guilty.

Pam finally thought of a convincing lie: "I've got a dental appointment, Miss Catting, so Amy and Vie are accompanying me, to the bus stop." Apparently satisfied with Pam's explanation, she closed the window and drove off.

"That was a close thing," Amy gasped with relief.

"The only problem is, we've got Catty first lesson this afternoon for history," Vie pointed out as they continued to the bus stop.

"How sickening!" Amy exclaimed, "that means you and me, will have to go back to school." So, in the end, only Pam escaped for the rest of the afternoon.

Thursday morning dawned, and Amy awoke with a feeling of euphoria. As she brushed away the cobwebs of sleep, she realised why: The last day of term had arrived. "Hooray!" she yelled and leapt out of bed, for once eager to get to school.

Fluff brought her record player and set it up in the form room, so instead of lessons, they danced to records, mostly the Beatles LP, all morning. Every girl brought her share of food and drink, and the presents were given to Mrs Butler. She was delighted with the brolly and teddy bear the girls had bought for her and the baby. In return, she gave the girls a large box of assorted chocolates to share.

Most of 5G2 were appointed as heads of table for lunch the following term, which meant being in charge of the new influx of first years. This didn't impress Amy much. They went into the canteen for their last school dinner of the term.

"Imagine having to sit with a bunch of puny first years every lunchtime," Amy said despondently. "We won't be able to chat together like this over dinner anymore."

Pam ducked as a lump of mashed potato whizzed past her ear. "Perhaps we can arrange to sit at the end of the rows of tables, and that way, we can still speak to each other," she reasoned.

Meanwhile, the food fight breaking out among the exuberant upper-sixth, who were leaving school, started to get out of hand. Stodgy snowballs of mashed potato were catapulted around, and large dollops smacked against the walls.

Mrs Snake came down from the mistresses' table, her dark eyes flashing dangerously. She was furious at having her lunch interrupted. She eventually restored order by bellowing ferociously now that detentions were no longer viable.

After lunch, everyone trooped into the jive session in the gym for a riotous hour of dancing and letting off steam. The school leavers did the rounds, asking everyone to autograph their skirts and blouses. A lot of blouses got torn up as souvenirs in the process. Miss Finley spoiled the fun by turfing out everyone who wasn't wearing the regulation plimsolls in the gym, including Amy and Pam.

They wandered across the road to the Manor courtyard, where they discovered a group of girls giggling and pointing upwards at a petticoat brazenly flying from the top of the flagpole. Mrs Slater, arriving on the scene, spotted it and promptly flew into a purple rage.

"I want someone up that pole immediately to fetch that garment down," she shrieked hysterically, stamping her foot. Miriam Cooper reluctantly scaled the pole since the petticoat on display belonged to her.

Pam and Amy went down onto the lower lawn, where they heard giggling and laughter coming from the potting sheds bordering one side of the lawn. A lot of surreptitious drinking was taking place there. Spirits were getting higher and wilder among the leavers, including Frudge. A voice that sounded like Frudge's yelled: "Let's have a ceremonial burning of our rotten berets," and a cheer went up.

The sheds emptied as everyone rushed towards the murky pond in the depths of the Manor grounds. A bonfire was soon made and lit in the large herbaceous flowerbed next to the pond. All the leavers flung their berets symbolically onto the pyre while dancing around it, whooping and chanting like red Indians. Pam and Amy joined in with the dancing, and then someone started letting off fireworks.

A furious Mrs Snake thundered onto the scene, appearing through the bushes, her face red with rage, just as Frudge was throwing a banger. It nearly hit Mrs Snake's foot, and she had to leap sharply out of the way as it exploded. This was no mean feat for a woman of Mrs Snake's ample proportions.

"You have gone too far this time, Francis," she yelled, "I shall report you to Miss Hardacre for trying to murder me with a firework."

"Oh, but Mrs Snake, it was only a banger," Frudge protested. "I didn't throw it at you on purpose."

Mrs Snake wasn't listening; she had spotted the burning berets. "What is the meaning of this wanton destruction of school uniforms?" she snarled, her eyes bulging as if they were about to pop out. "This is the last straw!" She turned on her heel and stomped off in search of the headmistress.

Miss Hardacre heard Mrs Snake's version of events hard on the heels of a prefect reporting the discovery of a den of booze in the potting sheds. With the school leavers well and truly out of control, Miss Hardacre felt she had no alternative but to call in the police.

Frudge found herself expelled on her last day for unruly and dangerous behaviour, which she proudly considered an excellent way of exiting from school life. The school finally closed for the holidays under a cloud of disgrace.

Yvonne had also been drinking in one of the potting sheds with some of the upper-sixth, becoming progressively sulkier. Amy decided not to go to the club with her that evening, so she rang

Yvonne's mum on the way home and left a message for Yvonne saying she couldn't make it.

The first day of the holidays found Amy in a good mood. She offered to prepare the runner beans for dinner and had just started on them when Coral turned up and begged her to go shopping with her instead.

Ditching the beans, Amy changed her clothes, and then they walked into town. Coral bought a white blouse, while Amy bought some face powder and a pan stick in a dark shade which she hoped would hide her freckles by making her skin look suntanned.

After lunch, Amy attempted to make some sponge drops while her mum was visiting Aunt Ruth. They turned out flat and rubbery, so she resorted to digging a hole in the flower border and burying them, so Mum wouldn't find out. Hercules kept whistling at her from the building site, but she ignored him, aware that he was married, though that didn't stop her from fancying him.

Saturday morning at Woolies, Amy was disappointed to be put on the same nappy counter as before. She didn't see Vie all day because they had to take different lunch breaks. Up in the canteen, a boring salad was the dish-of-the-day, much to Amy's disgust. Mrs Pluckthorn, one of her neighbours with peroxide blonde hair and black roots, was busy serving the food. Amy kept her head down as she collected her salad, but Mrs Pluckthorn still recognised her and started chatting. Amy had rarely spoken to her before, so she politely escaped as soon as possible because she was conscious of the impatient queue gathering behind her.

Vie met Ricky after work, so Amy hobbled home alone, her ingrowing toenails making every step torturous after being on her feet all day. She spent the evening soaking in the bath to recuperate.

Dad's workmate and his wife came to Sunday tea. He was tall and lean with stern bushy eyebrows that guarded a twinkle in his eyes. His wife was tiny with a list to starboard caused by a spinal deformity.

After tea, her eyes lit up when she saw the piano in the lounge. She could play very well and didn't take much coaxing to rattle off a medley of tunes. Amy watched her fingers rippling over the keys with a mixture of fascination and depression, starkly aware that her own feeble efforts were amateurish in the extreme by comparison.

In her bedroom later that evening, Amy experimented with her new make-up. She ended up with a glowing bright orange face – not the tanned effect she was hoping for.

The following morning, Coral and Amy walked over to the local shops, where Amy bought some pale orange lipstick to match her face. She returned home to find Mum, armed with wooden tongs, struggling to get a dripping sheet out of the copper and through the mangle. Being Monday, she had converted the kitchen into the weekly laundry room, full of steam and wet washing. Amy got roped into hanging out the washing on the line, which provoked a volley of wolf whistles from the builders working on the garages.

Dad, his shift at work finished for the day, pushed his motorbike down the alleyway and into the back garden. "I've ordered a bale of straw for the guinea pigs," he said between puffs as he heaved his bike backwards onto its stand and removed his goggles and beret.

"I hope it doesn't take too long to get here – I've got no straw left, so I can't clean them out until it arrives," Amy said with difficulty as a wet pillowcase slapped her face.

Dad came over to help by holding the peg bag. "You'll be glad to know that we'll be having our usual fortnight's holiday in Suffolk, visiting Grandad and Uncle Ron. I booked the time off from work this morning. It's a pity the new Dartford toll tunnel won't be open until later this year, in November. It will be a big improvement to the journey, making it much quicker and easier."

'Just for once,' Amy thought, 'it would be great to have a normal holiday staying in a hotel as other people did.' But Dad always held to the notion that hotels were far too expensive and insisted his offspring would show him up because they didn't know how to behave. Amy was well aware of her father's true reason, which inevitably was monetary. Every year they got to visit the grandparents because it was a cheap holiday which suited his pocket. She knew it would be pointless to complain. Instead, she opted for a compromise. "I think you should allow Pam to come with us. Then I shan't get so bored spending two weeks in the middle of nowhere."

As a child, Amy had regarded Ivy Cottage's grounds and the surrounding meadows and fields as an adventure playground. But as a teenager, the appeal had diminished somewhat.

"There's plenty of interesting things to do at Ivy Cottage, pet, and you always look forward to seeing Grandad. As for taking Pam with us, we'll have to ask Mum what she thinks about it first." With the washing line full, he handed the peg bag back to Amy and went indoors.

That afternoon, from the lounge window, Amy watched Mr Whippy's ice cream van pull up at the kerb across the green. She was positive she caught sight of Graham in a white hat and jacket serving cornets and lollies, but she didn't want to venture out in case it was him.

She crawled out of bed in the morning when she heard Dennis leaving for work and leaned out of her bedroom window. "Can I borrow your records, Den?" she called down to him.

He grinned. "'Course, you can." He went back indoors and brought round an armful of his LPs, EPs and singles.

Amy dashed downstairs and opened the front door. "Thanks, that's great!" she said, her eyes sparkling as she took them off him.

"I'll want 'em back tonight, though," Dennis called out over his shoulder, walking back down the path. He turned at the gate with a lecherous grin. "By the way, I like your baby dolls."

Amy had forgotten to put on her dressing gown in her excited rush to collect the records. She blushed and quickly closed the door.

After breakfast, Amy went round to Corals and tried persuading her to help carry the weekly shopping back from town. But Coral had arranged to meet a friend in town, so Amy had to struggle home alone with two heavy bags of groceries. All she got was a 'thank you' for her trouble. Mum firmly believed that the school holidays weren't for idle play. Whereas Amy considered she had earned a lazy afternoon. She played Dennis' records until he arrived home from work and came round to collect them. He noticed her Buddy Holly LP. "I didn't know you liked Buddy Holly," he said in surprise.

"Of course I do. That was the very first LP I ever bought. You can borrow it if you like." Dennis went home happy with his records, plus the Buddy Holly LP tucked under his arm.

Amy sat on the back doorstep Friday morning, fraying the hems of her jeans to give them a new look. Hercules kept yelling across at her, so she waved at him a few times to keep him happy. She suddenly realised she hadn't done any piano practise all week. She dashed indoors to fumble on the keyboard in a vain attempt to get the pieces of music right before her lesson that evening.

The bale of straw was delivered during the afternoon. It took a lot of pushing and heaving to fit it into the old chicken shed next to the cages. Amy ended up feeling like a scarecrow with pieces of scratchy straw sticking out from her hair and clothes. She was pleased that at least the guinea pigs had plenty of straw because it meant she wouldn't have the grotty job of lugging home cumbersome sacks of straw from the pet shop.

Saturday morning, Amy met up with Vie, and walked to Woolies. She was still on the nappy and Fablon counter but was beginning to get used to it. One of the supervisors asked if she would work full-time the following week, which pleased Amy. She jumped at the opportunity of earning some extra money.

Vie took her breaks at different times to Amy and spent her lunch hour with Ricky. During the morning and afternoon breaks, Amy sat with

Luggett, a girl from Coral's class who looked more like a boy than a girl with her high shiny forehead and short dark hair swept back. At lunchtime, Amy joined up with Ross Kildare, a neighbour she didn't know very well because she lived further around the Crescent.

She arrived home exhausted, but at least her feet weren't hurting quite so much. She was content to spend the evening quietly watching television, as she felt so tired. Mum was pleased to learn that Amy would be kept busy working in Woolies all the following week. Amy was happy to have a genuine reason to get out of fetching the weekly groceries.

Dennis returned Amy's Buddy Holly LP the following morning and generously lent her all his records again.

The building site was deserted, being Sunday, but it made a good cricket pitch. Amy joined Ray and his mates for a rowdy game of cricket before dinner.

Mr Whippy's van arrived in the middle of the afternoon with its jingle jangling up and down the street. Amy jumped up and peered through the window at the tall person in the white hat leaning out of the ice cream van window. Again, she was almost positive it was Graham but couldn't be sure without venturing outside. She definitely didn't want to do that.

Amy walked part of the way to work on Monday morning with Dennis as they both left home at the same time. She promised to return his records that evening.

This would be her first full week at Woolies. As she changed into her overalls, she was pleased to see Vie arrive. She was also working a full week and looked really happy.

"You'll never guess what," she said, struggling into her overalls. "Me and Ricky have just got engaged!"

"That's great, Vie, but where's your ring?" Amy asked, grabbing her hand to examine it.

"We haven't got round to getting a ring because we've no immediate plans to get married for some time yet."

"So you'll finish your final year at school before you settle down?"

"Oh, I should think so," Vie said vaguely. Amy guessed she hadn't thought that far ahead. They headed down the stairs from the staff quarters and paused at the top of the stairs, leading down to the basement.

"I intend to do a lot of living before I think about settling down," Amy said, "still, if it's what you want, Vie, then I hope you'll both be really happy."

"I've got absolutely no regrets, Bat," Vie said and skipped off towards the sweet counter.

On the nappy counter, Joan was absent, so Amy had to cope alone. When she got busy, Cissie, on haberdashery, took pity on her and came over to help out. The manageress, Miss Morris, who Amy soon nicknamed Morris the Moo, was back from her holidays. Amy had been pre-warned about her stuck-up ways and tyrannical outbursts.

During lunchtime, Vie hurried off to meet Ricky as usual while Amy went on an important shopping trip. She hurried along the High Street to the record shop to buy the Beatles LP. New stocks were now in. At last, her very own copy was within reach. Her heart skipped a beat as she carried it back to work, her hands caressing it lovingly. She could hardly contain her excitement at the prospect of playing it.

On her way home from work, Amy stopped at the phone box to ring Jean and tell her the news of Vie's engagement. "As it's your half-day on Wednesday," Jean said, "I'll come over to see you if you like."

"I'll meet you at the station at two o'clock," Amy told her firmly, adding, "and don't be late!" But she knew only too well that it would be remarkable if Jean did turn up.

Joan was back at work in the morning but didn't look at all well. As they weren't too busy, Miss Morris sent Amy into the ticket cupboard under the stairs for the entire morning to tidy up boxes of price tags. She didn't mind because she could sit on the floor while she worked.

At lunchtime, she bought a bag of fruit at the greengrocers and went into the park with Vie and her friend, Rose, who worked permanently at the snack bar. Rose had greasy hair and a grubby, unwashed look. Vie had confided to Amy that Rose's family lived in abject poverty and squalor.

After swallowing a meat pie, Vie left to meet Ricky while Rose helped herself to Amy's fruit. Amy noticed numerous flaky scabs on Rose's hands and involuntarily moved slightly away. She couldn't help but wonder what customers at the snack bar thought of Rose's unkempt and somewhat odorous presence.

After lunch, Miss Morris told Amy to help on the shoe counter, where Gwyneth, a sweet little Welsh lady, showed her what to do. Amy enjoyed arranging the assorted shoes on the counter, not that any took her fancy, but they were more interesting than nappies.

Vie turned up unexpectedly on Amy's doorstep that evening to borrow her shoes as she was going to a dance with Ricky. This was the first time she had ventured near Amy's house since Mum had banned her, but she didn't risk coming indoors. She just took the shoes and hurried away, leaving Amy's mum none the wiser.

Wednesday morning, Amy and Bing, the section supervisor, were serving on three counters because Joan and Cissie were off sick. Luckily there were very few customers. Amy even found the time to assemble a plastic multicoloured striped door blind.

Woolies closed at one o'clock, so Amy and Vie met Ricky in the High Street. They went into Dimashio's ice cream parlour for a sandwich and a drink. Vie returned Amy's shoes, and then Amy hurried off to the station at the far end of town to meet Jean.

She nearly fainted with surprise when Jean stepped down from the train. They walked up the hill, and once back at Amy's house, they sat in her bedroom, playing records and chatting. Jean told Amy all about her holiday in the south of France, which sounded convincing, so Amy gave her the benefit of the doubt. Perhaps she had been abroad, though she didn't look very suntanned.

Jean was supposed to return home at 5 pm, but Amy persuaded her to stay for tea, so she didn't leave until eight o'clock. Amy walked to the station with her, and they arranged to meet in town the following Wednesday evening and go for a drink.

Amy arrived home to find Mum looking agitated. "While you were at the station, Jean's dad turned up here on his motorbike and thumped loudly on the front door. He said he was looking for his missing daughter because she hadn't arrived home at the right time. I mistook him for a coalman when I opened the door, which wasn't an unreasonable assumption because his clothes and skin were so grimy." Mum gave an involuntary shudder. "He was huge and very uncouth," she said. "I shouldn't want to get on the wrong side of him!"

"He didn't look as though he had just spent a fortnight lounging in the sun at a luxury villa in the south of France, then?" Amy asked.

Her mother gave her a withering look. "What sort of a question is that? Judging by the grease on his neckerchief, I shouldn't think he's removed it for weeks."

'So much for Jean's rich parents,' Amy thought as she hurried back upstairs to her bedroom, 'Jean's private life remains an enigma.'

Chapter Nine

August
Ivy Cottage

"Miss Brown, you are on gardening and crockery today."

Amy stopped in her tracks. She had been heading for the nappy counter in the basement when Miss Morris' imperious voice bore down on her. The gardening and crockery counter, adjacent to the nappy counter, was where Jane, a dumpy, elderly lady, worked full time.

"Don't forget to check for any chips by running your finger around the edges before you wrap up the tea and dinner sets in newspaper," Jane instructed Amy. "And remember to keep all the plants well watered." Amy enjoyed the new chores, which helped to make the time pass quickly.

"Roll on Saturday when I get my first full week's pay," she said over her shoulder to Jane as she trickled water onto the pot plants from a watering can.

"Well, mind you don't go and spend it all at once!" According to Jane, all teenagers were a scatty lot. Amy just grinned and daydreamed about what she was going to buy.

After lunch on Friday, she spent the afternoon going up and down in the lift to the stock room on the top floor, collecting goods to restock the shelves. This was her first time in the stock room which stretched across the top floor. There were no windows, only sparse bare light bulbs which threw spooky shadows along the dingy gangways. The eerie silence contrasted sharply with the bright, noisy bustle on the shop floor.

At the end of the day, Amy rushed home for a frantic practise session on the piano before hurrying to her lesson. She hadn't practised for the last three days but managed to muddle through her set pieces somehow. Mrs Falco was satisfied with her efforts because she gave her two new pieces of music to learn.

Amy struggled into her green overalls in the morning, thinking of Coral. She was now en route with her family for a holiday on the south coast. "Lucky devil!" she muttered, fumbling with the buttons as the bell summoned her to the shop floor.

Miss Morris nabbed her as she ran down the stairs to the basement. "Miss Brown!" she shrilled, looking as though she had a bad smell under her nose. "I'm putting you on the gardening counter again today, and I also need you to work next week, as we are short-staffed due to holidays."

"Yes, Miss Morris," Amy said politely, pleased to be working another full week.

After an uneventful day, when non-stop rain kept most shoppers at home, Amy received her first full week's pay packet. She sat by her locker and carefully counted it: three pounds, seventeen shillings and eleven pence. She didn't notice her aching feet as she skipped home. Feeling generous, she gave her mother the odd seventeen shillings and eleven pence towards her keep. This seemed to be expected once a full-time wage was earned.

Pam came round that evening as the rain had eased up. They headed for the fairground in Central Park. The ground was still slippery and boggy after the downpour earlier, so they picked their way carefully between the puddles. They were disappointed to find no-one there they knew.

"Let's have one ride and then go," Pam said, climbing up the steps of the Waltzer. They sat, pinned to the seat by a metal bar, waiting for the other seats to fill up. "By the way, I've finished with Den," Pam said, rubbing absently at a mark on the metal bar.

Amy was surprised at Pam's casual attitude. "That's a bit sudden, isn't it? I thought you were so keen on him."

"We had an argument the other day. I told him I didn't want to see him anymore and stormed off. It must have been over something really daft because I can't even remember what we were arguing about."

"Well, you can't have liked him that much to let a petty argument split you up." Suddenly the Waltzer took off, disrupting any further conversation as squeals and screams took over. They clung to each other, revelling in being tossed around as the Waltzer twirled at high speed. The music blared out, and the lights overhead became a blur of sparkling colour. At the end of the ride, they staggered off, still clinging to each other for support until the dizziness wore off.

"Let's go to the Wimpy for a coffee," Amy suggested. They sat at their favourite table in the window where they could keep an eye on passers-by.

"I forgot to tell you – I've got a Saturday job starting next week," Pam said excitedly.

"That's great, Tibs. Now we'll both have some money to spend for a change. Where did you find it?"

"Dad arranged it for me since he's the manager of Macfisheries supermarket. I'll be filling shelves and packing customers' bags during late-night shopping on Friday evening, and all day Saturday. I'll get paid thirty-seven shillings and sixpence, which isn't bad, is it?"

"Wow, Tibs, you lucky devil. I wish I had a cushy job there instead of working for stingy Woolies with miserable Morris the Moo breathing down my neck all day. Still, at least we can meet up at lunchtime because you'll be just along the road from Woolies."

"Sorry, Bat." Pam sighed. "I'll only be getting half an hour for lunch – just enough time to eat a sandwich and gulp down a cup of tea in the staffroom."

"Never mind – think of all that money you'll be earning. It's still a better deal than working at Woolies."

Amy told Pam all about Jean's visit on Wednesday, with the unexpected arrival of her furious dad on the doorstep. "I'm amazed she actually turned up for once, and her dad definitely doesn't fit the picture she's described of a high-flying executive type," Pam declared.

She walked the three miles to Amy's house the following afternoon. As they lounged in the bay window, drinking coffee and listening to records, who should come along but Mr Whippy playing a noisy jingle. Amy grabbed her handbag and searched for her purse. She thrust a few shillings into Pam's hand. "Tibs, go and buy a couple of lollies, then you'll be able to find out where Graham has got to – that's if it really was him. I haven't seen him hanging out of the van window lately."

"But I thought you weren't interested in him anymore," Pam protested.

"I'm not, but I don't like not knowing whether he'll turn up outside my house."

Pam went unwillingly and returned five minutes later with two ice lollies and the news, gleaned from Robin, the driver, that it was Graham and he had left some time ago.

"Well, that's a relief. At least now I don't have to worry when I hear that jingle coming up the road."

The following day, as Amy left to walk over to Pam's house, she was puzzled to see the alley gate leaning against the shed in the back garden.

At Pam's, they had the house to themselves as her family had gone for a day trip to the seaside. They messed about in the kitchen, making a large batch of chips for their lunch and then spent the afternoon at the fair, which had arrived in the next town.

They had a great time riding on the Whip and the Waltzer, but by the time they came off the Octopus, they were feeling giddy and sick and regretting their lunch of greasy chips.

"I need a cup of coffee," Pam gasped, hanging onto Amy. They headed for the Wimpy Bar in the High Street and ordered recuperative cups of coffee. They enjoyed listening to the Beatles belting out 'Twist and Shout' from the newly installed EP on the jukebox. After half an hour, they felt sufficiently recovered to walk back to Pam's house.

"We've just got time for some beans on toast for tea, and then we must get ready for the Scala," Pam said, rummaging in the bread bin.

An hour later, they were on the bus heading to the Scala. As they walked in, the first person Pam saw was Den. He was there with a new girlfriend on his arm.

"She's welcome to him!" Pam snapped and dragged Amy off to a table on the opposite side of the dance floor. Amy caught a glimpse of the lovely Ken vanishing down the steps into the gents. She realised she still fancied him, despite trying to forget about him.

"You must admit, Ken is rather dishy," she said, craning her neck as she waited impatiently for his return.

But Pam was absorbed in her own thoughts. "I would love to go out with Dan again," she said wistfully. "I've not met anyone else as sweet and gorgeous as him."

"That could be a problem since your mum forbade you from ever seeing him again. I know I'd never forgive my mother if she tried to stop me from seeing a boyfriend who I was madly in love with," Amy declared emphatically.

"Dan's name is taboo in our house these days," Pam said ruefully. "I suppose Mum was right when she said I lost all interest in school and exams because of him. I can't believe it's been a whole year, and I still miss him like mad and think of him all the time."

As they were leaving, they paused to ask the doorman if the Beatles were still booked to appear there on Wednesday evening.

He chuckled. "Someone's been spreading false rumours. You're the umpteenth ones to ask me that," he said.

Amy groaned as her hopes were dashed. "I thought it must be too good to be true." They linked arms and walked down the street, trying to console each other.

Amy was back on the nappy counter with Joan the next day. She was pleased she managed to get through the day without a single mistake on the till. Dennis popped in for a chat, as did his mum later on.

Pam turned up, still preoccupied with Dan. "I'm determined to find him again even though he's moved house, and I don't know where he lives now," she said as she absently folded and refolded a nappy.

"We'll have to think of a plan of action, Tibs," Amy said matter-of-factly. "Perhaps if we hang about the town centre, we might bump into him." Pam nodded but was unconvinced that it would work.

"I'll see you tomorrow afternoon as it's my half-day – we can meet up at Dimashio's for lunch. Afterwards, you can help me choose a pair of new shoes," Amy said, trying to cheer her up. Then she spotted trouble heading her way. "Look out, Morris the Moo is strutting towards us – you'd better go." Miss Morris didn't permit her staff to stand around chatting. She glared at Amy but was too busy to stop and reprimand her.

Later, Mum came in and smuggled a packet of sweets to her. With all her visitors, Amy found the time passed quickly for a change though she had to be constantly vigilant for Miss Morris popping out of the woodwork. Eating behind the counter was also strictly forbidden. Amy pretended to be tidying the bags under the counter so she could eat her sweets.

Dad became embroiled in a row with Mr Parks when he left for his night shift that evening. His neighbour was complaining about him removing the alley gate. Amy could hear their raised voices drifting in through the open lounge window.

"How am I supposed to sleep during the day, with your kids continually slamming the gate beneath my bedroom window?" Dad demanded.

"You've got no right to take that gate off its hinges," Mr Parks growled.

"It'll stay off and in my back garden until I finish my stint of nights," Dad shouted over his shoulder as he pushed his motorbike across the green. Indoors, Amy's attention was diverted to the television because Bern Elliot and the Fenmen were appearing on the 6.25 show.

Wednesday, being half day, Amy finished work at one and met Pam at Dimashio's. They enjoyed an ice cream sundae and coffee while trying to devise a plan for finding Dan. Unable to come up with alternative ideas, they left and crossed the road to the bus stop, where they caught the bus to the next town.

There were several good shoe shops in the High street to explore. Pam and Amy searched through the shelves trying on loads of shoes in the process, but despite the wide selection on offer, Amy couldn't find a pair she liked. "I think I'll give up for now," she said, thrusting a pair of black suede high heels back onto the shelf. "Mum wants us to meet her and Mrs Hamilton back at Central Park for a picnic."

"Can't remember the last time I had a picnic," Pam said, "maybe we could have a paddle in the pool, too," she added with a mischievous grin.

"First, I need to pop into a phone box and ring Jean. We agreed to go for a drink this evening, so I'll arrange for her to meet us later in the Wimpy Bar."

Amy and Pam emerged from the phone box, both dubious about whether Jean would keep to the arrangement. They caught the bus back to Central Park and strolled through the grounds beside the beautiful flower beds and large fish ponds. They crossed the ornamental bridge and passed the bandstand and tennis courts to reach the far side of the park, where they found Mum and Mrs Hamilton in the covered seating area next to the paddling pool. The pool was crowded with noisy children, being such a warm day. They were shrieking and splashing in the murky water.

Pam gazed at the unsavoury-looking water and shook her head. "I don't fancy paddling in that!"

A river meandered nearby along the park boundary, shaded by trees growing on the bank. Some more adventurous children had opted to play in the icy cold river.

Pam and Amy sat munching sandwiches while watching two small boys. They had no notion of modesty as they dropped their trunks and peed into the flowing water, trying to sink a plastic boat as it drifted past. Mum, nibbling daintily on a sausage roll, suddenly spotted their bare-bottomed antics. She became hot and flustered, worried that Mrs Hamilton's refined sensitivity would be offended. She thrust a box of sandwiches under Mrs Hamilton's nose to distract her, pointing out the various fillings on offer.

Pam and Amy got a fit of the giggles, which earned them a grimace from Mum. After grabbing a slice of chocolate sponge each, they wandered off towards the town centre, hoping to see Dan. They discovered Vie and Ricky holding hands and gazing deeply into each other's eyes, outside Dimashio's ice cream parlour. Feeling somewhat de trop, they only stopped briefly to chat, then continued along the High Street to the Wimpy Bar, where they drank coffee while waiting for Jean. As expected, she didn't show up. The lovely Ken walked past the window causing Amy to choke on a mouthful of coffee, but there was no sign of Dan.

"Our plan of action for meeting Dan seems a little flawed," Amy said after they ordered their third cup of coffee. "Maybe we need to rethink it."

Unable to think of any better strategy, Amy met Pam after work the following day. They once again went into the Wimpy Bar to drink cups of coffee. After an hour of scrutinising every passer-by, they finally gave up and left to head home. Then their luck changed when they suddenly spotted Dan walking briskly along the High Street in the opposite direction. Pam became flustered and too nervous to approach him, so they followed him instead. He jumped on a bus, and they were about to hop on after him when they realised, just in time, they had spent most of their money on coffee and didn't have enough left for the fare. Feeling disgruntled, they had no choice but to give up and walk to Amy's house.

Pam stayed for tea as Mum had cooked a panful of bacon and mushrooms, and the aroma wafting through the house was irresistible. Afterwards, they returned to the town centre, with their confidence revived to continue their search for Dan even though it proved to be fruitless.

They met Dennis ambling along, looking the worse for drink. He was carrying an LP under his arm. "You'll never guess what I bought today," he said, flinging his free arm around Amy's shoulder and brandishing the LP triumphantly in her face. To her amazement, it was the Beatles LP.

"I thought you didn't like them," Amy said scornfully.

"I don't – they're a bunch of poofters, but I like their music, even though it ain't a patch on Elvis."

Amy laughed. "Perhaps I'll make a Mod of you yet."

"Never!" Dennis shouted as he slouched off.

Friday arrived, and Amy was pleased because so far that week, she hadn't clocked up a single over-ring ticket on her till. On her way home after work, she passed Macfisheries. She saw Pam enthusiastically packing groceries into carrier bags on her first day at the checkout and almost packing her long hair too! Amy hopped on a bus as she didn't feel sufficiently energetic to walk up the hill. As the bus passed the Wimpy Bar, she was amazed to see Dan sitting at their favourite table by the window. He spotted her on the bus and gave her a wave.

'Would you believe it,' she thought, waving back trance-like. Should she jump off the bus and run back to the supermarket to tell Pam? But the bus picked up speed, and her feet were aching, so she opted to stay put.

There was an air of excitement in the Brown household that evening. “We're going to have our own car at last – a black Standard Ten,” Dad announced proudly. “Harry found it for me, and he's taking Mum and me for a test drive after tea.”

“I'm sure it will be an excellent car if Harry has recommended it,” Mum declared with conviction. Suffering from travel sickness as she did, Amy had misgivings about swapping the fresh air on a motorbike for the stuffy confines of a car.

They arrived home later that evening full of praise for the little car. It had passed its test drive with flying colours.

“I can collect it next Thursday evening,” Dad said triumphantly. “Harry has promised to have it serviced and polished ready for me.”

Pam persuaded her dad to let her have an hour off for lunch on Saturday so that she could meet Amy. Once more, they headed for the Wimpy Bar, hoping to see Dan. As they approached, Amy noticed the lovely Ken sitting at a table near the doorway. She grabbed Pam's arm and dragged her into the shoe shop next door. “I'm sorry, but I can't go in the Wimpy while Ken is there,” she said. “Help me find a pair of shoes instead.” After a lot of searching, the only pair she liked was out of stock in her size, so she conceded defeat.

They emerged from the shop to discover that Ken had left the Wimpy Bar, so they could sit for a short while, gazing out of the window, drinking coffee until the time came to return to work.

Amy cheered up that evening when she finished work and received her second full week's pay of

£3. 17s. 11d. After tea, she caught a bus to the Residents Club, where she met Pam. They chatted with a couple of boys, Stewart and Vick, who asked them for a dance. Stewart, the better-looking one, made a beeline for Pam, so Amy found herself lumbered with Vick, who she thought was OK in a weedy sort of way. The boys walked them home to Pam's house. Amy arranged to see Vick the following Saturday as he told her he was going away on holiday the next morning for a week.

Amy stayed overnight at Pam's, but as usual, didn't get much sleep, squashed into Pam's single bed with the dog insisting on lying across both girls. Amy had his tail wagging in her face, which was no improvement on doggy-breath. He'd been scrounging leftovers from the plates that obviously didn't agree with his digestive system, judging by the ominous odours that occasionally wafted up her nostrils.

"Tibs, your rotten dog, keeps farting in my face," she complained after unsuccessfully trying to push him off the bed.

But Pam was preoccupied with other, more important matters. "Perhaps I should try to forget about Dan," she said, "after all, this Stewart I met tonight is rather dishy."

"Well, at least he's tall enough for you to look up to him. Vick only reaches my height because he wears Cuban-heeled boots." Amy screwed up her nose and gave the dog a shove. "Monty, please aim your rear end elsewhere!"

Over breakfast, Pam showed Amy the card and letter she had received from Yvonne. She was in Dundee staying with her gran.

"Sounds as though she's bored out of her skull up there," Amy commented after reading the letter. "We might have been enjoying ourselves in Bognor if it hadn't been for her rotten parents."

After breakfast, Amy caught the bus home and left Pam to spend the rest of the day getting ready for her date with Stewart at the flicks.

Amy sat in the bay window after lunch, enjoying the entertainment on the green. She watched Mr and Mrs Denton attempting to put up a new tent they had just bought for a camping holiday. The innovative invention fitted onto the roof rack of their car. It was erected like an umbrella from the roof rack, and then, the car could be driven out of the pitched tent. The theory sounded easy but putting it into practise was another matter entirely. They were experimenting in the middle of the green where they had parked their car. Mrs Denton, with arms akimbo, was bellowing instructions to her browbeaten husband. He was busy scurrying around, pegging down the guy ropes. Then came the moment of truth when he drove the car out through the tent flaps. But the ropes caught on the front wheels, leaving the tent in a mangled heap on the ground behind him. Mrs Denton's face turned red, then purple, and she looked in danger of exploding. Mr Denton sheepishly climbed out of the car and spotted Amy grinning through the window. He gave her a wink and a wave. He knew his wife's bark was a lot worse than her bite, which was just as well.

Amy was up early in the morning, her wages burning a hole in her pocket. At last, she had enough money to buy her heart's desire – *a transistor radio*! She hurried into town and bought the white one she had seen in the TV and Radio shop window. It came with a brown leather case and an earphone, costing £4. 19s. 6d. This was one of the cheapest she could find, as it was all she could afford. She had wanted one for so long, and now she was flat broke but happy.

Pam called for Amy that evening to go to the Scala with her. She had arranged to meet Stewart there at seven-thirty.

"I really don't fancy playing gooseberry all evening to you and Stewart," Amy grumbled, "besides, I'm broke after buying my transistor."

But Pam wouldn't take no for an answer. "I'll pay for you to get in, and I promise to dance with Stewart no more than twice, so come on, we'd better go, or we'll be late." Amy relented as she didn't like to let her friend down. They walked, arms linked, down to the Scala to meet Stewart.

"We had a smashing time last night at the flicks," Pam told her as they reached the town centre. "I'm really looking forward to seeing him again tonight." They arrived at the steps outside the Scala as Alan Starling came sauntering along.

He stopped for a chat. "How about us going out again sometime?" he asked Pam with a cheeky grin.

"No thanks," she replied coldly, "I've got a new boyfriend now who knows how to treat a girl properly!" She turned her back on him, so Alan shrugged and went inside. Then, who should come ambling along but Fred Bloggs. He smiled, obviously recognising the girls after all this time.

"Are you two lovely young ladies coming inside?" he enquired as he joined them on the steps.

Amy stood there awe-struck, but Pam smiled sweetly and told him they were waiting for Stewart Ramsbottom. "He's supposed to be meeting us here."

"I know Stewart," Fred said, "I'll have a look for him inside and send him out to you if I find him." After he'd gone in, Pam's cousin, Colin, arrived and generously insisted on paying for both of them to get in, so they gladly accepted.

Once inside, they found Stewart chatting with Fred, which annoyed Pam, especially when he didn't even bother to apologise for not waiting outside for her. Colin, apparently, also knew Fred and Stewart. Someone suggested going for a drink, at the Black Lion pub, about a mile out of town. Despite just arriving, they collected passes at the door and then piled into Colin's van. Pam sat on Stewart's lap in the front while Amy found herself squashed against Fred on the floor in the back amongst various toolboxes. She didn't mind in the slightest because she was in ecstasy. Fred cracked jokes with Colin and Stewart, but Amy could only gaze at him in adulation and smile stupidly like the proverbial Cheshire cat because she didn't want him to notice her chipped tooth. After a quick round of drinks, they returned to the Scala, and Fred vanished for the rest of the evening, causing Amy to lose interest in her surroundings.

At the end of the evening, Stewart took Pam home, and Colin gave Amy a lift home in his van. He had an irritating habit of digging his bony finger into her ribs to emphasise his point. How she wished it had been Fred who had asked to take her home.

There were arguments over the breakfast table in the morning. Amy was furious with her mother for insisting that Pam couldn't go with them to Suffolk.

"You didn't object to Katy Bullen going to Suffolk with us," Amy pointed out.

"But you were a lot younger then," Mum explained. "The old Morris Eight we briefly owned back then could accommodate three children on the back seat. There simply won't be room in this car for Pam and all her luggage. It's only a small car, so it will be a squeeze as it is."

A frosty silence remained between Amy and her mother when they caught the bus into town. In the Co-op, Amy chose a pattern and expensive burgundy wool to knit a school jumper. She relished watching her mother foot the bill.

That evening, Amy carefully cast on the stitches for the back of her new jumper while listening to Luxemburg on her transistor and daydreamed about the gorgeous Fred asking her out.

A card from Coral arrived in the morning post. Her holiday sounded pretty dull. She was stuck on a large municipal caravan site which definitely didn't appeal to Amy.

Pam came round that evening to show Amy her beautiful new handbag made of brown leather. "This cost me the whole of my first pay packet. I got a right telling off from my mother, for squandering all my money. She was peeved because she didn't get a penny of it."

Amy carried her record player out to the kitchen so they could listen to her Beatles LP in peace.

"I bumped into Vick in town, and he told me he was only now about to leave for his holiday," Pam said, pulling herself up, to sit on the kitchen table.

"That's a bit different to the story he told me last Saturday," Amy said in disgust. "I don't know whether I'll bother to meet him on Saturday night.

I quite like him, but he sounds like another Jean!" She sighed. "Besides, I can't stop thinking about Fred."

"Me too," Pam said dreamily, "he's so dishy." She noticed Amy's face drop. This obviously wasn't what Amy wanted to hear, so Pam tactfully changed the subject. "I had another letter from Yvonne today. She can't wait to get home again. She's fed up with her gran's constant nagging."

"Maybe she'll appreciate the company of her friends a bit more," Amy remarked, handing Pam a mug of coffee.

Thursday morning, Dad took £150 to work with him. He caught the bus because, that evening, he would be collecting the Standard Ten from Mr Hamilton's garage. He eventually arrived home in his shiny new car and drew up next to the green.

Everyone rushed out to scrutinise and admire the neat little car. His friend, Gordon Williams, looked envious because he couldn't drive.

After breakfast Friday morning, the family jumped into their new car, conscious of their neighbours' eyes watching them. Mum settled herself regally in the front seat, and Amy half expected her to give a majestic wave as they left. Dad drove them down to the river estuary, where they sat watching the boats sail past while the rain beat a tattoo on the roof.

"This is better than getting soaking wet on the motorbike," Dad remarked, beaming at everyone. Amy wasn't so sure. Already she was beginning to feel slightly ill as carsickness began to take hold.

Vie left for a three-week holiday at Butlins on Saturday morning, and Yvonne had returned from Scotland. Pam and Amy met up with her at the town hall that evening. The place was deserted as the group hadn't turned up, so they caught a bus to the Residents Club instead. This appeared to be the favourite haunt for the in-crowd to hang out; hot and jam-packed to bursting with a great group pounding out terrific music. They sang a powerful version of 'Poison Ivy', which they repeated several times due to popular demand.

"I'm definitely going to try and get a copy of that song," Amy said to Yvonne, who had arrived at her side cuddling a boy she had just met. The group started up again, so Yvonne quickly swept him away for a dance. Neither Vick nor Stewart appeared all evening.

"I've had enough of that Stewart messing me around," Pam said tetchily. "I intend to have nothing more to do with him." Amy agreed. She felt the same about Vick. As they were leaving, a fight broke out in the street. They had to run to get out of the way as fists began to fly. A youth with blood down the front of his shirt staggered past them. The unpleasant experience left them feeling shaky. A car pulled over, and a couple of boys offered them a lift home, but they declined. They felt in need of a walk in the fresh night air. When they reached Pam's house, Amy decided to catch the bus home, despite Pam's pleas for her to stay the night. She didn't want to hurt Pam's feelings, but she couldn't stomach a repeat of the previous Saturday night, sharing Monty's flatulence.

Amy lazed in bed all Sunday morning and got up to find her mother in a bad mood. "Just look at the size of this bruise I've got coming up on my knee," she declared, pulling up her skirt to reveal a purple lump. "That damn cockerel from next door kicked me!" Amy tried to keep a straight face and look suitably sympathetic.

The Parks were fattening up a cockerel for their Christmas dinner. The cockerel had other plans and tried to escape at every opportunity. "I saw it running amok in Dad's cabbage patch," Mum explained. "He'd wring its neck if he caught it, so I went out to try and recapture it, but it's a right bad-tempered bird. I would never have believed it could give such a vicious kick until I picked it up to return it, to its own garden." She did a lot of pronounced limping for the rest of the day to extract the maximum amount of sympathy.

Amy caught the bus into town on Tuesday and asked for 'Poison Ivy' in the record shop, but they hadn't heard of it.

"Perhaps it's an old song," the assistant remarked thoughtfully, scratching his chin. Disappointed, Amy stocked up with several batteries for her transistor in readiness for her holiday buried in the depths of rural Suffolk. As she headed for home, she saw Ton-Up Slater on her moped, the ear flaps on her leather helmet fluttering in the wind behind her as she roared by at twenty miles an hour. Amy was reassured by the thought that her dad no longer had to dress in his awful mac, beret and yellow goggles now that he was driving a respectable car.

She called at the cobblers to have new tips put on the toes of her new blue sling-backs because she didn't trust her dad to do it to her liking. Then she stopped at the hairdressers as her mother wanted an appointment for a trim the following morning.

Dad took Ray into town in the morning, dropping Mum off at the hairdressers. Amy now had the freedom to put on her Beatles LP at full volume in the lounge, so she could hear it clearly while upstairs lying in bed.

Back from her holiday, Coral arrived bearing a present of cream perfume. She lounged across Amy's bed. "Sorry I haven't been to see you before, only I've been doing a lot of catching up with Mick," she said with a smirk.

"I bet you have! Your romance is still going strong, then?"

"Well, they say that absence makes the heart grow fonder," Coral declared, "and I definitely agree with that sentiment!" Coral refused to appease Amy's curiosity by divulging more details.

Friday morning, Mum went into town to do the last bits of shopping before they went on holiday. Once again, Amy took advantage of her absence to play her LP really loud. She thought she heard a muffled banging on the wall from the Denton's house, but she couldn't be sure as the Beatles were crashing out 'Please please me'. She watched from the bay window and turned the volume down when she saw her mother coming along the street laden with shopping bags.

"What's the matter with Marge Denton?" Mum demanded, dropping the shopping bags on the kitchen table. "She's playing that flippin' 'Wimoweh' by Karl Denver at full volume. Doesn't she realise that the noise comes straight through the wall from their dining room into our kitchen?"

Amy looked innocently at her mother. "Oh, I expect she's just enjoying her music."

"If she doesn't turn it down soon, I shall have to bang on the wall because it will give me one of my migraines."

Pam turned up after lunch. Amy had been getting quite worried about where she had got to all week.

"I've been a bit preoccupied with a new boyfriend," she explained. "His name's Andy, and he's got a smashing scooter covered in mirrors."

"Wow, you lucky thing." Amy was dead envious. "How did you meet him?"

"I've been doing some extra hours at the supermarket this week, which is why I haven't been to see you. He got chatting with me when he was going through the checkout, and after work, he was waiting for me on his scooter and offered to give me a lift home. How could I refuse?"

Amy switched on the kettle for coffee. "So what's he like then, this Andy?" she asked, getting the mugs out of the cupboard.

"He's a right Mod with a Beatle haircut and wears a parka and beret when he's riding his scooter. We've been out twice so far, but he's a bit quiet - doesn't say a lot." Amy fervently hoped that Andy would take Pam's mind off Fred.

"What's that noise coming through the wall?" Pam asked, suddenly realising she had to raise her voice to be heard.

"That's Mrs Denton. She's left Karl Denver singing 'Wimoweh' at full blast while she's out shopping. I think she's doing it to get back at me for annoying her with my Beatles LP."

Pam picked up her mug of coffee. "Let's get away from this awful din and sit in the lounge where we can listen to the Beatles in peace. With Amy's mum across the green having tea with Mrs Williams, they could turn up the volume with impunity.

After tea, Pam left for her evening shift at Macfisheries. Amy walked to her music lesson, where Mrs Falco dropped a bombshell. “I would like to enter you for the third-grade preparatory exam in music. I think you are ready for it.”

“Oh, I don’t know about that – I’ll have to think about it,” Amy said, flustered. This wasn’t why she wanted to learn to play the piano. She hated the thought of playing to a critical audience of examiners.

On her way home, she stopped at the pet shop to stock up on oats for Bobby and Patsy, plus some mixed corn for Rubenstein, enough to last for two weeks.

That evening, she sat engrossed in her knitting, her mind brooding over the music exam. ‘I’m sure it will be character forming,’ she told herself, ‘so I must try to be positive and then perhaps I can believe that I can do it.’ Despite her misgivings, she decided to face up to the challenge and take it on.

Amy woke to torrential rain in the morning, so Dad took her to work in the car. She met Pam for lunch as she had persuaded her dad to let her have a whole hour. They went for coffee and a plate of chips each in the Wimpy.

“I’m not going out with that nerd Andy anymore,” Pam said crossly.

“That didn’t last very long. What went wrong?” Amy asked in surprise.

“I saw him give Miriam Cooper a lift on his scooter yesterday evening. The cow was snuggling up to him on the pillion.”

“Perhaps there was a perfectly innocent explanation for it,” Amy said hopefully.

"No chance! I saw him turn and give her a peck on the cheek as she climbed on his pillion."

"Never mind, Tibs, it's these quiet ones you've got to watch."

Amy was feeling fed up at the prospect of going away on holiday with her family for two weeks. She arranged to meet Pam in town that evening for a quiet drink at the Railway Tavern to cheer themselves up. For once, neither of them was in the mood for dancing.

"Wish I didn't have to go to flippin' Suffolk," Amy said as they sat at the bar with a vodka and lime each.

"Why not come and stay with me? Mum and Dad won't mind as they really like you, though it will mean squeezing into my bed for two weeks."

Amy pulled a face. "I don't think I could take fourteen nights of your dog farting in my face! And did you know you grind your teeth in your sleep?"

"Oh, I'm sure I don't," Pam protested. "I expect it's Monty."

"Anyway, there's no way Mum will let me stay behind 'cos she'd be afraid I'd wreck the house with wild parties."

Pam grinned. "Yeah, we could have a great time."

"Forget it – it's not going to happen. I'll be bored to tears for two weeks in the middle of nowhere."

Sunday was spent in frantic activities: Cleaning the animals' cages and packing the suitcases ready for the journey to Suffolk the next day.

In the morning, Dad gave Amy a lift to Coral's house with Rubenstein as she had agreed to look after him. Their neighbours, the Williams, were going to feed the guinea pigs and Toots the cat.

With their four-legged family catered for and the car packed, they finally set out at ten minutes past two on the start of their holiday with Grandad and Uncle Ron in Suffolk. Mum got all excited and light-headed at the prospect of seeing her dad again. Ignoring the groans coming from the back seat, she burst into song at the top of her voice, something she rarely did.

In previous years they had endured an arduous journey by train to Ipswich station. Uncle Ron would meet them in Grandad's wheezy old Austin, with its smelly leather seats and side indicators that flapped out like orange fingers pointing the way. The engine would complain at the slightest gradient, as did the gearbox, crunching every time he changed gear.

Being a poor traveller, Amy took a travel sickness tablet before leaving home, which sent her to sleep for most of the journey. Ray nudged her awake for the last lap along the bleak open lane with deep ditches on either side. She rubbed her eyes and peered out at the rural landscape with the occasional stunted tree flashing by. A car honked its horn as it careered by on the wrong side of the road.

"I'd hate to come along here in winter when there's ice on the road. I bet loads of cars end up in these ditches, judging by the reckless way the locals drive around these narrow lanes," Amy commented. They passed the thatched cottage still called Turner's Milk Parlour. Nan once came there for her milk though it had long since ceased to supply milk. The tiny red letterbox was set in the wall outside, and as they drove past, they knew there was only one more mile to go. This was Dad's signal to sing out the well-worn refrain at the top of his voice to the tune of 'Polly put the kettle on.'

"Grandad put the kettle on........ we're nearly there!"

The five-bar gate had been propped open in readiness for their arrival. The little Standard Ten turned into the yard at 5.40 pm. Dad felt chuffed with his new car's performance on its first long journey.

The yard of Ivy Cottage was reminiscent of a bygone age. They drove along the rutted track with the pigsties on the left, which now housed chicken manure. The deep, forbidding pond on the right was hidden from view by thick bundles of faggots, placed side by side like ranks of soldiers standing to attention. An opening gave access to steps cut into the mud that led down to the water's edge. The water-filled ditches drained into the pond, and Grandad used the water for his two hundred or so chickens that he reared for eggs. He was very proud of his eggs. No supermarket shelf would see these eggs. They were of such superior size and quality that they were destined for the tables of the rich and famous staying at the best hotels in London.

Mum had her usual panic attack as they passed within feet of the murky duck pond. "Lou, do be careful. One slip, and we'll all end up in that awful pond." She tugged at his arm nervously, almost causing him to lose control of the steering wheel. "Lou! Stop messing about!" she shrieked as the car suddenly lurched towards the pond. Dad laughed. He enjoyed teasing her, but she was in too much of a tizz to notice he was only pulling her leg. The car drew up beside the old ash tree in front of the cowshed that now housed bales of straw and the lawn mower.

Grandad came shuffling out of the large main shed wearing the same clothes he always wore: His waistcoat with its fob watch, shirt sleeves rolled up to his elbows, exposing arms and hands tanned as brown as the soil and his flat, grubby cap that hid his full head of jet-black hair with hardly a hint of grey. He pulled his cap off and wiped an arm across his forehead. His eyes watered with emotion as he watched his family tumbling out of the car. Grandad was pleased to see them, especially his daughter, because she would free him from the hated household chores for two weeks. He was looking forward to escaping into his beloved garden all day and tending to his chickens. He had no qualms about handing over the housework and cooking reins. But it meant Mum's vacation became a bit of a busman's holiday, not that she minded as she realised how happy it made her dad. Since Nan died three years ago, he had struggled to cope with the housework. By his standards, this was strictly women's work and always would be if he had his way!

Before they could take their cases indoors and unpack, Grandad insisted on the annual ritual of leading them around the neatly manicured, lawned paths in the garden that intersected the vegetable plots and flower beds in order to solemnly admire the marvellous displays of brightly coloured flowers massed in profusion and the crops grown to magnificent proportions.

"That be all the feed they get from the chicken manure that make 'em grow so big," Grandad said proudly in his broad Suffolk dialect.

Dad was very envious of these prize-winning specimens. "If only I could grow vegetables like this, I'd be able to show Gordon who's got the greenest fingers," he said to Amy. With the luxury of now owning a car, Dad had the means to get a heap of this miracle manure back home. He realised he'd need to be extremely careful not to let his wife find out, or his plan would be scotched.

In the innocence of her youth, Amy marvelled at the wonders Grandad could perform with his bare hands. One of his tricks was to kill wasps by clapping his hands together to squash them without getting stung. Another was pulling up stinging nettles without feeling a thing. Now Amy was older and a little wiser, she realised that over the years, hard manual work had made his hands as tough as cured cowhide and impervious to stings. However, it still made a good party piece to show to a naive friend.

Ray and Amy's obnoxious cousin, Norman, was also on holiday at Ivy Cottage until the following Saturday. He was a year older than Amy, with slightly eccentric habits and an unpredictable temper that could flare up for no reason. "I intend to keep out of Norman's way as much as possible. You can keep him company if you like," she told Ray as they struggled to carry their cases up the tiny steep staircase that led to the bedrooms from behind a door in the kitchen.

Amy didn't like the row of interconnected bedrooms because of the lack of privacy, as the indoor toilet facilities only extended to a chamber pot under each bed. Uncle Ron's bedroom was open-plan on the landing at the top of the stairs, so everyone walked through his room. Grandad's bedroom was at the top of the stairs on the right, and Mum and Dad's bedroom was at the opposite, far end, so they were the only rooms to enjoy any privacy. They didn't have to put up with a route march through their bedrooms. At least Amy had her own bedroom. Ray had to share Uncle Ron's double bed, and Norman was relegated to the uncomfortable horsehair chaise longue in the dining room. Amy loved the old-fashioned iron bedsteads with their thick feather mattresses. When she was small, to get into bed, she had to climb onto a chair and make a flying leap into the middle of the well-fluffed bed, having first pulled back the sheets and then sunk at least a foot as the soft downy mattress enveloped her, making it as comforting as the dip in her bed back home.

The outdoor toilet facilities were almost as primitive as the indoor ones.

A small shed discreetly shrouded in honeysuckle at the end of the footpath next to the large main shed housed a wooden bench with a hole. Beneath stood a large bucket. The bench was smooth and white from constant scrubbing with the benefit of feeling warm against bare flesh. A pile of newspapers and magazines were heaped at one end of the bench. It didn't pay to relax as the door had no lock, so the sound of approaching footsteps signalled the need to start whistling or singing to make it known that the toilet was occupied.

Tuesday morning, after a breakfast of fresh eggs and bacon cooked on the quaint paraffin stove with its gurgling noises in the egg room adjacent to the dining room, Grandad was happy to be back in his old routine. With his grubby flat cap clamped to his head, he worked, bent double, amongst his vegetables. He'd pause now and then to check the time on his trusty fob watch. At 10.30 precisely, he shuffled to the back door with two hand bowls filled with freshly dug or gathered vegetables and expected his beaver to be ready for him.

"Amy, come and start scraping these potatoes," Mum said, emptying a hand bowl into the sink. Amy groaned but knew she couldn't get out of this chore. She could have deliberately peeled them too thickly, if they had been old potatoes, then she would have been quickly banished from the sink. She was well aware that Grandad abhorred waste. Today they were new potatoes, so there was no escaping the interminable scraping that caused unsightly brown stains on her fingers.

'It's not fair, just because I'm a girl,' she thought for the umpteenth time as she scrapped. Ray and Norman were free to spend the morning in the meadow adjacent to the cottage, making a den in a dry ditch hidden by the overhanging hedge. Amy didn't mind too much because it kept them out of her hair. She glanced at Grandad, sitting on the three-legged stool next to the old range sipping his cup of chicory coffee and munching on a plain biscuit. She realised that habitual routines seemed to dominate the lives of country people. Grandad was absorbed in watching Mum paring the runner beans very thinly. She knew he would check the peelings discarded in the chicken feed bucket outside the kitchen window to ensure there was no undue wastage. He had been brought up to appreciate frugality and could not abide waste.

The baker's van drew up in the road, the first of three visits per week. Amy was excited to see a dishy baker's boy coming towards the open back door, delivering the bread. 'He could almost pass for a young Elvis,' she thought as she watched him set down his large wicker basket on the dresser in the kitchen. 'He does look a bit of a Rocker, though, but then what else can you expect in the depths of the country,' she reasoned. He sat down on a chair, and Mum quickly made him a coffee as he had arrived in time to join Grandad for his beaver. Amy wished she had the self-confidence to speak to him instead of discreetly ogling him from the kitchen sink. 'If Yvonne was here, I know she'd be chatting him up right now,' she thought ruefully.

Uncle Ron was Mum's youngest brother, a bachelor still living at home. He was even more useless than Grandad when it came to housework. His sole contribution to the upkeep of the cottage and garden consisted in looking after the greenhouse and raising the annual bedding flowers from seed. He worked at a farm about two miles up the road, and being August, he was busy getting in the harvest, which involved spending long hours in the fields.

Mum put down the vegetable knife and busied herself, filling a glass bottle with cold tea. "I want you to take Ron's beaver up the field to him. I'll pack some bread and cheese to go with his tea. There's nothing so refreshing as cold tea on a hot summer's day," she declared, handing the bottle to Amy, who grimaced at the thought of cold tea. She screwed up her courage to give the baker's boy what she hoped was an alluring smile. He smiled back, and Amy noticed his deep blue eyes. 'Oh, I think I'm in love,' she thought as she dashed out of the kitchen door feeling flustered.

She walked up the road to Last's farm, still daydreaming about the baker's boy. She stopped to stroke Mrs Last's horse as it stood, with its head bowed over the gate of the field adjoining the farmyard. Mrs Last was a typical farmer's wife – a friendly, plump little lady. Amy wondered how she managed to get onto her large horse, let alone ride him.

Further along the road, she arrived at Stanley's farm and picked her way up the partly harvested field, the stubble scratching at her ankles, making them bleed. There was no mistaking Uncle Ron's bright red face beaming down from the top of the combine harvester, a picture of health from years of working outdoors. She'd never seen anyone else with such a vivid, ruddy complexion. Amy could easily pick him out at a distance if he was working in a group of farm labourers, by his black beret perched above his round red face. A tractor and trailer half full with sacks of corn stood next to the combine harvester. Uncle Ron and another worker in the trailer were busy filling sacks with the corn from the tank on the harvester. It was hot, dusty work. Amy could see the dust motes swirling above the trailer, trapped in the shafts of sunlight. The harder he worked, the redder Uncle Ron got. In her younger days, Amy had worried that he might actually explode.

He grinned, pleased to see her bringing his much-needed refreshment. His Suffolk accent was even broader than his dad's. It took Amy most of the two weeks' holiday to get her ears tuned in to understand some of what he was saying. Today, she could only catch the odd word.

She didn't hang around, leaving him to enjoy his cold tea and snack in the shade of a hedge. She picked her way through the vicious stubble and felt relieved when she reached the lane again.

Everyone had to be indoors on the dot at 12.30 for dinner. Grandad was a stickler for punctuality. Uncle Ron pedalled home, face aglow, eager to appease his gargantuan appetite. This was a brief respite from a long day in the fields. He would take his tea meal back to work, as he'd be harvesting until dusk.

Grandad and Uncle Ron always had a large nobble of bread with their dinner. They indulged in a fragmented conversation between mouthfuls, their dialect broader than ever. No one else, except Mum, could understand much of what was said. Today the subject appeared to be how the harvest was progressing.

Suddenly, without warning, Grandad gave one of his legendary, loud sneezes. Norman was so surprised that he jumped, causing his chair to tip backwards, gouging a hole in the hardboard partition that separated the dining room from the hallway. Grandad muttered something unintelligible. Amy and Ray got told off for giggling, whereas Norman didn't get reprimanded for the damage he had caused.

"Never mind, it was only an accident," Dad said, "I'll soon get that repaired."

Amy was at a loose end after breakfast the following morning. Feeling bored, she grudgingly offered to help Ray and Norman finish making their den in the meadow. They found some pieces of a tree trunk to improvise as seats.

"How about we stock up with some booze?" Norman suggested.

"And just how do we do that?" Amy demanded.

"If we all chip in with some money, I reckon I could pass for eighteen at the Greyhound pub," Norman said as he puffed out his chest, hoping it made him look older.

"It's worth a try, I suppose," Amy said dubiously, "the worst that can happen is you get chucked out of the pub."

"He'll get away with it," Ray confidently predicted. "We'll get some bottles of beer this evening, but we'd better head back now 'cos it must be dinner time."

After dinner, Dad drove them to the seaside at Felixstowe. Ray and Norman promptly vanished into the fairground all afternoon, so Amy browsed around the souvenir shops. She bought a crested teaspoon as a present to take back for Coral. Meanwhile, Mum bought bread rolls from a small bakery in the town. She also bought some ham and cakes. Everyone eventually met on the beach for a picnic tea on the pebbles.

"We must pop in and pay our respects to Aunt Rene on the way home as she lives nearby," Mum said, packing up the remains of the picnic. Amy gave a groan which Mum ignored. She continued: "She lives alone, so she'll be glad to have some visitors."

The car drew up outside a small end-of-terrace cottage. Aunt Rene's face lit up as she opened the door and saw her niece and family standing there. Although Mum called her aunt, she was actually her step-grandmother, having married her grandfather after he was widowed. She had been quite a lot younger than him. Aunt Rene was so thrilled to see them. Her neat silvery white hair was pulled back from her shining rosy face into a bun at the nape of her neck, and she wore a wrap-around pinafore. She ushered them into her tiny sitting room dominated by an enormous grandfather clock with a loud and steady 'tick tock.' Amy had the misfortune of sitting next to it. She felt uncomfortable under the gaze of numerous eyes boring down on her from the faded sepia photographs of ancient relatives set in dark wooden frames that covered the walls. She drifted into a daydream while the adults droned on about their latest ailments, and Ray passed the time swapping fag cards with Norman. She was rudely jolted back to the present by the grand old clock shuddering into life with a cacophony of bells clamouring out the hour. The noise made Mum realise that it was time to leave.

Back at Ivy Cottage, the adults headed for the kitchen and a cup of tea, so Norman signalled to Ray and Amy to follow him. He jumped over the five-bar gate and loped off towards the meadow next door. Amy and Ray quickly caught up with him.

"Right, you two, let's have some money so I can get the beer," Norman said impatiently. They dug into their pockets and handed over their meagre savings. Norman counted it and snorted. "Well, we're not going to get drunk on this, are we?" he grumbled.

"It's all I can spare," Amy said, "and besides, we can hardly stagger home drunk, can we?" Norman just pulled a face and then jogged off down the lane while Amy and Ray went across the meadow to the den in the ditch to wait.

Dusk had fallen by the time Norman returned with three bottles of beer. "I passed for eighteen, no problem; knew I would – oh, and I remembered to get these as well," he said, tossing down a packet of mints. "We don't want to go indoors stinking of booze." Norman hit the bottle caps off on a large stone, and they sat on the tree trunks swigging the warm beer and relishing the vague feeling of decadence.

'I must be bored out of my mind to be sitting in a ditch drinking beer with my lousy brother and poxy cousin,' Amy thought despondently. 'Pam would never believe it.'

The morning dawned bright and sunny, so after breakfast, Dad and Amy walked up the road to Last's farm to give Mrs Last's horse some sugar lumps. He was in his field, hanging his head over the gate, and enjoyed the handful of treats. Afterwards, they wandered around the farmyard, but the place looked deserted because everyone was busy harvesting in the fields where they had been since daybreak. Just as they were leaving, Mr Last emerged from the depths of a cow shed pushing a wheelbarrow overflowing with fresh manure. He recognised Dad from previous years when he visited the farm, so he put down the wheelbarrow and came over for a chat.

"You remember old Billy Rookyard, who looked after the cows?" he said. "Well, he's retired now, so I'm doing all the milking."

"Even Horner?" Amy asked in amazement.

Mr Last looked puzzled, then smiled. "Oh, you mean Patsy. Yes, she grudgingly lets me milk her now but to begin with, she would kick the bucket over if she got half a chance."

Billy Rookyard had worked at the farm for as long as Amy could remember. Mr Last's workers obviously didn't belong to any union because Billy had milked the cows seven days a week and could never take a holiday because of Patsy. She was an extremely cantankerous cow who only allowed Billy to milk her. Amy and Ray had nicknamed her Horner because she had a twisted horn growing around her forehead with its point aiming straight for her temple. Billy would push a penny between the horn and her head to reassure them that it wasn't digging into her. He always kept a few sweets in his pocket for Amy and Ray in case they were playing in the meadow next to Ivy Cottage when he came to round up the cows. Sometimes they wandered up the fields to watch him on his tractor, busy ploughing or planting depending on the time of year.

Amy sighed. She would miss his friendly face and cheerful greeting: "Hello there, young Tommy and Mary." He liked to tease them by pretending he had forgotten their names.

Back at Ivy Cottage, Amy wrote a short letter to Pam and then wandered down the gloomy path behind the tall conifer hedge, which screened the eastern edge of the garden. She watched the man next door take the honeycombs out of his beehives, using only a smoke puffer for protection. Grandad bought a regular supply of honey from him as this was Uncle Ron's favourite spread on his bread at teatime.

With dinner over, Mum dragged them off to visit Hilda, her old school chum. She lived several villages away in a quaint thatched cottage with low, beamed ceilings and an enormous inglenook fireplace. Her thin, lanky husband had to walk around indoors with a permanent stoop.

Unlike Mum, Hilda had never moved away from the area, so she also spoke with a broad accent, which was difficult to understand. Like Uncle Ron, she also had a very ruddy complexion.

There was hardly any garden behind the cottage, so they grew vegetables in the large front garden. Cauliflowers and cabbages lined the path to the front door. They weren't as pretty as flowers but far more practical.

Hilda led them from the lounge down a few steps into the vast flag-stoned kitchen dominated by a huge oak table, bleached white from years of scrubbing. It stood solid and majestic in the centre, while an Aga at the far end gave the room a cosy atmosphere. This was evidently the hub of the home. There was a television in the corner and a settee against the wall. They sat around the table drinking tea, overhead an assortment of cooking utensils dangled from the beams.

Afterwards, Hilda took them on a brief tour of the cottage. Amy was fascinated by a child's nursery, which could only be entered by a small secret door camouflaged with wallpaper to make it blend in with the bedroom wall. She felt like Alice in Wonderland as she bent double to fit through the doorway.

Back at Ivy Cottage after tea, the Browns prepared to leave in their car as Ray wanted to visit a schoolfriend who had recently moved to Ipswich. Just as they were driving through the five-bar gate at dusk, they almost ran over Mum's older brother, George, and his wife, Molly, who had arrived on their bikes to pay them a visit. They had cycled for over ten miles, so the Browns had no option but to cancel their plans and re-park the car.

George and Molly had never been blessed with children. George talked with a nervous catch in his voice due to his ordeal as a prisoner of war, during the Second World War. His younger brother, Jack, had been less fortunate. As the pilot of a Lancaster bomber, he was shot down over France and became the only member of his family to lose his life during the war. His picture on the parlour wall in Ivy Cottage depicted an exceptionally handsome young man. Fate had dealt him a cruel blow as he was newly married just before being called up for duty.

Aunt Molly was a petite, northerner and, as such, had never been too popular with Nan when she was alive, especially as Molly smoked constantly. Though not very old, her face was already a mass of wrinkles, and she spoke with a rasping, dark brown voice, but she had a wicked sense of humour. Amy liked her because she didn't entirely conform to what was regarded as proper by her sanctimonious in-laws.

The evening dragged by for Amy as another discourse ensued on the ever-popular subject of illness which Mum enjoyed getting her teeth into. She was the undisputed champion of the surgeon's knife. She liked to think no-one else had endured quite so many operations or suffered the variety of illnesses that she could lay claim to. Meanwhile, Norman sat in a corner and sulked all evening.

"I reckon he's in a mood because we didn't take him with us earlier," Amy whispered in Ray's ear.

Norman was still sulking in the morning. He slunk off to the den in the meadow while Dad drove Amy and Ray into Ipswich to do some shopping.

They combined the shopping trip with a visit to Ray's schoolfriend and invited him back to Ivy Cottage for tea, but he came up with the lame excuse that he was going shopping.

"He's always been terribly shy," Ray explained on the way home. "He won't mix with anyone he doesn't know."

Norman had stopped sulking and was his usual moody self. After tea, he grudgingly joined them to visit yet more ancient relatives in the form of Grandad's sister and brother. They lived adjacent to each other in a pair of small semi-detached cottages surrounded by fields.

As Dad drove along the winding lanes, Mum reminisced about her aunt and uncle's rural way of life. "They rarely venture into town; the last time Auntie Hattie made the journey was to have her eyes tested by the opticians. She was amazed at her first-ever glimpse of traffic lights. They still live in a bygone age where the pace of life is taken at a slow stroll and 'help thy neighbour' is put into daily practise. If any essentials are needed in town, rather than taking the bus themselves, they give the bus driver a list of their needs. They then collected them from him on his return journey later in the day. Uncle Bert's wife, Edith, once handed the driver a brown paper bag containing Uncle Bert's dentures with instructions to take them to the dentist for repair. He was given strict orders not to forget to collect them from the dentist's surgery before he started his homeward journey. They were the only set Bert possessed, and he wouldn't be able to eat his tea without them."

"I know how he felt," Dad chipped in, giving everyone the benefit of a gummy grin.

Mum ignored him and continued. “Auntie Hattie has led a very sheltered life as a spinster. She still lives in the same cottage where she was born. It’s only a one-up, one-down affair with a lean-to scullery tagged on the back. Yet, somehow my grandparents managed to bring up thirteen children there, including your grandad, Uncle Bert and Auntie Gertie. Not many people could do that these days.”

“Not many people would want to try!” Amy said scornfully.

“Uncle Bert, who lives next door with his wife, has a black and white cat which is very special to him because he has trained it to the gun.”

“Oh, come off it,” Norman scoffed. “That’s not possible.”

“It’s true, I tell you,” Mum reiterated, annoyed by the interruption, as she was getting into her stride. “He stands at his back door and shoots at the rabbits that munch on the crops in the surrounding fields and his vegetable garden, then sends the cat off to retrieve them.”

“I’ve heard of gun dogs but never a gun cat before,” Amy remarked.

“Uncle Bert is very proud of his beloved cat. All his trousers have holes in the knees. The cat likes to lie on his lap and pluck at the material.” Mum sniffed. “And Uncle Bert is daft enough to let him,” she added disapprovingly.

Auntie Hattie was excited to have so many visitors. She ushered them into her tiny sitting room. Everyone ducked to get through the front door. Once inside, Amy sat on the black leather chaise longue, squashed between Ray and Norman. Mum and Dad sat on the dining room chairs beside the damask-covered table that took up most of the space in the room. Auntie Hattie had her own rocking chair by the fire. It was always lit, summer or winter, but the room never seemed hot or stuffy. She wore a woollen shawl around her shoulders. Amy couldn't help staring, shocked by the sight of her gnarled and knobbly hands, crippled with arthritis, clutching the arms of her chair. Amy had never seen such badly deformed hands before. Auntie Hattie's poor eyesight didn't allow her to read, and her hands prevented her from knitting. She spent her days sitting in her chair, gazing out of the small-paned window across to the fields opposite. With neither radio nor television for entertainment, she only had her thoughts and memories for company.

'No wonder she loves having visitors pop in for a chat to break the monotony,' Amy thought.

Occasionally, when Mum was in one of her rare communicative moods, she would drop hints about Auntie Hattie's past concerning a soldier in the First World War. There were rumours of a daughter who, she presumed, was fostered out or adopted. Perhaps Auntie Hattie hadn't led quite such a sheltered life after all. Amy wished she could ask her about her memories, but this was yet another family skeleton that must stay firmly locked in the cupboard. Amy wondered if the rumour was true. 'It's so sad,' she thought, 'illegitimacy was such a taboo in those days, and even now, nearly fifty years on, things still haven't improved that much.'

Like Grandad, Auntie Hattie still possessed a full head of thick black hair with hardly a grey hair. She wore it swept into a bun resembling a large cow pat on her head. Amy tried to calculate how long it would be if it were unravelled. She suspected her great-aunt had never visited a hairdresser in her life. These country people knew all about living a frugal existence. They didn't believe in the unnecessary expense of hairdressers. When she was alive, Nan's hair was a case in point. She wore her long silvery hair in plaits, wound neatly around her head. If Amy got up early in the mornings, she loved to watch, fascinated, as Nan stood in front of the parlour mirror, brushing out her straight hair, which reached well below her waist. Amy had often resolved to grow her hair as long as her nan's, and now, since her disastrous perm, she was even more determined to leave it to grow as nature intended.

Auntie Hattie always had chocolate bars for any children who visited her. She kept a store of them in the top drawer of the heavy chest that lurked in the shadowy corner of her room next to the chaise longue. She never forgot to hand them out when the time came to leave. This almost made the boredom bearable of an hour or so of the adults discussing their favourite topic of health, or to be more accurate - their lack of it!

Before leaving, they visited Uncle Bert and his wife next door. Like his brother and sister, Bert also had a good head of dark hair, and there was a strong family resemblance. Today he was in bed suffering from lumbago, so they didn't stay too long. Edith was a short, dumpy woman with a high forehead. Amy considered her one of the least attractive women she had ever seen. But her pleasant manner compensated for her looks.

The rain pelted down all the way home, reducing the countryside to a blur. They arrived at

Ivy Cottage just as the mobile chip van pulled up in the lane on its fortnightly visit.

"Dad, please treat us to a fish and chip supper," Ray begged. "It'll make up for such a boring day." Dad didn't need much persuading, and even Grandad enjoyed the unaccustomed luxury.

Living conditions at Ivy Cottage were improving year by year. Now that electricity had recently been installed, there was no more fumbling in the darkness when returning home late at night. Unlocking the outside door into the dining room and finding the matches to light the oil lamp left in readiness on the table before leaving. And no more taking a candle to light the way up the stairs to bed. Mains water had been promised but as yet hadn't arrived. Every morning, Grandad cycled up the lane with a pail suspended from each handlebar to collect drinking water from a tap positioned awkwardly in a ditch opposite Last's farm. The pails had lids and stood on the flagstones in the pantry beneath a shelf, as it was the coldest room in the cottage. Next to them stood a third pail with milk bottles dunked up to their necks in water to keep them fresh. Outside the kitchen door, a large water butt collected rainwater for washing and washing up. Down the path, near the main shed, another two galvanised tanks collected rainwater for the weekly laundry session.

Norman didn't want to go home Saturday morning, so he ran off and hid in the cornfield behind the meadow. After a lot of searching and calling, he was eventually found. Dad drove him straight to the station and deposited him safely on the train. Then Norman's frantic face appeared at the window just as the train began to pull away.

"Uncle Lou, I've lost my watch. It must be in the cornfield," he yelled as the train gathered speed.

"Don't worry, we'll look for it and post it on to you if we find it," Dad yelled, waving at the fast-disappearing train. He drove back to the cottage and galvanised everyone in a hunt for the missing watch.

"I wouldn't be surprised if Norman said he'd lost his watch just to get us wasting our time searching for it in vain," Amy said crossly, "he's probably wearing it and laughing all the way home." After a whole morning spent searching the cornfield, they were forced to give up because it was like searching for the proverbial needle in a haystack.

After lunch, Amy and Ray were hauled off to visit the next lot of relatives. Aunt Bea and her family ran the Buck's Head pub several villages away. The adults settled down to another round of boring talk over cups of tea, so Amy wandered out into the back garden and made friends with a tortoiseshell cat.

"Her name's Tammy," a voice said. Amy turned to see Aunt Bea's daughter, Penny, emerging from a nearby shed. They had never met, but Amy guessed she must be a couple of years younger than her. She gave Amy a friendly smile.

"We've got one very spoilt cat called Toots," Amy told her. "He goes a bit cranky at times – it might be something to do with his love of curry. He eats it 'til the tears run down his face."

Penny laughed. "Tammy's a fairly normal cat though she's usually very nervous of strangers and runs away to hide. You've obviously got the knack of putting her at ease," she said. "How about we go into the public bar for a game of darts while it's empty?" Amy thought her suggestion sounded like a good idea. On the way, they popped into the kitchen to invite Ray to join them. They found him visibly drooping over a game of solitaire, on the kitchen table.

The public bar was a dingy room. It had nicotine-stained walls and curtains, and it stank of stale beer and cigarette smoke. Penny poured three lemonades behind the bar, then thrashed them easily at darts.

"This isn't fair," Ray complained. "You've had plenty of practise." He didn't like being beaten, especially by a girl. Amy was relieved to get out into the fresh air once more when it came time to leave before the pub opened for the evening session.

Teatime at Ivy Cottage meant the inevitable large plate of buttered Suffolk rusks on the table as they were a traditional dish. Amy was puzzled why they were so popular when she found them pretty bland. Grandad always started his meal with bread and butter or bread and jam.

"It's far too extravagant to have both at once on your bread," he said, glaring at Amy's plate of bread spread with butter and topped with a generous helping of home-made jam.

'Grandad is even more tight-fisted than my flippin' father,' Amy thought, 'I bet Dad hero-worships him.'

"Would you like a tomato, Dad?" Mum asked with a wicked twinkle in her eye as she held out a large dish of red tomatoes.

Grandad looked at the dish with deep suspicion. "Bloomin' poisonous, they are," he growled. "You won't catch me growing foreign things like that." Grandad strongly disapproved and despaired of modern, decadent ways. He would never normally entertain tomatoes in the house. They were only in the house now because he knew how much his daughter enjoyed them. He regarded them as highly dubious imports along with oranges, though bananas, for some reason, he accepted.

After tea, Grandad announced that he wanted to visit his nephew, Willie. They stood in the yard debating whether to take one or two cars, when who should turn in at the gate but Uncle Willie himself, driving an expensive-looking car. He invited everyone back to his house for the evening, and his car could comfortably accommodate everyone. He owned a lovely big house, which commanded magnificent views over the surrounding fields and churchyard. Two black Labrador dogs and two cats greeted them. Like Grandad, Uncle Willie owned loads of chickens. Unlike Grandad's chickens, which were free-range, Uncle Willie's chickens were cooped up day and night in tiny mesh cages inside large sheds.

"Battery hens!" Grandad muttered in disgust to Amy as though it was something to be ashamed of. She found herself moved and very saddened by the plight of the restricted chickens.

Uncle Willie's daughter, Sylvia, was about Amy's age. She was another cousin who Amy barely knew. She took Amy into the study to play with her two kittens. Once Amy discovered she was an ardent Beatles fan, she quickly warmed to her. "I've named the kittens Paul and George after you-know-who," she said proudly, handing Amy a black, fluffy Paul to cuddle.

Back at Ivy Cottage, Saturday night meant one thing – bath time! Down in the shed, an enormous black pot nestled on the fire set in the wall, heating the water while the egg room was temporarily converted into a bathroom. A galvanised tin bath was brought in from the shed where it had been hanging on the wall. Towels were carefully laid on either side of the bath to mop up any water. There ensued the inevitable dispute over who could be first. Neither Amy nor Ray wanted to bathe in dirty water, and it was considered far too wasteful to have two baths full of water. Tonight, Amy lost the argument.

"It's late, and since Ray is the youngest, he needs to get to bed quickly," her mother reasoned. Amy could only sulk as she waited for her turn.

Chapter Ten

September
Season of Fruitfulness

Amy enjoyed a relaxing Sunday morning listening to Easy Beat on the radio while playing a game of Ludo with Ray. He went off in a sulk after being well and truly beaten. At four o'clock in the afternoon, Amy shut herself in the parlour and tuned the radio to Pick of the Pops, as she did without fail every Sunday at home. She made a careful copy of the Top Ten in her chart book, converted from an old exercise book.

Mum came in and tutted her disapproval. "When I was a child, we were only allowed to read the Bible on a Sunday – nothing else was permitted apart from attending Sunday school. If your Grandad finds you listening to that racket, he'll complain that I'm not bringing you up properly." Amy pretended to be so engrossed, writing in her book, that she hadn't heard her mother.

Monday had always been Nan's busy laundry day in the shed, and now it had become Mum's chore. Early in the morning, Grandad lit the faggots under the large, circular stone copper to heat the water for boiling the whites. More water was heated on the fire set in the wall, which also heated the brick oven behind it that was no longer used. There were several galvanised baths filled with water for washing and rinsing, one with a blue rinse for the whites and one with Robin starch added. The final stage was feeding the clean washing through the mangle. Then the washing was put in a large wicker basket and carried down to the long linen lawn beside Grandad's vegetable garden for pegging out to dry on the line.

To avoid being roped into helping with the Monday wash, Amy went to Ipswich with Dad and Grandad. Grandad had an appointment with the dentist. She wandered along the High Street and bought a sixpenny picture of the Beatles. Further along, she paused to gaze into a shoe shop window and drool over a beautiful pair of Mod shoes, but the 39/11d price tag meant they were far too expensive. She sighed and dragged herself away as it was time to meet up with Dad again.

They arrived home in time for dinner, and then Amy helped Mum cut some roses from Nan's rose garden to take to the churchyard for her grave. They walked through the meadow and along a little used footpath at the side of the cornfield where Norman had lost his watch. At the far end of the field, they reached a track that led to the quaint little church where Amy's mum and dad had been married. Mum got nostalgic on seeing the church and recalled the difficulties of getting married during the war. "That's why there were no wedding photos." She sighed. "It's a pity I don't have any pictures of my big day."

They walked round to the graveyard with Mum carrying the roses and a pair of shears while Amy was entrusted with a large bottle of water.

"Grandad said Nan's headstone should soon be ready," Mum said as she carefully arranged the roses in the urn. "It's taken long enough." Amy handed her the water and watched her mother fill the urn, then fuss over the grave, clipping the overgrown grass around the edge. Amy gazed at the makeshift little wooden cross. Three years had passed since her nan died, but Grandad had never adjusted well to living without her. When she was alive, he had always insisted he would shoot himself if she died before him. After her funeral, Uncle Ron had taken time off from work to keep a close watch over him day and night for several weeks and hid his shotgun to be sure he didn't carry out his threat.

Mum wanted to go inside the church for some quiet contemplation, so Amy wandered off for a stroll. Next to the churchyard was a large meadow that rose to a small summit. She pushed open the five-bar gate and walked up the incline to the top, where a dead tree lay on the grass. The sun beat down from a cloudless sky. As she reached the tree, she could see the rest of the meadow falling away to a stream that sparkled invitingly in the sunlight. Over to one side was a clump of trees and a few bushy areas near the stream. As Amy began to walk down the slope towards the stream, she caught sight of some movement under the trees. She stopped and looked across into the shade and could make out several young pink piglets rooting around. Then she noticed the mother pig coming into view through the trees. She either hadn't spotted Amy or didn't object to her presence since she seemed unconcerned. Amy was unsure whether to continue down to the stream when suddenly, her mind was made up for her. An enormous brown boar emerged from behind one of the bushes, obviously daddy pig. He definitely disapproved of Amy's presence so near his family. He looked ferocious, and Amy saw the evil glint in his eye before he lowered his head and charged straight for her. Her legs turned to jelly as panic welled up inside, but somehow she managed to turn and flee, desperate to put the fallen tree between herself and the boar. She didn't bother to run around the tree but instead threw herself over the trunk, landing in a heap on the other side. The boar came stampeding up the slope and stopped suddenly, eyeing the tree with a terrified Amy peering over it. She picked herself up and gradually backed away, keeping the boar in sight with the tree between them until she was halfway down the slope to the gate. When she could no longer see him, she turned and ran for her life. She rushed through the gate and slammed it shut. Only then did she stop to catch her breath. She looked back and saw the boar with an air of victory about him, standing in front of the fallen tree.

Amy hurried back to the church just as her mother emerged from the doorway. She kept her frightening experience with the boar to herself as she suspected she would get little sympathy from her mother.

The postman brought Amy a letter from Pam in the morning. She wrote that she had been going around with Yvonne, but not a lot had happened. Amy didn't feel like she had missed out on too much.

During lunch, Dad proposed an outing to the seaside in the afternoon. Mum wanted to wash the kitchen floor, so she didn't accompany them.

On arriving at Felixstowe, Amy wandered off on her own to do some souvenir shopping in the town. She bought Jean a small shell ornament and tried to get Pam a big picture of the Beatles, but they were sold out, so she bought her a Bambi ornament with a mirror instead. Back on the seafront, she bought some postcards to send to Pam, Coral and Jean before meeting up with her dad and Ray on the pebbly beach. Dad had a tray of tea and some packets of biscuits bought at the nearby cafe. Ray lounged on the shingle swigging at a bottle of lemonade because he hated tea. He claimed it made him feel sick. With the tea drunk and the biscuits eaten, it was time to head back to Ivy Cottage.

Mum insisted Amy help with the housework the following morning. With no vacuum cleaner in the cottage, Amy had to hang mats and carpets over the linen line and beat the dust out of them. This was hard work, with the hot sun making it even more uncomfortable. As she thumped at a mat, it suddenly occurred to her that Katy Bullen's birthday was the day after next, and she hadn't got a card for her. There was no convenient shop she could pop along to. 'Oh well, I shall have to send a belated card this year,' she thought resignedly, giving the mat an extra hard thump.

That afternoon, a welcome light rain fell, cooling everything down. After tea, boredom proved to be the mother of invention. With nothing better to do, Ray and Amy laid a row of crab apples across the road. Then they sat on the five-bar gate and watched them get splattered by the passing motors. They gathered the apples that had fallen from the crab apple tree that grew beside the gate and piled them up by the roadside, ready to replace the squashed ones.

Dad appeared briefly and leaned on the gate. "You'd better leave a gap at either end so cyclists won't fall off their bikes trying to negotiate the apples," he advised before wandering back to the cottage.

As they sat on the gate, enjoying their home-grown entertainment, Ray yelled suddenly as a crab apple bounced off his head. A second one hit Amy on the shoulder. Looking around, to their surprise, they spotted Uncle Ron crouching behind the wall of a pigsty with just his red face beaming out. This was totally out of character for him to play silly games, but if that was what he wanted, they were only too happy to join in. A full-scale crab apple war broke out as they leapt down, gathered up handfuls of apples and sent them whistling over the pigsties. They heard the occasional satisfying grunt as an apple found its target. They pressed home their advantage and, being two against one, soon had Uncle Ron taking refuge inside one of the pigsties. He scrambled onto a shelf and tried to protect himself under a pile of sacks with plenty of ammunition to keep Amy and Ray at bay. Unfortunately for him, he had spent his usual hour in the kitchen after tea, washing, shaving and Brylcreeming his hair, getting himself pampered and ready for his nightly trip to the local pub. With harvesting finished, he planned to meet his mates again for a drink and a game of darts. But his best clothes were now definitely the worse for wear, being impregnated with the aroma of pigsty mingled with chicken manure which completely overwhelmed his aftershave. Uncle Ron only had himself to blame for his predicament.

Then Dad arrived on the scene, curious to know the cause of all the noise. "Oh, come on, you two, stop picking on your poor uncle. Call a truce so he can get to the pub for at least one drink before closing time."

"He started it," Amy protested, but Dad refused to believe that Uncle Ron would have started the bombardment in the first place. Uncle Ron quickly made his escape while they were still arguing.

The end of the holiday arrived the following morning. Amy helped to cram clothes back into suitcases and load up the car. Uncle Ron, penitent after the previous evening, gave Amy and Ray five shillings each. Grandad gave them a half-crown and a bar of chocolate each, plus an early Christmas present of a tin of Quality Street to share. Amy could foresee the inevitable arguments looming over who had what. Grandad also bestowed a large box of assorted fruits from his orchard.

Dad came over with a suitcase. Now was the time to put his plan into action. "Amy, keep Mum busy indoors while I fill the remaining space in the boot with a bag of chicken manure. Grandad said I can have as much as I want for my allotment, but Mum mustn't find out or she'll go bonkers."

"Don't you think the smell might be a bit of a giveaway?" Amy asked with a grin.

Ray sauntered out of the shed, so Dad called him over. "Ray, go and pick a large bunch of honeysuckle from around the toilet shed and spread it along the dashboard." Ray, looking puzzled, just shrugged and wandered off to do as he was told. "That should solve the problem of the pong," Dad said, looking pleased with himself. Amy wasn't so sure, knowing her mother's keen sense of smell.

After lunch, they said farewell and Grandad's eyes welled up as he waved them off. Amy's eyes watered a little too, but that was due to the contents of the boot! Dad's subterfuge went well on the homeward journey as long as they kept on the move. They bowled along at a steady speed until they reached the town centre of Chelmsford, where everything ground to a halt with road works causing a long traffic jam. By then, the manure had heated up, simmering gently in the boot. The unmistakable pong began to filter through the car until everyone was engulfed by the pungent stench. All the windows were quickly wound down. Ray and Amy hung their heads outside to gulp mouthfuls of fresh air while Mum buried her nose in the honeysuckle. They received some odd looks from passers-by. The smell was awful, but at least it helped Amy forget about being travel sick.

Dad duly copped a right verbal ear bashing from Mum, but he remained unrepentant. "It'll be worth it when I grow prize-winning vegetables to rival Grandad's," he said.

"I just hope the vegetables appreciate the sacrifice that we are making for them!" Mum retorted from behind her bunch of honeysuckle. Dad was the only one who seemed to relish the robust smell permeating the car. They eventually arrived home after four hours of very smelly motoring.

Amy found her GCE 'O' level art result waiting for her. "I've failed!" she groaned, "all because I painted in the staging under that stupid still life."

Dad gave Amy a lift to work in the morning. She discovered that glassware had been added to the crockery counter. "And that's not all," Jane said with a grimace, "we'll soon be having goldfish as well! Blinking daft idea if you ask me."

Pam popped in during her lunch hour to tell Amy she had passed her art 'O' level.

"I knew you would. Art has always been your best subject, and at least you had the sense not to paint in the staging."

"Perhaps this means I'm on my way to becoming a commercial artist one day," Pam said reflectively, "it's what I would really like to do."

Amy envied Pam's positive career attitude. She was still struggling with the dilemma of what she wanted to do in the workplace. "I'll come over this evening, and we'll celebrate at the Residents Club," Amy told her.

She stopped at Coral's on her way home to collect Rubenstein. Coral was out, so she left her present with her mum. She insisted on taking Amy to the kitchen to show her Coral's new baby hamster – a ruby-eyed cinnamon, the same as Rubenstein.

"I hope Coral makes sure it is really hibernating if it decides to go to sleep all winter," Amy said with a grin. Mrs Manser didn't appear to see the funny side, so Amy grabbed Rubenstein's cage and beat a hasty retreat.

After tea, she caught the bus over to Pam's. They walked to the Residents Club only to find it closed, so they returned to Pam's house, and Amy stayed the night as she had okayed it with her mother.

Pam got the cards out, and they played rummy while she told Amy all about her new boyfriend – another Alan, who also had a scooter. "Yvonne invited me to a party at her cousin's house. He was there and kept asking me to dance."

"You and Yvonne are so lucky where boys are concerned," Amy said with a sigh. What she wouldn't give for a decent boyfriend, let alone one with a scooter.

That night Amy had her usual struggle with Monty for a small portion of the bed while Pam went straight to sleep, turned over and took all the blankets with her. Amy was left with just the dog for meagre warmth.

On her way home after breakfast, she called in at the newsagents next to the bus stop to buy the Beatles monthly magazine for 2/6d. She spent the rest of the day drooling over it while Dad busied himself in the kitchen, making six pounds of plum jam with some of the fruit brought home from Ivy Cottage. He hoped this would get him back in his wife's good books.

Before going to bed, Amy weighed herself and found, to her disgust, that she had gained while on holiday. 'I must go on a crash diet right away,' she vowed.

The Browns returned from holiday to discover they had acquired new neighbours. The Parks had departed, and the Jones, with their three children, had moved in. They were yet another Welsh family in that corner of the Crescent. Dad went to introduce himself to Mr Jones and discovered a kindred spirit who also hailed from the valleys of South Wales. Their eldest son, David, was slightly younger than Amy, and although quite presentable, she realised he wasn't her type. He had two sisters: Joyce was a mere toddler, and Vera was about the same age as Ray. Amy was optimistic they would be an improvement on the noisy Parks mob.

She began her diet in earnest with just half a grapefruit for breakfast before returning to bed until the afternoon to avoid lunch. She eventually got up and busied herself dusting her bedroom and sticking up pictures of the Beatles on the bedroom wall to keep her mind off food. She discovered an article in a magazine claiming lemon juice was suitable for removing freckles so she resolved to try it out.

During dinner, Amy stuck to just a few vegetables. Afterwards, she occupied herself by getting her things ready for school. Still trying to keep busy, she made three and a half pounds of greengage jam and was pleased with the result. 'Every bit as good as Dad's,' she thought after licking the spoon. With hunger pangs gnawing at her insides, she opted for an early night.

The start of the autumn term found Ray unhappy with his first day at the new secondary school. He had to tolerate the trauma of being transported from the top year of junior school to the bottom year of secondary school. He would probably be enduring 'silly little first-year' ringing in his ears for the first week of term.

Coral was staying with her friend, Annabelle, for a week, so Amy had to walk to the bus stop alone. At school, her class was now 6G2, and her form room was the art room in the New Building because their form mistress was the art teacher, Mrs Host.

Now the girls were sixth-year students, they were each allocated a seat at the head of a table for lunch with the first and third-year students. This term was the first time the school had taken in eleven-year olds as first-year students. They looked so small and young to Amy. Previously the starting age had been thirteen. 'Was I really that small at eleven?' she mused as she gazed at her flock of nervous youngsters. Pam sat at the head of the adjacent table, on Amy's right, and Vie sat at Amy's left, so at least they could still talk occasionally.

Amy stopped at the greengrocer's to buy a lemon on her way home. That evening she rubbed half of it over her face, then waited expectantly for the results to take effect. She listened to her Beatles LP before heading for bed, even though she wasn't tired. She tossed and turned until after midnight, her tummy complaining loudly from lack of food as she was still subsisting on only fruit and vegetables.

Mrs Host brought in a large bag of eating apples from her garden. The girls were getting along pretty well with her, though they realised they would not get away with similar pranks to those they carried out under Mrs Butler's nose.

"She's fine so long as you keep on the right side of her," Yvonne told Amy at registration, "but she won't tolerate any nonsense. I've seen her lose her temper. When she's angry, she has a formidable

Scottish temper." Amy noticed that Yvonne seemed to be back to her usual friendly self now that her new friends in the upper-sixth had left school before the summer holidays.

Their first lesson was French with Miss Hardacre. During a pronunciation exercise, she told Yvonne to stand up and form some French words using a guttural sound in her throat. Yvonne gave it her best shot, but the sound she achieved was more like a duck being strangled. Everyone started to giggle, which sent Yvonne into one of her uncontrollable fits of laughter. She laughed so much that tears rolled down her cheeks; then she lost her balance and toppled into the aisle between the desks, writhing in hysterics, her feet kicking the air. The rest of the class exploded with laughter while Miss Hardacre remained unamused, her face reddening with mounting anger. She tried, in vain, to regain a semblance of order to her lesson and eventually exacted her revenge by giving everyone extra homework.

"What a miserable old cow!" Amy grumbled to Yvonne as they filed out of the classroom at the end of the lesson.

Yvonne grinned. "Och, but at least I did na pee me breeks for once."

Amy sat munching moodily on one of Mrs Host's apples for her tea. 'I flippin' well had better soon feel the benefit of all this dieting before my resolve weakens,' she thought, trying to ignore the others tucking into steak and kidney pie.

That evening, she rubbed the other half of the lemon over her face for half an hour, but the freckles stubbornly refused to show any sign of fading. 'Perhaps I need to persevere for longer,' she thought, peering hard at her face in the dressing table mirror.

The following afternoon, Amy found her dad waiting at the gates with his car when she came out of school with Vie. She knew her dad could hardly give her a lift without offering Vie one too, so they both jumped in the back seat. In town, they collected Mum laden down with bags of groceries. She ignored Vie as she flopped down on the front seat, and they headed off to Ray's school.

"I'm glad Ray's settling into his new school now," Mum said, glancing round at Amy. Vie didn't seem to mind being snubbed; she was just glad to be getting a lift home. Ray was waiting with a mate who also wanted a lift. By now, Dad's little car was getting very crowded. Ray perched on his mate's lap while Amy and Vie squeezed up to make room.

"I hope Dad doesn't see anyone else who needs a lift," Amy whispered to Vie, "this car can barely struggle uphill as it is."

That evening, Amy listened to her transistor and munched on more apples. She was over the moon when she heard 'Poison Ivy' by the Rolling Stones at long last.

Before going to bed, she got the Jiff lemon juice from the kitchen cupboard and rubbed it on her face with cotton wool. Being more economical than fresh lemons and also concentrated, she hoped it would be more effective.

After morning registration, 6G2 were given their new homework timetables. Miss Hardacre came in and insisted on inspecting them. She stood over Amy, peering down at her timetable and tutted. "You seem to have far too many study periods, Amy

Brown. We shall have to do something about that," she said and walked off.

'What an old cow,' Amy fumed under her breath. 'She's really got it in for me.'

Amy was relieved when Friday arrived. All week the girls had been subjected to vile dinners. At least she hadn't been tempted to eat them. Being head of table, she enjoyed making the first years eat everything and clear their plates.

Her last lesson of the day was music. She came out at the end of the lesson to find Dad, Mum and Ray waiting for her in the car. She had forgotten, they had arranged to visit Mrs Bullen, Katy and Charlie in their new flat.

Mrs Bullen still talked wistfully of the good old days when she lived a few doors away from the Browns. She hadn't been able to settle for long in one place since she moved away from the Crescent.

Katy eagerly told Amy all about her wedding plans for the following year and showed her some dress patterns so she could choose a style for her bridesmaid's dress. She wanted two older bridesmaids, two younger ones and a page boy. Mrs Bullen had agreed to make the dresses in lemon satin.

As they were leaving, Mrs Bullen called out: "We'll come and spend a long weekend with you before too long. It'll be great to be back in the Crescent with all my old neighbours."

"Er, yes, you must do that," Mum said, trying to sound enthusiastic. As much as she liked Mrs Bullen, she didn't particularly relish the prospect of a weekend of non-stop chattering.

Amy caught the bus to work alone the following morning because Vie had arranged to get a lift from a neighbour. Miss Morris called her over as soon as she emerged from the lockers. "I'm putting you back on the Fablon counter in the basement today," she said in her posh, bossy voice. Amy didn't mind, because this was Joan's last day. She was leaving to work in a hospital canteen.

"I shan't miss all these nappies and rolls of Fablon," Joan declared, carefully folding and arranging a pile of nappies next to the till.

"I don't envy you slaving away all day in a hot, steamy kitchen," Amy said. "I did it once on a Sunday – never again!"

Joan laughed. "Oh, I shan't mind, and I expect there'll be plenty of free food."

By lunchtime, Amy was starving, so she succumbed to a canteen meal of sausages, chips, peas and tomatoes, followed by pink and white ice cream with peaches. 'Bang goes the diet,' she thought as she swallowed another mouthful of ice cream.

Feeling fed up with her lack of willpower, Amy stayed in bed on Sunday until the afternoon. When she finally got up, she started altering her jeans into the latest fashion of ankle swingers. She sat in the lounge and took them in, shortening them, so they came straight down to just above her ankles. 'All in need now is a pair of brightly coloured socks, preferably fluorescent, to emphasise my ankles,' she thought, then shook her head, 'or maybe I'll give them a miss!'

Dad came in and peered over her shoulder at her handiwork. He had been next door watching Mr Jones making home-made wine. "Mr Jones has promised me a few bottles of wine to try," he told her.

"I don't know why you bother showing an interest since you're practically teetotal these days," Amy said.

"It's just my way of getting to know our new neighbours," he explained, "after all, we ought to be friendly."

On Monday morning, Coral and Amy met up with Vie on their way to the bus stop.

"Me and Mick had a very cosy date last Wednesday," Coral confided. "I went to his house while his parents were out, and we sat on the sofa listening to records."

"I bet that wasn't all you were doing," Amy said with a grin.

Coral giggled. "Well, we did do quite a lot of cuddling, and then his hands started to wander..."

"He seemed such a nice boy," Amy said, putting on a shocked expression.

"Being a well-brought-up, church-going girl, I naturally had to put him in his place," Coral said with a toss of her head.

But Amy detected a twinkle in her eye. "Well, that's your story. We'll believe you, won't we Vie?" Vie just nodded. She was preoccupied with a niggling toothache that was bothering her.

Amy arrived home from school fuming. She stomped into the kitchen and flung down her satchel. "Four flippin' homeworks!" she shouted.

Mum was making a pot of tea. "Have a cup of tea, dear. It can't be that bad, surely."

"Huh! I managed to do my arithmetic in school during the break but that still leaves three! It's worse than slave labour!"

After tea, she started her geography homework but didn't get it finished until 10.30. Then she worked on her French until 11.15. She finally took her English learning to bed and studied it until she fell asleep.

Amy had her arithmetic homework ready to hand in the following morning. The new maths teacher had already acquired the nickname of Breezy Bertha because she was such a fresh-air fiend. She bounced into the classroom in the Manor with long swift strides, her short, straight, dark hair held back with a red ribbon and her cheeks glowing with health. Her ample bosom seemed to have a life of its own, trying to free itself from the constraints of her tight cardigan. She didn't restrain herself with a bra or a blouse, and her legs were bare beneath her tweed skirt, which appeared to be the only skirt she owned. Ankle socks and sandals completed her outfit. Along the route march to her desk, she paused at each window to fling it wide open so the class could all benefit from the fresh air. Those unfortunate enough to have seats next to the windows felt the benefit more severely than everyone else.

She began the lesson by gulping deep breaths and flinging her arms out to the sides. She invited the class to do likewise, but they preferred to watch her antics in disbelief. "Fresh air is good for the brain," she assured them. They sat and shivered through a whole hour of double maths.

Amy only managed three sums during the entire period, "I think my brain has seized up solid from the cold," she complained to Jean, sitting next to her.

Jean giggled. "D'you think she preserves her hubby in cold storage at home by keeping all the windows open in all weathers?" she whispered.

Amy grinned. "Perhaps he's turned on by her sandals and white socks, or maybe it's the ribbon tied in a fetching bow on top of her head." She glanced up and saw Bertha glaring at them from her desk at the front of the classroom.

"Stop that chattering, you two, and get on with your work," she bellowed.

Amy stared at the maths problem on her desk while pondering the enigma of teachers. Was it their weirdness that made them decide to become teachers, or the trauma of teaching, that made them weird? She shook her head, unable to decide, and concentrated on the less complex problem in front of her.

Class 6G2 received a letter from Mrs Butler at registration in the morning saying how quiet her life had now become.

"I think she actually misses us," Pam said. She sounded surprised after reading the letter. "Perhaps we should all club together and buy another present for the baby when it arrives?" Everyone agreed with Pam.

After lunch, the girls were herded off to the playing field for a hockey match during double games. It involved a ten-minute walk to get there. Amy and Pam chose positions out on the wing where they were seldom disturbed and could chatter to their heart's content.

"How's Alan? Are you still seeing him?" Amy asked.

"Oh, it's all going swimmingly; he took me to the Residents Club on Saturday evening. We had a good time there, and then he took me to the flicks on Sunday."

"Come on, you two, join in the game," Miss Catting yelled, running up to them and prodding them into a slow jog with her hockey stick. Their lack of enthusiasm forced her to give them up as a lost cause, so she dashed away to referee a bully off.

The route back to school took them through an orchard full of pear trees. The girls discreetly stuffed the ripe fruit down their shirts, bras and knickers. They arrived back at school looking very lumpy, with knickers sagging from the unaccustomed weight. In the changing room, while Miss Catting was in the staff changing room, they quickly transferred the pears into their kit bags so they could be taken home.

Amy stopped at the newsagents on her way home from school to buy the latest Beatles magazine. She spent the evening ogling the pictures in it before putting on her nightly facial of Jiff. She studied her face closely in the mirror but didn't like what she saw. 'I've been putting Jiff on my face for a week now, and those flippin' freckles are still there. I hate them!'

Amy took her Beatles magazine to school the next day, and the girls all drooled over it during the morning break as they lounged on the bales of straw in the stables.

"How about all six of us go to the flicks to see 'Billy Liar' next Wednesday evening?" Pam suggested. Everyone thought this was a great idea, though they all knew who wouldn't be turning up.

Saturday at Woolies, Amy was on the nappy and Fablon counter again, where she met Jenny. She had started there full-time on Monday, and being a quiet, pleasant lady, Amy got on with her straight away. “I enjoy working with nappies and Fablon,” she told Amy. “I’m sorting out what stock I need, so it would be a great help if you could go up to the stock room and collect the things on my list.”

Amy was only too glad to spend the day going up and down in the lift to the stock room on the top floor, where she could skive amongst the gloomy rows of shelves stacked high with merchandise.

During her lunch hour, she went to another chemist searching for Lergyll’s Birch Balsam but with no success. She consoled herself with some cleansing milk and face cream instead. That evening she sat before her mirror, applying the milk and face cream. ‘I believe the freckles are fading a little,’ she thought as she scrutinised her face, ‘or is it just wishful thinking?’

Yvonne turned up unexpectedly on Sunday afternoon with her mum and stepdad. They invited Amy for a picnic as the weather was so warm and sunny. Yvonne’s stepdad drove them out into the countryside. He selected a triangle of grass in the middle of a road junction as the ideal site for a picnic. Fortunately, the roads were little used. After they had finished eating, Yvonne and Amy took off for a walk across the fields and succeeded in getting lost. Halfway across a field, where a large cow was grazing, they discovered on closer inspection, to their dismay, that it was actually a bull.

“Quick, there’s a gate over there – let’s run for it,” Yvonne said, trying to stay calm. They reached the gate and leapt over it, falling down on the other side before realising that the bull hadn’t even noticed them. They eventually found their bearings and arrived back at the car just as Yvonne's parents were starting to worry about them.

A letter from Kathleen arrived in the morning post. She sounded a bit fed up with her school life. Amy read the letter over breakfast while relishing Ray receiving a good telling off from Dad. He had caught him smoking in the shed before breakfast.

At school, Amy finished her French homework in the Manor toilets. She had Miss Hardacre first lesson for two French verb tests, and much to her surprise, and Miss Hardacre's, she managed to achieve full marks in both tests.

That evening, Amy wrote back to Kathleen and tried to cheer her up. She told her about her holiday in Suffolk, mentioning the fiasco with the chicken manure in the car boot. She wasn't sure Kathleen would find that sort of thing amusing.

On Wednesday morning, the class helped Mrs Host set up the stage in the hall. They arranged the enormous display of fruit and vegetables everyone had brought in, ready for Harvest Thanksgiving on Thursday.

Fluff came in and put a large basket of apples on the stage. "Sorry, girls, but I shan't be able to go with you to the flicks this evening as I'll be babysitting my younger brothers and sisters."

Yvonne stomped past carrying a tray of carrots and parsnips.

"That's a pity, Fluff," Pam said, glancing across to where Yvonne was busy arranging carrots. "Yvonne's not going either. She's got the hump, but nobody knows why 'cos she won't talk to anyone."

Amy had arranged to meet Jean at the station at 7.30 pm but, as expected, she didn't show up. 'What an unreliable cow!' Amy fumed as she went to meet the others. Vie arrived with Ricky, and Pam turned up with Alan, so they changed their plans and went to the Scala instead, as tonight was a free entry.

"Alan seems to be a nice, considerate boy," Amy whispered to Pam as they queued to get in. "You're so lucky to have found someone like that." Pam clung onto Alan's arm tightly as though worried Amy might try to prise him away from her.

Once inside, two gorgeous Mod boys came over and asked Amy and Vie to dance, but Vie refused as she knew Ricky would be none too pleased. However, being free, Amy jumped up and danced with both of them, which evolved into a comical version of the mad Mod dance. Alan couldn't resist coming over and joining in the fun while Pam looked on disapprovingly and disowned them. Amy thoroughly enjoyed the rest of the evening, dancing non-stop with a couple of Alan's mates.

Jean was absent from school Thursday morning, as expected, after letting everyone down the previous evening. During assembly, the whole school had to endure a long, boring sermon on Harvest Thanksgiving from a peculiar old vicar. Afterwards, a small group from 6G2, including Vie and Amy, were chosen to distribute the food to the old people's homes in the area. Amy and Vie had to cram into Miss Catting's Mini to deliver the food to some almshouses in the town centre. A good-looking photographer from the local rag turned up to take their picture. They posed on the driveway in front of the Grange, along with Miss Hardacre, holding the heavy boxes and smiling sweetly as though they loved standing there looking like right nerds. The photography session set Miss Catting all of a twitter, making her quite pleasant for a change, and she even gave the girls a load of apples in payment for all their hard work.

"I reckon she fancied that photographer," Vie muttered to Amy as they returned to school for lunch, "that would explain her good mood."

Tired of all the humping of heavy boxes, Amy conveniently lost her plimsolls and socks. Therefore she couldn't participate in double P.E. and was allowed to laze around during the lesson, watching instead.

She called in at the newsagents on her way home from school to place a regular monthly order for the Beatles magazine.

Friday morning found just Amy and Yvonne putting in an appearance at school as Vie had gone to London for a job interview though Mrs Host didn't know this. Pam and Fluff had skived off, no doubt, to avoid the science test, and Jean was absent yet again. Amy still hadn't got to grips with her new timetable. She wandered across the road to the Manor for a history lesson, then realised everyone else had gone to the Grange for French. She stuck out her tongue at the grinning faces as she walked into the classroom late, feeling a right twit.

Yvonne was in a better mood than she had been all week, so Amy went to the jive session during the lunch hour with her. Amy was still smarting from the horrid science exam. "I wish I hadn't bothered to come to school today, but there was no way I could have persuaded Mum to let me stay home unless I was at death's door."

"I know what you mean, Bat. I have the same problem with my mother," Yvonne grumbled. "But cheer up – how about we go to the flicks tomorrow evening as we didn't go during the week?" Amy agreed and arranged to meet Yvonne after work.

Saturday in Woolies was a busy day for Amy, but she didn't mind as it made the time fly by. During her lunch hour, she went to Sherry's and bought a pattern for an empire-line dress, some salmon pink material and red bias binding.

After work, she met Yvonne, and they caught the bus to the next town to see 'Billy Liar.'

Dad, for some reason, thought they had gone to the Scala, so he stopped off there on his way home from work to give them a lift. When Amy arrived home, she was immensely relieved that she hadn't been there after he told her what had happened.

"I was wearing my ambulance uniform, and the man on the door said I could go inside to look for you. As my eyes adjusted to the smoky gloom and flickering lights, people kept asking me if there had been an accident. I waited patiently through several numbers, expecting the dancers to gradually rotate around the floor....."

"You weren't watching ballroom dancing, for goodness sake!" Amy cut in scornfully.

"Well, I couldn't understand why they chose to remain in the same place and just jig around. As a last resort, I had your name broadcast over the loudspeakers, but that also drew a blank, so I had to give up and come home."

"I would have died of embarrassment if I'd been there," Amy declared. "Please don't ever do that again."

Vera and Joyce, the two little girls from next door, came round to watch Amy cleaning out her guinea pigs' cages the following morning. They were thrilled when she let each of them hold a guinea pig.

Afterwards, Amy was busy cutting out her new empire-line dress on the lounge floor when she heard yelling from the dining room. She rushed in, still clutching the scissors, to find out what the rumpus was about.

"Get out!" Mum screamed at her, "and give me those scissors – I need them." She grabbed the dressmaking scissors before thrusting Amy from the room. Amy could only watch through the keyhole and try to make sense of the apparent madness occurring in the next room. She could see Ray lying on his back on the dining room table, writhing in agony and yelling with pain. Dad was holding him down while Mum's panic-stricken voice tried in vain to calm him as she hacked at his jeans with the scissors like a demented surgeon in an operating theatre. Mum later confided to Amy that Ray, during a careless moment in the toilet, had caught himself in the zip of his jeans. Despite the painfulness of the situation, Amy couldn't stop a giggle from bubbling to the surface.

"It's no laughing matter, my girl," Mum reproached her, "he's nursing a very sore blister, but don't you dare let him know that I've told you."

Jean was back at school Monday morning, but nobody spoke to her. They were so fed up with her unreliability that they had elected to send her to Coventry. There was still no sign of Vie. The girls wondered if she had been offered the job in London.

Amy stopped to buy a Valentine magazine on her way home as there was a gorgeous picture of the Beatles on the front cover. At home, a letter was waiting for her from Kathleen. She sounded much happier, and Amy hoped her letter had helped.

She finished sewing her empire-line dress at 7.30 pm and proudly wore it to the Scala at 7.35 pm. She met Pam, Alan and Fluff on the steps outside, and they all enjoyed a great evening. Some advertising notices were handed around, so Amy gathered a pile of them as Alan wanted to demonstrate his origami skills. He showed Amy how to make moving paper men, aeroplanes and confetti, which ended up all over the floor and Pam, again, disowned them.

Amy was disappointed to discover that the neck of her dress bagged out when she leaned forward, so she would need to alter it before wearing it again.

On her way home, she met up with Dennis. He was merrily staggering homeward after an evening spent boozing. He burst into song at the top of his voice and invited Amy to join in.

“Do be quiet, Dennis,” she hissed, “our slumbering neighbours definitely won’t appreciate you serenading them!”

Chapter Eleven

October
Ready Steady Go

Amy had been in a bad mood all day because her Beatles magazine hadn't arrived. Coral and Mick came round that evening to borrow her Beatles LP and left 'She Loves You' in exchange which helped to cheer her up a little. She treated her parents to a demonstration of the mad Mod dance. They tried to look suitably impressed, but Dad soon lost interest and switched on the television to catch the news.

Amy gave up and retreated to her bedroom to spend the next hour sticking more pictures of the Beatles on her bedroom wall before going to bed feeling fed up.

The same gorgeous conductor took her fare on the bus to school, giving her hand a slight squeeze. Amy flushed – he had made her day. Little did she realise that their paths would cross again in years to come.

In the Manor cloakroom, she met up with Yvonne, who appeared to be preoccupied; something was obviously bothering her. Amy got out her books and began to scribble down her English homework. Yvonne sat beside her and rummaged in her satchel, searching for her English book.

Amy paused for a moment. "I don't know about you, Yvonne, but I find it difficult remembering that we're not on speaking terms with Jean. Perhaps we should give her another chance."

"Well, maybe we could just try ignoring her irritating habits," Yvonne suggested, peering over Amy's shoulder in order to copy her English.

Amy agreed. "But it won't be easy."

During the lunch hour, Amy and Yvonne went to the Manor to get some reading books from the library, which was Amy's favourite room. Octagonal in shape, it had oak-panelled walls, gothic-shaped lattice windows and a solid, carved oak door. Situated in the far corner of the Manor, the library was approached along a gloomy oak-panelled corridor. Elba Coots from 6G2 helped in there, every spare moment she could as she desperately wanted to be a librarian one day. If she wasn't busy sorting out books or picking her nose, she was diligently crocheting yet another cheval set.

They had reached the library door before Amy realised her satchel wasn't on her shoulder. She had put it down somewhere and forgotten where so she and Yvonne stayed out of class for the first lesson after lunch looking for it. They eventually found it in the Manor toilets at the end of the first lesson, so they remained there for the second lesson, as it was boring history with Miss Catting.

"I've got something important to tell you," Yvonne said as they sat down on their satchels to protect themselves from the cold stone floor in a corner beside the washbasins. "But you must promise not to breathe a word to anyone about this." Amy duly promised, curious to know what could be so deadly secret.

Yvonne leaned close and whispered: "I phoned Alex yesterday evening, and his mum answered the phone, sobbing. She told me the police had arrested him for murder!"

"No!" Amy exclaimed in shocked surprise.

"Apparently, it happened about two weeks ago when he got involved in a fight outside a pub. According to Alex, the other chap fell and hit his head on the kerb."

"He seems to make a habit of getting into fights," Amy remarked. She was puzzled as to why a decent, well-dressed, well-spoken bloke from a wealthy family living in the better part of Chelsea had such an apparent penchant for trouble.

"I've calmed down now, but last night I was so upset, as you can imagine. I've given the matter a lot of thought and intend to stand by him, and I will wait for him to get out of prison if he's convicted," Yvonne said with a hint of heroism.

"You must think a lot of him to do that," Amy said. "I suppose it's inevitable that he'll end up in prison as he was bound over to keep the peace earlier this year."

"I'm keeping my fingers crossed that the court might be lenient with him, but I'm not very hopeful."

"Don't worry, I'm sure a good solicitor will prove it was just an unfortunate accident," Amy said, trying to reassure her friend.

"Remember, I don't want anyone else to know about this just yet," Yvonne reminded Amy, who once again promised to say nothing.

She arrived home from school to find her father busy pickling red cabbage. "Are you off out this evening?" he asked, prodding shredded cabbage into a large preserving jar.

"No, I'm staying in. Pam and Fluff are going to the flicks to see 'Billy Liar' because I told them how much me and Yvonne enjoyed it on Saturday.

Saturday night still rankled with her father. "I wasted a lot of time waiting for you at the Scala," he muttered.

"Well, I can't help it if you got it all wrong, can I?" Amy retorted and stomped off to her bedroom.

The girls hid in the Manor toilets the following morning to avoid double games. Yvonne produced a pack of cards, and they played rummy squashed into two cubicles with the cards placed on the floor in the gap under the partition.

The afternoon was devoted to a careers talk for everyone in the sixth year. Amy, Pam and Fluff didn't fancy attending as it sounded boring, so they sneaked off and caught an early bus home.

'I needn't have bothered going to school today,' Amy thought as she strolled home, enjoying the warm sunshine of an Indian summer. 'It's been a whole day wasted.'

Fluff walked into the classroom at registration and made a surprising announcement. "Vie has definitely left school for good. I met her mum yesterday evening. She told me that Vie has found a job in London doing dress designing for six pounds, two shillings and sixpence a week starting from Monday."

"I don't blame her," Pam said, "it sounds a lot more interesting than school work, and at least she's getting paid for her efforts."

"Her mum asked me to tell the teachers," Fluff added.

"Tell the teachers what?" Mrs Host asked sharply. She had just walked into the room, so Fluff repeated what she had just told the others.

Mrs Host sighed and shook her head. "She'll be sorry. The day will come when she will regret having no GCEs to fall back on – you mark my words."

"I think Vie will be quite content once she gets her first pay packet," Amy muttered to Pam.

"I don't see what she could hope to gain by staying on at school for 'O' levels anyway," Pam whispered back.

At Amy's music lesson that evening, Mrs Falco got out her metronome and set it ticking on the piano. Amy trailed hopelessly behind, unable to keep up with its rhythm, no matter how slowly Mrs Falco set the tempo.

She went home feeling disillusioned with music and set about altering the neckline of her empire-line dress to take her mind off her dismal piano playing. She put bias binding around the hem, then found she didn't have enough to hem around the sleeve edges.

Saturday morning, Dad gave her a lift to work. There was no sign of Vie, so Amy assumed she was getting ready to start her new job on Monday. 'She doesn't need the paltry wage of fifteen shillings and ninepence for a hard day's slog in Woolies anymore,' Amy thought as she trudged down the stairs to the nappy and Fablon counter in the basement.

Miss Morris came strutting up the stairs and stopped to speak with her. "Miss Brown, could you work an extra hour after school each evening next week? I need to get the Christmas cards priced up and put out, and there is other extra work waiting to be done." Amy said she would, as it meant an additional ten shillings in her pay packet next Saturday.

During her lunch hour, she posted a twelve-shilling postal order for a large Beatles poster and bought a battery for her transistor.

Sunday wasn't a good day for Amy. Vera and Joyce from next door, once more, came round and watched her cleaning out the guinea pigs' cages. She let them hold the guinea pigs again, but when her back was turned, they put them down on the lawn to eat some grass. The guinea pigs spotted far tastier food next door. They dashed under the fence into the Denton's garden and began tucking into Mr Denton's lettuces. It took quite a while to round them up. The guinea pigs didn't relish surrendering their newfound freedom, while Vera and Joyce thought it was all good fun.

"Mr Denton won't be very pleased when he sees his chewed lettuces," Amy told the girls as they shut the guinea pigs back in their cages, "but at least we didn't get bellowed at by Mrs Denton! She must be out – thank goodness."

Amy had arranged to meet Pam at the Scala at 8 pm that evening, but her bus didn't turn up, and by the time the next bus arrived, it made her half an hour late. There was no sign of Pam outside the Scala. She waited until 9 o'clock and then caught the bus back home as she didn't want to risk paying to go into the Scala if she wasn't in there.

At school, Amy discovered that Pam, Alan and Fluff had been in the Scala the previous night, after all. They arranged to meet again that evening, and Amy promised not to be late.

She wore her salmon pink empire-line dress to the Scala, where she met Pam, Alan and Fluff outside right on time.

"I think I shall pack up Alan 'cos he's just too immature for me," Pam said as they handed in their coats at the cloakroom.

"I thought you were pretty keen on him," Amy said.

"I was, but I'm fast going off him."

Later in the evening, while Pam and Fluff went to the ladies, Amy sat at a table with Alan showing him how to make a moving Martian man out of an empty cigarette packet.

"That's a good trick," he said, "let me have a go." He was so engrossed in folding the packet that he didn't notice Pam and Fluff return and sit down.

Pam glanced at Alan and nudged Amy. "See what I mean?" she whispered. Amy just nodded. She couldn't very well tell Pam that she had encouraged him.

At that moment, a contest was announced over the loudspeakers. Patrick Kerr, Amy's celebrity neighbour from the Crescent, and his fiancé had arrived to choose fifty girls and boys to audition for Ready Steady Go on Friday.

"I want everyone on the floor dancing while Patrick and his fiancé wander amongst you making their selections."

Pam and Fluff refused to get up and dance, so Amy and Alan jumped up and joined in. All over the dance floor, everyone was desperately trying to out-dance everyone else. Then disaster struck. Amy caught the heel of her shoe in the hem of her dress. It ripped, causing her to lose her balance. She hurtled down the steps into the ladies' toilet and landed on the floor. She was shaken but unhurt, except for her pride. While she was down there, Alan, unaware that his partner was missing, continued jigging away merrily and got himself selected. Somehow, Fred Bloggs was also chosen.

Amy emerged from the ladies and slumped onto a chair back at the table, feeling fed up. "How on earth did Fred get chosen when all he can manage is a slow shoe shuffle?" she asked crossly. She was peeved at missing out on being selected.

Alan returned to the table beaming. "This could be my big break when I appear on the telly," he said excitedly. Pam just grunted non-committally and suggested it was time to go home.

After school the next day, Amy went into town and asked at the record shop if the Searchers EP had a track on it entitled 'Love potion number nine.' She was told it did. "In that case, I'll bring some money with me on Thursday and buy it," she said and left feeling elated.

At Woolies, she worked from 4.30 to 5.30 on the cosmetics counter upstairs as Miss Morris wanted her to rearrange the stock beneath the counter. Dennis the Menace came wandering through. He spotted Amy and leaned over the counter for a chat.

"I thought I recognised you bendin' over down there," he said with a grin.

Amy straightened up, clutching a box of lipsticks, and glared at him. "You were drunk and disorderly the other night, you great steaming nit!" she said crossly. Too late, she realised the floor manager was standing close by earwigging their conversation. He came towards them, scowling, so Dennis quickly slunk away.

"Miss Brown, you are here to work and not chat with boys. I shall have to report you to Miss Morris," he said icily, then turned on his heel and walked off. Amy stuck out her tongue at his receding back. Before long, Miss Morris appeared and gave her a predictable telling-off. Amy doubted if all this hassle was worth it for the extra ten shillings.

Wednesday was half-closing day so there was no evening work at Woolies. Amy arranged to meet Pam and Fluff in the next town after tea, and they went to see 'Tom Jones' at the flicks. Amy bought ten cigarettes as they intended to enjoy themselves.

"Has anyone heard from Vie since she started work in London?" Pam asked, stubbing out her cigarette when it was only half-smoked. She had suffered from tuberculosis as a child and consequently, she was now wary of smoking too much. She never took the smoke down into her lungs – just blew it straight out through her nostrils. Nobody had heard from Vie.

"I don't know about you two, but I'm getting extremely irritated by Jean and her tall stories about her rich and famous relatives," Amy said as the B film came to an end.

"Yeah, me too," Pam agreed. "I've had about as much as I can take."

"Why do you think she does it?" Fluff asked.

"Who knows? Probably to get attention," Amy said. "If she imagines we're all going to think she's great because she tells us she's got famous relatives, then she's sadly mistaken."

"We have got to do something about her," Pam declared. "Tomorrow we'll talk it over with Yvonne." Amy felt a sharp prod on her shoulder. She turned around and glared at the two old fogies sitting behind them.

"You girls are doing far too much chattering," one of them complained. "we can't hear the film."

"The film is only now about to start," Amy pointed out crossly, and they settled down to watch 'Tom Jones.'

As Amy walked home from the bus stop that evening, a Mod pulled up beside her on his scooter and offered her a lift. He looked rather dishy, and she would have loved to jump on his pillion, but caution got the better of her, so she just smiled sweetly and declined. She soon forgot about what might have been when she arrived home in time to drool over the Beatles on the telly.

The girls took Yvonne down onto the lower lawn in the Manor grounds before assembly in the morning. Jean hadn't arrived at school yet, so they had a chance to discuss the problem of Jean with Yvonne.

"You know I'm as fed up with her as you are," Yvonne said. "I vote one of us must tell her to stop annoying us with her constant fibbing." But they couldn't agree on who should be the one to tell her.

"We must draw straws," Fluff declared, "it's the only fair way to do it." The others agreed but with no straw to hand, they used blades of grass instead. Fluff picked the shortest, so they unanimously voted her as spokeswoman.

During the lunch break, Fluff drew Jean away from the group to speak to her. She wasn't relishing the task she had been given.

"Jean, I've been asked to tell you, on behalf of the other girls, to stop telling lies, as you have absolutely no reason to do so, and we have had enough of your fibs and tall stories."

Jean said nothing but turned very white and pretended she hadn't heard. All afternoon she sulked and spoke to nobody.

Amy bought the Searchers EP in town after school before going to work. She walked to Vie's afterwards to collect her geography textbook for Miss Finley. Vie was out, so she chatted with her mum for a while and learnt that Vie was pleased with her job and didn't have any regrets about leaving school. But for some reason that Amy couldn't fathom, Vie was in her mum's bad books because her mum had cancelled Vie and Ricky's engagement party.

Coral returned Amy's Beatles LP on the bus to school the next day. Amy wasn't surprised when Jean failed to put in an appearance. She assumed Jean was still nursing her bruised ego. Pam and Fluff were also absent.

Amy was furious when she discovered a nasty scratch across her LP as she inspected it during registration. "Coral didn't even have the decency to apologise!" she ranted to Yvonne as she tried to remove the scratch with a bit of spit and polish.

Yvonne and Amy managed to sneak into the jive session for free at lunchtime and practised a new dance craze called the 'hitchhiker.' Amy glanced across to the door and saw a white-faced Coral being led out of the gym. She went over to a classmate of Coral's to ask what was wrong with her.

"She felt sick after morning break, and Catty Catting has just told her to go home," the girl explained. Amy found it difficult to rustle up much sympathy towards her after what she had done to her Beatles LP.

After her hour of work in Woolies, Dad met Amy and gave her a lift to her music lesson. It was half an hour earlier than usual because the girl before her was absent.

She raced home afterwards in time to watch Ready Steady Go. Linda Gosling in 6C2 won an LP for her dancing. Amy spotted Fred Bloggs and several others she recognised from the Scala, but she couldn't see Alan anywhere.

Watching Ready Steady Go reminded Amy that her pink dress needed repairing. She spent the evening stitching the hem and taking it in on the side seams to make it fit better.

On the bus to work in the morning, Amy found Linda Gosling sitting upstairs, proudly showing off her LP. She had been able to swap the LP she had won for the Beatles LP.

At the end of a long day, Amy received her pay packet containing £1. 5s. 8d. Miss Morris stopped her as she was leaving and asked her to continue working evenings up to Christmas. She agreed because the extra money would come in handy.

Amy had arranged to meet Yvonne and Pam at the town hall at 8 pm, but after tea, while washing her hair, she developed a stomach ache, so she had a bath and went to bed instead.

She came down late the next morning feeling a lot better. Ray entered the kitchen holding a large wooden cage with YMCA in bold letters across the front. "I bought these six mice at a jumble sale," he announced proudly, putting it down on the kitchen table. "The man who sold them to me said they are all males."

"I hope he's right," Amy said, peering in at the heaving pile of bedding in the corner where the occasional tail or nose emerged and then vanished.

Just then, Mum came into the kitchen, took one look at the cage on her kitchen table and immediately banished it and its smelly contents to the shed.

Later, as Amy cleaned out her guinea pigs' cages, Dave from next door came and leaned on the fence for a chat. He gave her a fag which she quickly hid in her pocket. "Mum and Dad are taking your two sisters out for a drive this afternoon," Amy told him as she returned from the manure heap.

"Yeah, they're quite excited about going to the countryside," Dave said, puffing on his cigarette.

"Don't your parents mind you smoking?" Amy asked, surprised at his openness with fags. "Mine would do their nuts if they caught me smoking in public or private, for that matter."

"Yeah, mine would too, but I keep a sharp lookout."

With the house to herself that afternoon, Amy could listen to her records and smoke her fag, in peace. Pam arrived in time for tea and wanted to know where Amy had got to the previous evening.

The Beatles were on the telly, so they spent fifteen minutes swooning over them. Then they turned their attention to practising another new Mod dance which left them exhausted by the end of the evening.

Amy ambled along the upstairs corridor in the New Building, heading for morning registration in the art room when she met Pam, Fluff and Yvonne loitering by the lockers.

"Hey, Bat!" Yvonne said and beckoned her over. "I think Jean is absent today, no doubt still suffering from the shock of being told she's a liar."

"Yeah, so we were just thinking up some more ways of getting the message home to her that we are all fed up with her fibs," Pam chipped in.

Amy grinned. "Have you come up with anything?"

Fluff started giggling. "We've just rearranged her locker. When she opens it, all the books will fall out."

"And we've put an anonymous note on top of them asking her to stop telling lies," Yvonne added.

Just then, Lundy arrived in a hurry to get to her locker. In her haste, she opened Jean's locker by mistake and took the full brunt of the books on her head. She gave a yell as the books clattered to the ground around her. The girls groaned, their handiwork undone. Now they would have to carefully rearrange it all over again. Lundy looked dazed as she staggered off to the classroom.

Mrs Host came striding along. "Hurry up, you girls. Get that mess cleared up quickly and come into registration, as you are late."

"Yes, Mrs Host," they murmured demurely in unison.

After school, Amy headed for Woolies and immediately received a telling-off from Miss Morris for arriving at the counter five minutes late. She spent a boring hour pricing Christmas cards until she could finally escape at 5.30.

She called in to see Coral on her way home as she had been absent from school since being sent home feeling sick. Amy found her propped up in bed, looking fed up and feeling sorry for herself. She didn't have the heart to moan at Coral for scratching her record. Instead, she promised to call the following evening.

Jean put in an appearance at school the next day. The girls watched discreetly as she opened her locker but were disappointed when only two books fell out. Jean found the note but didn't comment on it. The girls made a point of avoiding her all day, and nobody spoke to her.

Amy spent another tedious hour pricing more Christmas cards after school and afterwards popped in to see Coral again. She found her no better, and she had developed a cough, so Amy didn't stay long.

As she walked around the Crescent, she met up with Dennis and told him off for getting her into trouble with Miss Morris the previous week. He just grinned and gave her a fag by way of a half-hearted apology.

Amy was delighted to find the five-foot poster of the Beatles had arrived when she got home. She wasted no time in sticking it on the wall beside her bed. Standing back, she admired the gorgeous four clothed only in Victorian bathing costumes. 'That looks great!' she thought with satisfaction. There was now hardly any spare wall left that wasn't covered with pictures of the Beatles.

Ray and Amy had dental appointments the next day, so Dad met them after school. This was only a check-up, and they were relieved to get the all-clear. Amy was puzzled why Ray managed to get away with no fillings, knowing how rarely he brushed his teeth.

On the way home, they stopped at the Hamilton's and found Rosamund there for her half-term. She showed Amy her collection of Beatles pictures, ones that Amy didn't have. "I'll try and get hold of some for you," she promised, leading Amy to the kitchen to show her a newly acquired stray tabby cat sprawled out on a cushion, acting as though he owned the place. Then she took Amy down the garden path to the shed, where she was surprised to find a young guinea pig rummaging under the hay in a large cage.

"I didn't think you girls were interested in keeping pets."

"Kathleen has been enthusiastic about guinea pigs ever since she helped you with yours, so now she has managed to persuade Daddy to buy us one. I do find it hard work, though, especially cleaning the cage. At least we only get to do it during the holidays."

Yvonne found herself in trouble the next day during the double games lesson. She had forgotten to bring her maroon knickers to change into, so she wore her transparent nylon panties under her games skirt. Miss Catting didn't notice, and Yvonne would have got away with it if she hadn't been so enthusiastic during the hockey match. She dribbled the ball at full speed down the field, oblivious to the chorus of wolf whistles coming from the usual crowd of spectators standing on the sideline. They were pupils from the nearby boys' Tech., who weren't participating in the football match in progress on their pitch in the adjoining field. Yvonne's skirt had popped undone and dropped off at the other end of the field, giving the boys an unexpected eyeful. It slowly dawned on Yvonne that she was no longer fully clothed. The situation struck her as excruciatingly funny. She collapsed on the pitch in hysterics, laughing uncontrollably until she peed her breeks. A furious Miss Catting ordered her back to the changing hut at the far end of the field for the rest of the lesson and gave her a detention.

In town, Amy called at the chemists and bought a can of glowing gold tinted hair spray for four shillings and five pence before going to Woolies to price up tins of cat food for an hour.

She stopped at Coral's and found her out of bed but still coughing. "Doesn't sound like you'll be back at school until next week."

"Mum thinks I should be OK by Monday," Coral spluttered between coughs.

Friday evening, Yvonne headed for her detention and Amy returned to Woolies, where she was again stuck in the grocery department pricing various items. She didn't mind as there was a little more diversity than with the Christmas cards.

After tea, Amy washed her hair and tried out the spray tint. To her disappointment, her hair only turned a shade lighter, but the instructions on the can indicated that the colour would show up more after a couple of days. Hearing an argument breaking out in the kitchen, she went to investigate.

Ray had come in and announced that his 'all male' mice had just given birth to a dozen babies! A horrified Mum insisted they had to go, but Ray was adamant that they should stay.

"You must split up the males from the females, then they won't have any more babies," Mum stipulated, "and I still want them gone as soon as possible."

Saturday proved to be unusually quiet at work for Amy. She met Pam briefly at lunchtime, and they each bought the latest fashion of a navy nylon mac with matching headscarves in the Army and Navy Store.

"I've heard the Swinging Blue Jeans are appearing at the Scala Monday evening, Bat. We'll have to go," Pam said as she paid for her mac, and Amy wholeheartedly agreed.

Amy and Pam met Yvonne off the bus after work, and they walked up the hill to Amy's house for tea. Afterwards, they walked to Vie's house, but she was out, so they chatted with her mum and dad for a while. Apparently, Vie was still enjoying her job, and all was going well with Ricky. He was allowed to co-habit with Vie in her bedroom, much to the girls' surprise.

"I can just imagine what my mother would say about that!" Amy said as they headed back to her house.

Pam nodded. "Mmm – mine too!" Amy fished her transistor out of her pocket, and they listened to Luxemburg as they walked along. They played records back at Amy's and practised their new Mod dance. Pam and Amy tried teaching the steps to Yvonne, but she had as much coordination as a three-legged duck.

In the morning, Amy wore her hair in a half-bun and noticed the golden tints gleaming back at her from the mirror. 'I'll have to change that colour,' she thought, 'it's starting to look a bit too red.'

She needed to return to Vie's to collect a book, and the rain was a good excuse for her to wear her new mac and scarf. She arrived at Vie's to find her out yet again. Her mum let her search in Vie's bedroom for the English textbook she needed. Amy rummaged around but couldn't find it among all the clutter from Ricky and Vie's clothes and belongings, so she had to give up.

She returned home and stuck more pictures of the Beatles, on her bedroom wall. In the lounge, she browsed through the paper and found an advert for a free illustrated catalogue of Beatles pictures. She wasted no time in sending off for it.

Mum saw what she was doing and groaned. "You've already got dozens of pictures on your bedroom wall. You'll be sticking them on the ceiling next."

Amy's eyes lit up. "That is a good idea, Mum. Then I can lie in bed and gaze up at the Beatles as I fall asleep." Mum shook her head in despair at her daughter.

Monday morning, Ray discovered his white guinea pig, Snowy, lying dead in his cage. He wasn't all that upset, which didn't surprise Amy as she had been looking after it for over a year since Ray lost interest.

Amy came home after work and buried Snowy in the flower border beside the pear tree without ceremony. She hadn't mentioned the death to Coral because she knew she would want to come round and perform the last rites. She would have given Snowy a full funeral service, no doubt, with Dennis in attendance offering sarcastic sympathy over the fence.

Afterwards, she got ready and left to meet Pam. They were thrilled at the prospect of seeing the Swinging Blue Jeans at the Scala. Once there, they managed to work their way through the crowd into a prime position near the stage so they could drool over the group when they appeared.

"Ooh, I think they're really gorgeous," Amy gasped, applauding vigorously as the group left at the interval.

Pam agreed. "They're much better live." She glanced across the room. "Look out, here comes mad Graham."

He swept Amy away for a dance before she had time to argue. He was as mad as ever as he cavorted around the floor with her. Meanwhile, Pam disowned them and went upstairs to the bar for a drink, where she met her cousin, Colin and Fred. Amy joined them later, still breathless from being danced at top speed around the floor. She stayed with them for the rest of the evening to avoid another dance with mad Graham. Colin and Fred gave the girls fags, and at the end of the evening, offered them a lift home.

Amy went indoors, her head once more in a spin over Fred. 'He is absolutely gorgeous!' she thought.

She saw him on her way to school in the morning, but he didn't see her. She resolved to speak to him if she saw him again the following morning.

But the next morning held only disappointment with far worse to come. She didn't see Fred, which was just as well because when she got to school, Pam was bursting with excitement at her news.

"Hey, Bat, I saw Fred yesterday evening and guess what?" She didn't wait for her to guess. "He made a date with me for Thursday!"

Amy smiled, but her heart was aching. "That's really great for you, Tibs," she said, trying hard to sound sincere, but she spent the rest of the day in a black hole of depression. She had always expected that Pam would be the one to get him eventually.

School closed early, as it was Speech Day. Dad arrived at the school gates to give Amy and Coral a lift home. They had to return to school at 7.30 pm for the speeches. Amy wore her navy blue mac and put her hair in a bun. She took her transistor and plugged the earpiece in to listen to Luxemburg instead of the boring speeches. The local MP was the guest of honour and presented certificates for outstanding work to all the goody-goodies.

During Thursday morning's assembly, Miss Hardacre made a couple of announcements. "The school governors have granted an extra day, added to the half-term holiday. So the good news is that there will be no more school until next Wednesday." Then she scowled. "Now for the bad news: Some girls helped themselves to a lot of the food left over from the Speech Day yesterday evening. Therefore I want everyone to bring in twopence on Wednesday to help pay for it."

"What a flippin' cheek!" Amy exclaimed grumpily as she and Pam headed for the bus stop after school. "I wouldn't mind paying if I'd eaten some of the food." Pam didn't care because she was too preoccupied, thinking about her date with Fred that evening.

Amy arrived home and told her parents about the extra day's holiday, but they refused to believe her, so she changed the subject. "Is there any chance I can go on the school trip to Germany next year?"

"We're not made of money," Dad promptly reminded her, "we shall have to think about it once we know what costs are involved." Amy didn't hold out much hope of persuading them as they said the same thing every year when the school trip was announced and always came up with a reason why she couldn't go.

She went to bed with a cloud of depression hanging over her. 'Tibby is with Fred tonight, but I shan't allow it to bother me,' she lied and absorbed herself in her Beatles magazine to stop from brooding too much.

Amy felt a little better in the morning when she saw a glum Ray trudging off to school. Her mother was still highly suspicious about her extra holiday and persisted in asking a lot of questions. Amy cheered herself up by re-tinting her hair back to blonde.

That evening, after pricing Christmas cards in Woolies, Dad gave Amy a lift to her music lesson. Mrs Falco's husband was in hospital, having an operation, so Mrs Falco dismissed Amy promptly, at the end of the lesson, as she needed to visit him.

Saturday night, Pam was out with Fred again, which made Amy thoroughly depressed. She watched the Beatles on Lucky Stars to cheer herself up and take her mind off thinking about what Pam and Fred were doing.

Dad was busy setting the clocks back one hour as Amy climbed the stairs to bed. “You can have an extra hour in bed tomorrow,” he told her.

She groaned. “But that means we’re back to dark evenings again.”

After Sunday lunch, Amy caught the bus over to Yvonne’s, as she had asked for her help to make a Christmas cake. Yvonne weighed and added the ingredients to a large mixing bowl while Amy stirred with a wooden spoon. They carefully poured the cake mixture into a prepared tin and put it in the oven. Then they decided to walk around town and stopped at a cafe for a coffee.

“Have you heard any more news about Alex?” Amy asked as they sat at a table in the window, sipping cappuccinos.

“Only that, his case won’t come up in court until the new year, so we must all wait on tenterhooks until then. His parents have found a solicitor, who comes highly recommended, so maybe he’ll have a chance of getting off.” Yvonne sighed and took a swig of coffee.

Back at the house, they walked in, just after Yvonne’s mum had arrived home. They realised, too late, that they had forgotten to set the oven timer when they saw Yvonne’s mum removing a black, dry cake from the oven. “The cost of this wasted cake will come out of your pocket money, my girl,” she shouted, glaring at Yvonne. Amy made a hurried exit and headed for the bus stop.

Pam arrived for tea Monday evening and tactfully refrained from mentioning her dates with Fred. The girls walked down town to the Scala, where they met Fred outside. He greeted Pam with a kiss, and Amy's heart hit the pit of her stomach. "I'll wait out here for Colin, so you two girls go on inside," he said.

They had a few dances and then walked around looking for Fred and Colin. Two boys approached them and asked for a dance. As they couldn't find Fred or Colin, they agreed. Amy danced with a boy called Graham. He was quite dishy and not as nutty as mad Graham.

Afterwards, as there was still no sign of Fred or Colin, they agreed to accompany them to the Railway Tavern for a drink. They passed Dennis on the way, looking the worse for drink, so Amy ignored him.

After an orange juice and a fag, they returned to the Scala. Dishy Graham and his mate promptly vanished when the girls spotted Fred and Colin wandering around looking for them. Pam naturally didn't mention where they had been and with whom.

As Amy danced with Colin, she noticed Frudge doing a weird dance with mad Graham. Later, as she and Pam were coming out of the ladies, they saw dishy Graham and his mate. They spotted the girls and came over.

"There you are! We've been looking for you two all evening," he said, somewhat unconvincingly. "How about we take you home?"

"Sorry, we're going home with someone else," Pam said quickly and tugged on Amy's arm, pulling her away. "I didn't think much of his mate anyway," she whispered in Amy's ear. "Fred's much better."

Amy agreed with her, but she still fancied dishy Graham in his Mod leather jacket even though he looked a bit of a Rocker.

Colin gave them a lift home in his Dormobile, but first, they stopped at Fred's house for coffee before taking Pam home. Finally, Colin brought Amy home, and they sat snogging in the van for a while.

"I really like you – how about coming out with me on Saturday evening?" he asked, stroking her hand. Amy reluctantly agreed, but she wasn't very excited at the prospect.

'Perhaps it'll take my mind off Fred,' she told herself as she waved goodbye to Colin and went indoors.

Dad took Amy shopping in the morning and bought her a pair of black, round-toed, stack-heeled shoes – just the sort of shoes he approved of. He also bought a new hearthrug to replace the threadbare rug the hamster liked to chew on. Mum had put her foot down and refused to have one of his home-made rag rugs in the lounge.

When Amy arrived home, Ray took her to one side, looking pleased with himself. "I don't know if I should be telling you this, but Dave from next door told me, in confidence, that he fancies you," he whispered with a smirk.

"Is that supposed to impress me?" Amy snapped, irritated by her brother's gloating attitude. "You can tell him the feeling is definitely not mutual!" She stomped off to her bedroom but couldn't help feeling a little flattered.

Amy had finally finished the green cardigan with the cable pattern she had promised to knit for her dad after many months of surreptitious knitting. With only days to spare, until his birthday, she had persuaded her mother to sew it together. Later that evening, her mother presented her with the finished cardigan. She only needed to sew on the buttons and then wrap it up.

Amy was late for school Wednesday morning. She missed the bus and had to wait fifteen minutes for the next one. As she hurried from the bus stop to school, she saw Fred Bloggs. He was chatting to a group of Grammar girls when he spotted Amy and waved. She waved back and gave him a warm smile that belied the misery in her heart.

At school, she bumped into Coral, who was hunched over and heading for the medical room. "I've got pains in my stomach, so I'm going to lie down for a while," she told Amy.

'She always seems to be ill with something lately,' Amy thought as she climbed the stairs to her form room.

Pam and Fluff were both absent, but Jean was there. She greeted Amy with a friendly grin and invited her to her house Friday evening. Amy wondered, somewhat cynically, what excuse Jean would come up with to cancel the arrangement.

The weather had turned much colder, and Amy discovered she had developed her first itchy chilblain of the winter. Yvonne's poor circulation made her a martyr to them every winter. She saw Amy rubbing her foot, so she leaned across the gangway. "Bat, the doctor gave me a tube of ointment for my chilblains. Do you want to borrow it?"

"Er, no thanks, Yvonne, I can tolerate it as I've only got the one."

During their break, Yvonne wanted to know what Amy and Pam had been up to at the Scala. Amy told her and mentioned her date with Colin on Saturday night. "Didn't you go out with him a while ago?" Amy asked.

"Yeah, but only once. He wasn't much of a snogger, so I didn't bother seeing him again. How did you find his snogging?"

Amy flushed a little at the directness of her question. "Well, I suppose you're right there; he is a bit of a wet kisser," she admitted.

Pam was back at school the following morning, but Jean was absent. The rain pelted down all day, so the first lesson was indoor games which Amy and Pam avoided by getting Pam's games kit out of the lost property. It had languished there since she left it in the Manor cloakroom a week ago. They also claimed a pen each while they were browsing through the unclaimed items.

"By the way, Bat, Fred and Colin have arranged for us to go out in a foursome on Saturday. That should be fun, shouldn't it?"

"Er, yeah, 'course it will," Amy said, trying to sound enthusiastic. As much as she liked Pam's company, the thought of her snuggling up with Fred all evening while she was stuck with Colin didn't appeal to her, in the least.

Amy called in to see how Coral was doing on her way home, as she had been absent. She found her in bed. "I went to the doctor's yesterday evening, and he gave me some tablets and told me to stay in bed for a few days," she said. "They seem to be working because I feel much better already."

Coral's mum was in the front garden cutting flowers as Amy left. She thrust a large bunch of chrysanthemums into her arms. "Take these home for your mum," she said, "they'll look lovely arranged in a vase." Amy thanked her, surprised by the unexpected gesture.

Chapter Twelve

November
The Elopement

Jean and Pam were both absent from school the next day. Yvonne arrived with a message for Amy from Jean. "She rang last night and asked me to tell you not to go over to her house tonight because her mother's got scarlet fever."

"I bet!" Amy scoffed. "I knew she'd come up with an excuse to stop me from going."

That evening, after an hour spent pricing Christmas cards in Woolies, Amy walked up the long hill to her music lesson. Seeing Dennis ahead of her, she caught up with him. "Look at this," he said, rolling up his sleeve to proudly show off his latest tattoo. "I've just bin to 'ave it done, but I'm not courtin' anymore, so there's a blank space for a girl's name."

"Doesn't it hurt?" Amy asked, unimpressed. She didn't like tattoos as they were emblems of the Rockers.

"'Course not - I'm tough, not like your weedy Mods. They wouldn't be able to take the pain," he said derisively. "Play your cards right, and I'll 'ave your name tattooed in that space," he added with a lecherous grin.

"Er, no thanks, Dennis," Amy said, unflattered by his apparent generosity. She didn't believe for one moment that he was serious.

He shrugged and grabbed her satchel. "Oh well, at least I can do the gentlemanly thing, and carry your satchel up the hill for you." Amy glanced suspiciously at him, wondering what he was after. He wasn't usually so considerate.

Her piano lesson took second place to a vigorous discussion on religion with Mrs Falco. Being Italian, she was a devout Roman Catholic and easily shocked by Amy's atheistic views. Amy was just happy to be distracting her from the lesson.

Her monthly Beatles magazine plopped through the letterbox on Saturday morning, giving her a great start to the day.

During her lunch hour at Woolies, she succumbed to the latest fashion craze and bought herself a tartan skirt and knee-length dark green socks. She also bought a packet of Nicobrevin as an additional present for her dad's birthday in the hope that it might help him to give up smoking. This left her flat broke.

That evening, she wore her new clothes when she left to meet Pam, Colin and Fred at the park gates in town as arranged. She was horrified to see them roll up in Colin's dirty old coal lorry. "Sorry, Amy, but my car and van are both non-runners at the moment," he explained sheepishly, helping her up into the cab.

Amy sighed. Now she knew what he did for a living and it did her image no good. 'How can I go out with a coalman?' she thought, 'especially when he takes me out in his filthy coal lorry!'

"I just hope we don't see anyone we know," she grumbled as she squeezed in beside Fred, who had Pam on his lap. This was as embarrassing, if not worse, than Dad's old pop-pop motorbike and his ghastly garb.

"At least Colin has thoughtfully put plastic bags over the seats so we won't get covered in coal dust," Pam said, trying to stick up for her cousin. The cab was so cramped that Amy accepted Colin's offer to sit on his lap while he drove. She worked the clutch pedal and dip switch while he steered and operated the accelerator and brake pedals. This made driving conditions very difficult, so they endured an erratic journey with several hair-raising moments. Bends were taken far too quickly as they drove to a village pub for a drink. Luckily, they only drove along quiet lanes and didn't see a policeman.

After leaving the pub, they went to Fred's house for coffee, and Amy eventually arrived home at 11.30 pm. Her family had just got home from a firework party at the Hamilton's. Mum was hanging out of the front door, no doubt wondering what a coal lorry was doing delivering coal at that time of night, so Colin drove further down the street. He arranged to see Amy the following afternoon and promised to have his car working by then. "You just better, had!" she warned him as he helped her down from the cab.

Amy put the carefully wrapped birthday presents on the breakfast table beside Dad's plate in the morning.

He sat down and gazed at them dubiously. "What's this, then?" he asked, picking up the smaller present and examining it.

Amy grinned. "Open it and find out. Happy birthday, Dad!" She knew her father didn't like receiving presents. He felt uncomfortable knowing that someone had been spending their money on him. He quickly tore open the wrappings, muttered a brief thank you and shoved the Nicobrevin in his pocket. Amy hoped the tablets wouldn't end up tucked away in the back of his sock drawer, along with most of his other presents. He opened the second present and beamed with delight as he held up the long-awaited cardigan. Amy was pleased that at least he appreciated one of her presents. He thanked his daughter, knowing how much time and effort she had invested in making it.

Ray came in and sat down. He had forgotten his dad's birthday, as usual. "Have you heard what happened at the Hamilton's firework party?" he asked, grabbing a piece of toast and coating it with a thick layer of chocolate spread. "It all ended abruptly when a rocket went out of its planned orbit. It shot through the crowd and the open French doors into the dining room and exploded in red stars against the sideboard. It caused a lot of damage before it could be extinguished." He chuckled through a mouthful of chocolatey toast.

"That was no laughing matter," Mum snapped, coming in with cups of tea, "luckily no-one was hurt, but it turned out to be quite a costly party."

"But it was a bloomin' good do until that happened," Dad declared. "Can't be too careful with fireworks."

After breakfast, Amy went down the garden to clean out her guinea pigs' cages. Dennis spotted her and came out for a chat while she worked.

"I'm serious about wantin' to add your name to my latest tattoo."

"And I mean it when I tell you that I don't want my name tattooed on your body, thank you," Amy retorted.

Dennis sighed. "Any uvver girl would jump at the chance," he said and then rolled up his sleeve. "Look at this one." He proudly showed off his biceps, where a half-naked lady wiggled when he flexed his muscles.

"Quite a novelty!" Amy said sarcastically and then returned to scraping the cages.

Colin arrived late that afternoon, but at least he had his Humber car. "I've been working on it all day," he said, trying to excuse his lateness. He showed her his black fingernails as proof which didn't impress Amy. "Fred's invited us over to his house for tea," he said as he drove off. After Saturday night, Amy didn't fancy spending another evening watching Pam and Fred canoodling together.

Fred opened the front door and led them into the back room, where Pam was amusing Fred's baby sister, Louise. On the table, Fred's mum had laid out a delicious spread for them. After tea, they played a game of 'I Spy' with Louise before leaving for the Odeon to watch 'From Russia With Love'.

Colin put his arm around Amy and tried to kiss her, which threatened to spoil her enjoyment of the film, so she quickly stopped that. She couldn't possibly kiss Colin with Fred sitting so close to her. She was relieved to see that Fred was behaving himself, content with merely putting his arm around Pam's shoulders.

Colin drove Amy home and asked to see her the following Saturday. She agreed half-heartedly, unsure whether she really wanted to see him again.

Pam and Fluff were both back at school Monday morning. While they waited for Mrs Host to take registration, Pam showed Amy a letter she and Fluff had composed telling Jean they were all fed up with her lies. "I'm going to post it on my way home," she said.

But Amy wasn't paying much attention as she had something else on her mind. "When you see Fred, can you ask him to tell Colin that I don't mind going out with him to make up a foursome, but not as his girlfriend."

"Why don't you just tell Colin yourself?" Pam asked.

"I suppose I should, but I'm a terrible coward when facing up to something unpleasant."

"Fred is taking me to the Scala tonight. How about I try and find dishy Graham and arrange a date for you? I know you like him."

"Mmm, he is rather nice. You can try if you like."

November the fifth arrived with non-stop rain all day, soaking the bonfires. Pam arrived at school to tell Amy she had given her message to Fred, and he had promised to pass it on to Colin. "Both the Grahams were at the Scala last night, but I didn't manage to speak to dishy Graham because the place was broken up by hooligans. Me and Fred had to make a hasty exit."

Amy stayed in all evening listening to her records while the neighbours let off their fireworks and coaxed their damp bonfires into life. Next door, Mr Jones celebrated bonfire night by sampling his home-made wines. At 10 pm, Amy looked out of the back bedroom window. She saw him staggering around the dying embers of the bonfire with a bottle in one hand and a sparkler in the other, singing 'Men of Harlech' at the top of his voice.

Amy awoke to another rainy day. Dad sat, chuckling at the breakfast table. "That Mr Jones obviously brews a pretty lethal potion," he said. "He was discovered at one o'clock in the morning asleep in the dustbin at the bottom of his garden with just his legs and head protruding and nursing a bottle of wine."

Amy was buttering a slice of toast. "He looked well gone when I saw him last night," she remarked with a grin.

At school in the form room, as the class waited for registration, Pam was excited about the news she had received regarding Vie. "She's only eloped to Gretna Green with Ricky!" she announced. "Vie's aunt called at my house yesterday evening to ask if I knew anything about Vie's plans. I told her I didn't, but I'm not sure she believed me. She said that Vie's mum is frantic and has got the police out looking for them."

"Why, on earth, would they want to elope when they are already living together at Vie's house?" Amy asked.

"Maybe Ricky had an argument with Vie's mum, and she ordered him out of the house," Pam surmised. "I bet her mum could try the patience of a saint."

"I wonder what the Mormon church will make of Vie's escapade?" Amy mused.

"I reckon she might be excommunicated," Fluff said.

"Don't be daft, Fluff, that's the Roman Catholic Church," Pam said with a grin, "but I could be wrong."

Towards the end of the English lesson that afternoon, Miss Hardacre came in looking furious. She dismissed Mrs Slater and sent Jean out of the room before addressing the class. "I have received a serious complaint from Jean's mother regarding a malicious letter sent to Jean." She paused and peered hard at the faces looking back at her. "Does anyone here know anything about such a letter?" Her steely gaze came to rest on Amy. "What about you, Amy Brown, or you, Pamela Tibton?"

Amy felt indignant. How dare she jump to conclusions! She scowled but said nothing. She couldn't incriminate Pam.

Miss Hardacre was getting angrier the longer that no-one owned up. "I want the girl or girls responsible to stand up now, or I will put the whole class in detention."

A chair scraped behind Amy, and Pam stood up. "I sent the letter, Miss Hardacre," she said quietly, staring hard at the floor.

Another chair scraped, and Fluff was also on her feet. "We both wrote and sent the letter, Miss Hardacre. Amy had nothing to do with it. We only did it because we were so fed up with Jean's......"

"I don't want to hear any excuses," Miss Hardacre shouted, then turned to Amy. "As for you, Amy Brown, I owe you an apology since it appears you weren't involved." Amy's mouth dropped open in amazement. She could hardly believe her ears.

Miss Hardacre returned to addressing the whole class. "This victimisation of Jean must stop. I do not expect to hear any more complaints. You two will write a letter of apology and bring it to me tomorrow morning," Miss Hardacre said, glaring at Pam and Fluff as she rose and strode from the room.

As Pam sat down, Amy turned to her. "It's so unfair. She didn't want to hear about all the lies we've had to put up with."

Pam was looking relieved. "Oh well, it could have been worse; at least we didn't get detentions."

Fluff leaned over. "Fancy Jean, showing that letter to her mum. I never thought she would do that."

"I don't think she deserves to be in our gang anymore," Amy said, "we should chuck her out."

The bell sounded for home time. Jean entered the room to be greeted by a cold silence. She looked embarrassed as she grabbed her satchel and quickly left again.

Ray was in an obnoxious mood that evening. "Dennis tells me that he's having your name tattooed on his arm," he teased. "Are you going to have his name tattooed on yours?"

Amy glared at him. "'Course I'm not! It's a load of nonsense."

"I think you're secretly in love with him."

"Don't talk such flippin' rubbish!" Exasperated with her brother's taunts, she reneged on her New Year's resolution and thumped him just as her mother entered the room. She rushed over to protect her darling son and started hitting Amy.

"You're a vicious old cow!" Amy yelled, ducking to fend off the blows.

"How dare you talk to me like that. It's lucky for you that your father isn't here. Get to your room!"

"Don't worry – I'm going!" Amy shouted and stormed out of the door, "and I intend to leave home at the very first opportunity," she called out as she stamped up the stairs.

She threw herself down on her bed, fuming at the injustice of life. All round it had been a pretty abysmal day.

She wasn't on speaking terms with her mother the next day. They just sat and glared at each other across the breakfast table.

Coral was back at school, but Jean was absent as expected. Pam and Fluff took the letter of apology addressed to Jean's mum to Miss Hardacre for approval before posting it.

Later that morning, Miss Hardacre entered their study room upstairs in the Manor and bent over backwards, to be nice to Amy after making her wrongful accusations the day before. "How are you getting on?" she asked with a sickly smile. She grabbed Amy's hand and examined her nails. "I think your talons need trimming," she joked. Joking didn't come naturally to her. As she left, she paused to announce: "I shall give you all an extra French lesson next Thursday instead of your study period." She said it as though she was doing them a big favour and ignored the groans that greeted her suggestion.

Amy rushed home after her stint in Woolies to watch Town and Around on television as Bern Elliot and the Fenmen were appearing, playing at the Scala. They had achieved a little fame, with a record making it into the charts. Later the whole family settled down for the annual ritual of picking the winner of the Miss World contest. Amy cheered when her choice of Miss Jamaica won the title. Yesterday still rankled so she studiously ignored Ray and Mum all evening.

Amy made a heroic effort at school to overcome a bout of nausea. Something she'd eaten hadn't agreed with her. Jean was still away. As the girls strolled along the corridor to the hall for assembly, Mrs Slater pounced on them to give them a ticking off. "You four need to pull your socks up. You are always late for assembly."

"She doesn't have to finish volumes of homework before lessons," Amy whispered to Pam.

Amy felt well enough to head for the jive session with Pam at lunchtime, where they perfected their Mod jive.

"Fred says Colin's car has broken down again, so there are no arrangements for tomorrow night," Pam said, as they waited for the record to be changed on the Dansette in the corner of the gym.

"Can't say I'm very grieved," Amy said. "At least he's not suggested we all go out in his rotten coal lorry again. I wish Fred would get round to giving him my message."

"By the way, I popped round to see Vie's aunt yesterday evening to find out if there was any news of the runaways," Pam said. "Apparently, the police have tracked them down at Gretna Green. Vie has spoken to her parents on the phone and persuaded them to go to Scotland for their marriage. They made it clear that they are determined to go ahead with the ceremony regardless."

"It's a pity she's up in Scotland," Amy said. "I would have liked to go to her wedding." Then the music started again, and they twirled off into their jive.

Saturday morning, Amy woke up feeling much better, so she put her hair up in a half-bun for work.

As she climbed the stairs from the basement in Woolies and crossed the ground floor on her way to the canteen for her morning break, who should she bump into but Colin. "I'm sorry about tonight being messed up because of my car," he said, looking ill at ease, "would you mind if I brought my coal lorry again?"

Amy felt trapped. "Er, don't bother, Colin, I've made other arrangements, so I can't see you tonight." She turned and escaped through the door labelled 'Staff Only.' Obviously, Fred hadn't spoken to him yet.

Amy met up with Pam for lunch as she had been given a whole hour. They went into the Wimpy Bar for egg and chips. As they waited for their meal to arrive, Pam gave Amy the latest news on Vie that she had gleaned from Vie's aunt. "Vie's mum has changed her mind about going to Gretna Green. She spoke to Vie again on the phone and told her that she could get married to Ricky if they came home first. Vie agreed, so the police are bringing them back from Scotland."

"That's great! Maybe we'll get an invite to the wedding after all."

"According to Vie's aunt," Pam continued, "Vie's mum was quite happy for them to live together in Vie's bedroom, but the sparks began to fly when they spoke of getting married. She put her foot down, saying they were far too young."

"You were right about Vie's mum being at the bottom of it all," Amy said. "I wonder if they'll have a white wedding."

"I should hardly think so!"

Amy was rudely awakened that night by Dennis coming home drunk and singing at the top of his voice. She heard a blazing row erupt between him and his mother. It culminated in him being kicked out of the house. She dozed off, wondering where he would be dossing down.

Amy experimented with her make-up in the morning by carefully applying it to half of her face. She had read somewhere that this was the latest Mod look. Then she pulled on her jeans, rolled up to the knees, so they showed off her long green socks and went down the garden to clean the guinea pigs' cages.

Dad came strolling down the path. "I've managed to track down another piano that has a much better tone to it," he said, looking at her askance. "It's being delivered on Wednesday. What on earth is wrong with your face?"

"It's the latest fashion," Amy replied. He walked away, shaking his head.

That evening Amy was glued to the Royal Variety Performance, watching the Beatles. She went to bed in a state of euphoria. 'They were Great!!! Flippin' Fantastic!!' she thought as she sank into the comfortable dent in her mattress.

Jean appeared at school Monday morning so Pam and Fluff made a half-hearted effort to apologise to her. Jean looked somewhat embarrassed and remained apart from them and quiet for the rest of the day.

After tea, Amy put her hair up in a half-bun and lacquered it well to try and outwit the rain and gale-force wind. She headed for the Scala, wearing make-up on both sides of her face as she had decided she preferred it that way.

Pam was waiting for her on the steps outside. They went inside and had a dance while waiting for Fred to arrive. Colin walked past and ignored them. "Looks as if Fred has had a word with Colin," Pam shouted in Amy's ear.

"He doesn't seem to want to stay friends, though – not that I care," Amy shouted back. Halfway through the evening, Fred eventually turned up and took them to the Railway Tavern for a drink. Amy soon got fed up acting as gooseberry to the pair of them, so she left and walked home.

She kept her hair in a half-bun all night, and in the morning, it remained immaculate because of all the heavy lacquering. The gale continued to blow as she walked from the bus stop to school, but not a single hair moved out of place.

Jean appeared to be avoiding everyone and kept to herself as much as possible.

After lunch, all sixth-year classes were summoned to the hall for a talk by Flight Lieutenant Harris of the WRAF. She eulogised about the marvellous prospects of a career in the air force but didn't convince many people, let alone succeed, in recruiting anyone.

"You wouldn't catch me wearing an awful uniform or being ordered around," Amy declared as she walked to the bus stop with Pam after school.

"Mmm, nor me," Pam agreed. "It would be too much like school."

Amy left Woolies that evening and took Vie's school books to her house. She was back home again, so Amy hoped to chat with her and catch up on all her adventures.

But Vie's mum opened the door and glared at Amy as though she had been behind Vie's elopement. "Vie's not in," she snapped in answer to Amy's enquiry. She snatched the books, said a frosty goodbye and shut the door in her face.

Amy walked past the station on her way to school in the morning. She was surprised to find Jean lurking on the steps that led up to the platforms. She was waiting for her and seemed agitated. "Bat, can you tell Mrs Host that my mum has been ravaged by a mad dog and now she has forty-five stitches in her leg, so I must stay home to look after her."

"I think you mean savaged, not ravaged," Amy pointed out coldly, wondering how much truth her news contained. She suspected Jean was merely making an excuse to escape from the uncomfortable atmosphere at school.

"I'll come into school this afternoon to collect my schoolwork," she added.

"Sounds as if you expect to be absent for months," Amy said accusingly. "I don't know how you get away with it!" She stomped off before Jean could answer and mulled over the unfairness of life for the rest of her journey to school.

That evening Pam and Fluff arrived at Amy's house with Vie's engagement present - a set of coffee mugs.

"You must come with us, Bat," Fluff urged, but Amy had no inclination to see Vie's mum again.

"She was downright rude to me yesterday. You two go, besides I haven't got her a present yet."

"These mugs can be from all three of us if you like," Pam offered. "I'm sure Vie will be there this evening." They eventually persuaded a reluctant

Amy to accompany them. Again, Vie was out, and her mum was still in a foul mood.

She opened the door and scowled at Pam. “It’s all your fault,” she accused Pam. “You urged her to elope in the first place.”

“I did not!” Pam said indignantly. “It was Vie and Ricky’s decision to elope.”

“Liar!” snarled Vie’s mum. “I don’t want any of you at the wedding,” she shouted and slammed the door shut.

Fluff blushed with embarrassment. “Er, do you think we should leave Vie’s present on the doorstep?”

“No way!” Pam said. “These mugs would probably end up in the dustbin if Vie’s mum found them first.” They walked back to Amy’s feeling fed up and found Dad in the lounge, gaily tinkling the ivories on the new piano that had just arrived.

“Listen to the lovely tone on this piano,” Dad said, switching to a quick rendition of chopsticks. But Amy couldn’t muster much interest, so she turned on the television as the Beatles were due to perform. The girls squashed up on the settee, ready to swoon over their idols but were disappointed when Paul and George failed to appear because they had gastric flu. A disgruntled Pam and Fluff went home, so Amy tried out her new piano before retiring to bed. She had to admit that it did sound much better than the previous one.

Amy, Pam, Fluff and Yvonne were summoned to Miss Hardacre’s study after lunch the next day. She smiled at them as they entered, wondering what trouble they were in now.

"Right girls, I want four volunteers for gate duty this afternoon, and I'm sure you four would be only too glad to have a valid excuse for missing lessons."

"Yes, Miss," they chorused half-heartedly. Parents were coming to look around the school, and hanging around the school gates all afternoon waiting to direct parents sounded like a very dull and chilly job.

Amy stood at the first entrance to the carriage driveway of the Grange, with Fluff at the second. Pam stood across the road at the Manor gates while Yvonne was positioned down by the New Building. They could only gesture to each other as they were too far apart to chat. After standing around shivering all afternoon, they were thoroughly fed up because not a single parent bothered to turn up!

At Woolies, Amy was in trouble with Mr Roberts, the floor manager, when he caught her talking to Lynn. She had replaced Vie, after taking the obligatory maths test, working Saturdays and evenings for a brief stint in the run-up to Christmas.

"Miss Brown, you are here to work, not chatter," he said in his cold pompous voice.

'This place gets more like a flippin' concentration camp!' Amy fumed under her breath.

At the morning assembly, Miss Hardacre announced that she wanted to see all the sixth-year students in the hall at 2 pm.

The first lesson of the day was geography with Miss Finley. She set up the projector, so they could watch a travel film. Lorna Potter was sent to Miss Stevens, who would be teaching them for their second lesson. She had to ask permission for the class to be a bit late, as the film would slightly overrun the end of the lesson.

6G2 arrived at their biology lesson with Miss Stevens to find her in a bad mood. "I've got a good mind to keep you all in after school as you didn't ask permission to be late!" she ranted. Everyone looked blankly at her, but no-one dared to say anything.

Amy leaned over to Pam. "I've come to the conclusion that our teachers are all steaming mad!" she whispered.

At 2 pm, everyone gathered in the hall, wondering what Miss Hardacre wanted. She came striding in and stood on the platform, looking disconcerted.

"Please sit, girls. I have something of great importance to tell you." Everyone quickly sat down cross-legged on the floor. "It has come to my attention that one of my girls has foolishly absconded to Gretna Green. This has caused great anxiety to her family and a lot of work for the police who had to track them down and bring them home." Amy got a nudge in the ribs from Yvonne. Miss Hardacre had found out about Vie's escapade and appeared unaware that Vie had left school. She then went on to give a long lecture on the sheer folly of such conduct, ending with: "And woe betide any other girl who has the temerity to bring this school into disrepute by copying this despicable behaviour." She glared around the sea of faces looking up at her, and her eyes came to rest on Amy, who flushed uncomfortably under her steely gaze.

That evening as Amy was about to leave Woolies, Mr Roberts called her over to give her another ticking off for talking too much. 'I hate him!' she thought, seething with anger as she hurried to the bus stop, only to see her bus vanishing up the hill. Mr Roberts had caused her to miss it, making her arrive late for her music lesson, but Mrs Falco didn't seem to mind.

"You can come half an hour earlier next week as my pupil before you will be away," she told Amy. "I now have the date for your music exam. It will be held on Saturday, 7th of December." This news sent a shiver down Amy's spine. She dreaded the thought of playing in front of an audience of judges. Mrs Falco dug out the medals she had won over the years for her music. She proudly showed them off to Amy, but she had no ambitions in that direction. She couldn't even remember how she ever justified to herself the need to enter for this horrid exam. By pretending to take an interest in the medals, time soon passed, and very little piano playing occurred.

On the nappy counter Saturday morning, Jenny was playing cupid. She had heard all about Amy's brief but boring fling with Colin. "I know a nice boy called Bob. He's my boyfriend's mate. How about I arrange a date for you with him?"

Amy shrugged. "Why not? I've got nothing better lined up," she said half-heartedly. She didn't, for one moment, think that anyone Jenny knew would be her type, but she couldn't help being just a little curious.

Amy browsed in the music shop during her lunch hour and found a book of carols, reduced in price, so she bought it. That evening, she drove her parents to despair, practising carols for over two hours. They finally escaped to bed just as Ray came in.

Feeling in a generous mood, he gave his sister four fags. Amy could hardly believe her eyes. She grabbed them quickly before he changed his mind and hurried off to the toilet for a quick smoke. It entailed her usual stunt of balancing on the toilet seat to reach the window to blow the smoke outside.

Ray came down the garden path in the morning looking worried. He found his sister cleaning out her guinea pigs' cages. "I've just counted my mice, and there are another twelve babies! It's beginning to get out of control."

Amy grinned. "Your YMCA is getting overrun. What are you going to do about it?"

"Think I'll see if the pet shop will take them. I might as well go round there now," Ray said and hurried off.

Monday morning, Amy wore her hair down with the ends curled under. She no longer had curly hair now that the hated perm had gone. She arrived at school through the wind and rain to find her hair was straight again. She gazed in the mirror of the upstairs cloakroom in the Grange and sighed. "I don't know why I bother!"

"Cheer up, Bat," Yvonne said as she breezed in and saw Amy looking fed up.

"Wish I'd gone to London with Pam to look for a job," Amy said. "She's skiving off to do the rounds of the employment agencies. She says she's fed up with school, nagging teachers and homework. Aren't we all?"

"It's tough, but remember when I nearly made that mistake. I think she would be better off staying to get her GCEs."

Amy and Yvonne bought a load of tuck at break time, only to have Miss Hardacre catch them eating it during their study period. They received yet another lecture but were relieved there was no detention.

After the last lesson that afternoon in the Grange, Mrs Slater saw Amy and Yvonne coming down the stairs wearing their coats. They had put them on in the upstairs cloakroom. "Take your coats off and go and put them on again in the downstairs cloakroom," she ordered. The girls started to protest at this pointless exercise. Miss Hardacre came out of her room to see what all the fuss was about. For once, she actually sided with Amy and Yvonne. Mrs Slater turned on her heel and stomped off in a huff.

"See you later at the Astra, Bat," Yvonne called out as they headed for their respective bus stops. They had arranged to go to the cinema that evening to see 'That Kind of Girl' and 'The Fury of the Vikings'.

They met at the Astra and sat in the back seats to smoke fags and stuff themselves with popcorn. They concluded that the films weren't too bad as they parted at the end of an enjoyable evening.

Pam finally arrived back at school on Thursday. As she came through the large entrance door of the Grange, she met Amy and Yvonne in the hall. "I didn't manage to get fixed up with a job in London," she said, "so I'm going to look locally. I persuaded Fluff to go job-hunting with me, and she had better luck 'cos she's got an interview tomorrow."

"You must be daft to think of leaving school before the end of the school year," Yvonne shouted at her crossly, "can't you see your whole future is at stake here?"

Pam was taken aback by the intensity of Yvonne's words. "It's none of your business if I decide to leave school," she retorted. Miss Hardacre heard their raised voices outside her room. She came out to reprimand Yvonne for upsetting Pam without attempting to find out what the fuss was about.

Friday evening, Amy went straight from work to her piano lesson.

"I'm starting your lessons slightly earlier at quarter to six from now on," Mrs Falco told Amy. She was happy with this arrangement as it meant she could get home in time to see half of Ready Steady Go.

But today, she arrived home to find serious music playing on television all evening. President Kennedy had been assassinated in Dallas, Texas, that afternoon.

Mum was sitting in the lounge looking upset. "I think it is terrible!" she exclaimed, wringing her hands. "You couldn't imagine that happening in this country. They have far too many guns over there."

"Well, he's not the first president to be assassinated. Have they caught the person who did it?" Amy asked.

"No, they are still searching for the assassin who shot him in the head."

Amy tuned in to Luxemburg only to hear more serious music, so all she could do was play her records instead.

She received a visit from Mrs Tibton while at work in the basement at Woolies the next day.

She chatted with Amy for ages, her conversation interspersed with winks, while Amy just wished she'd go before she got Amy into further trouble. Mrs Tibton was probing for information, trying to discover who Pam was currently going out with, as Pam didn't tell her anything. Amy acted dumb and said she didn't know, but she suspected Mrs Tibton didn't believe her.

That evening, Amy met up with Yvonne at the town hall as the entry was free for all the girls. A crowd from school was already there, so they had a great time. "It's a pity Pam's not here," Amy yelled in Yvonne's ear. The group were crashing out their deafening rendition, of the Stones' latest hit, 'I Wanna Be Your Man'. "She would have enjoyed herself."

"Don't worry, I'm sure Pam will be enjoying herself with Fred instead." Amy had forgotten that Pam had a date with Fred. She forced a smile and tried to repress an image of the pair of them cuddling up together.

Coral turned up with her boyfriend, Mick, and sister, Susan, so at the end of the evening, they all walked home together while Yvonne caught a bus home.

At school Monday morning, Pam announced that Fluff had left school to work as a trainee assistant at a laboratory in London.

"She always did like science, so it sounds exactly like the sort of work she wanted to do. It should suit her," Amy said.

"Do you realise we are now down to four, that's if you can still count Jean," Yvonne said dejectedly.

"And don't forget, I'm still looking," Pam chipped in, "I've written off for a job at a local bank."

Yvonne sighed. "Tibs, I wish you wouldn't. I know you'll regret it. If you must get a job, you should look for something artistic – that's where your talent lies."

"I just need to get out of here and earn some money," Pam declared vehemently.

That evening, Amy met Yvonne at the station, and they walked to the Scala, where they were joined by Pam and Fred.

Mad Graham was there. He grabbed Amy by the arm and pulled her to one side. "How would you like to go to an all-night party in London next Saturday?" he asked.

"Huh, no chance of that with my stuffy parents."

"Can't you make some excuse – say you're staying at Pam's?"

"It wouldn't work – they'd find out." Amy wasn't keen to go with Graham, anyway. She had no intention of risking getting into trouble with her parents because of him.

Bern Elliot's record was played several times during the evening as they were the resident group, and it had reached the heady heights of number sixteen in the charts. "I'm not struck on their song," Pam shouted across to Amy and Yvonne as she danced with Fred, who was doing his usual shuffle.

Amy nodded. "I don't know how they made it into the charts."

At school after lunch the next day, the cold weather didn't tempt the girls outside. Instead, they packed into the large airing closet in the corridor next to the changing rooms because it was warm and cosy. Amy peered through the slatted door and spotted a man coming out of Miss Catting's changing room. She giggled. "Hey girls, Catty's been entertaining a man in her room."

"Let's go and have some fun with her," Yvonne said. "Accuse her of luring men into her room."

"I don't think that's a good idea. She doesn't have much of a sense of humour, so we'd probably end up with detentions," Pam warned them.

"I need to stretch my legs," Amy said, "I think we should move out of here." They tumbled out of the cramped cupboard just as Miss Catting emerged from her room. They quickly picked themselves up, expecting a tirade from Miss Catting. But she was in a good mood, so Yvonne had no qualms about pulling her leg regarding the mystery man, which amused Miss Catting, much to everyone's surprise. But she wouldn't be drawn into giving them an explanation.

Amy spent the evening practising her music as there was not much time left until her exam. She could now play each set piece straight through, but there was still plenty of room for improvement.

She persuaded her father to write a note excusing her from games as the weather was still so cold, and she didn't fancy freezing on the hockey field. He wrote that she had a pulled ligament in her left knee. "Don't forget to limp with your left leg," he told her, "and don't let your mother find out, else I'll be in the dog house."

The note didn't fool Miss Catting. "That's a good excuse," she said with a smile. She was still in a good mood, so she sent Amy to tidy up the skipping ropes and beanbags. Amy didn't mind as it meant staying warm indoors.

She bought a brown eyebrow pencil and a Beatles magazine in town before her evening stint at Woolies. She drooled over the magazine on the bus home, flicking through pages of dishy pictures.

That evening she removed her eyebrows with Veet 'O' hair remover. She had tried plucking them but found the procedure far too painful. Now she carefully pencilled in new ones that gave her a slightly surprised look. She found it difficult to get them to match. Much to Amy's amazement, her mother didn't notice any difference in her appearance.

Friday evening, Amy arrived at work to find that Lynn had brought in 'She Loves You' for her to borrow, She also had her new Beatles LP with her so they went to the record department and asked if it could be played on their turntable, but they refused. "What mean sods!" Amy said in disgust as she and Lynn headed for the Christmas card counter. "You'd think they might have a bit of Christmas spirit."

Dad was supposed to meet Amy from work to take her to her music lesson, but he failed to turn up, which was totally out of character. Amy caught the bus instead and arrived at Mrs Falco's ten minutes late. When she came home, she found her father looking very sheepish. "Sorry, love, I had an empty petrol tank."

Dad made up for his oversight by giving Amy a lift to work in the morning.

She discovered the range of goods on her counter had been extended to include ribbons, hats and contact paper. Then Gwyneth and her shoes were tagged on at one end, so Jenny and Amy found themselves rushed off their feet.

Today was Lynn's last day at Woolies, so she had to show Jackie, the new girl who would replace her, what to do. Amy went to lunch with them and found Jackie pleasant and easy to get along with.

The three girls met Pam in the High Street, and they all went to Dimashio's Ice Cream Parlour for a coffee. During their conversation, they discovered that Jackie knew John Preston, Pam's other cousin. According to Pam, he was far dishier than Colin. "I wouldn't mind meeting him," Amy said. "You've kept quiet about him."

"I'll try and persuade John to come to the Scala with Colin on Monday evening so that you can meet him," Pam said as they got up to leave.

"How come you're taking an hour, again, for lunch, Tibs?" Amy asked, glancing at her watch.

"It's amazing what you can get away with when your dad's the manager," Pam said with a laugh and hurried off to Macfisheries. The others walked back to Woolies to start their afternoon shift.

"I can get you the new Beatles LP for the wholesale price of one pound, five shillings and tuppence if you like," Jackie told Amy.

Amy was thrilled. "That would be great!" She returned Lynn's record of 'She Loves You', and they stopped at the record shop so Amy could buy her own copy of the Beatles' best seller.

"Do you fancy coming to a dance up in London tonight?" Lynn asked Amy at the top of the stairs as they headed for their separate counters. "It's at the Mormon church again."

"Yeah, why not. I'll give Yvonne a ring and see if she wants to come too."

Back on the nappy counter, Jenny told Amy she had finally arranged a date with her boyfriend's mate, Bob. "He's very keen to meet you and wants to take you to the cinema on Thursday evening."

"All right, tell him I'll meet him outside," she said, trying to sound keen.

Amy rang Yvonne on her way home, and she was pleased to be invited to the dance as she was bored. She arrived at Amy's house in time for tea, and then they walked to the car park at the local shops to pick up the Dormobile that would be taking them to London. The same young American Mormons were onboard, singing and playing their guitars. The dance was rather dull, so Yvonne and Amy decided to wander around the nearby streets. They soon discovered they were lost but eventually found their way back to the church just as the Dormobile was loading up to take everyone home. They hadn't spent much time dancing, and Lynn hadn't missed them because she had spent the entire evening dancing with a fairly dishy young man, who they presumed must be a Mormon.

They didn't reach home until 12.30 am, but Mum didn't seem to mind as she knew they were only out with the Mormons. Being so late, Yvonne stayed over, which meant both girls had to cram into Amy's single bed. Neither of them got much sleep that night as they both rolled towards the dip.

Chapter Thirteen

December
The Inferno

Yvonne left to catch her bus home after breakfast. Amy wandered out to the shed as she needed a shovel to clean out her guinea pigs. She found Dad busy cleaning out Ray's mice as he had lost interest in them now that their numbers were soaring out of control. Dad was muttering to himself.

"So, how many mice are there now?" Amy asked, peering into the large cage.

"I've just counted thirty-six," he growled.

Amy couldn't resist asking the obvious: "Shouldn't the males be split up from the females?"

"It's not that easy telling which is which, but something must be done with them. This state of affairs can't be left to continue unchecked."

Amy left him to get on with his cleaning and took the shovel down the shortened garden path to the chicken shed that housed the guinea pigs which now stood against the newly built garage wall.

Monday evening, she put her hair up in a half-bun for a night out at the Scala, spraying on plenty of lacquer to keep it in place. Bern Elliot was playing on stage. Fred stood watching as Amy and Pam danced their Mod jive. Amy spotted both Grahams standing by the tables and Colin hovering near the stage. She gazed around, looking, in vain, for someone who might be John Preston. Then Pam persuaded Fred to have a dance for a change, so Amy went over to chat with Colin, who was his usual friendly self again.

Just then, a dishy-looking bloke wandered over. Colin introduced his cousin John to Amy. With his Beatle haircut and black leather jacket, he was definitely an improvement on Colin. Amy gave him a warm smile. Pam was still dancing with Fred, so John asked Amy if she would like to dance too. She tried to act nonchalant but with difficulty as her heart was pounding nineteen to the dozen.

The evening drew to a close, and the only lift home on offer was from Colin with his coal lorry, so they had no choice but to reluctantly accept. Trying to fit five people into the cab was a tight squeeze. Amy sat on John's lap, and Pam sat on Fred's. They arrived outside Amy's house, and John took her to her front gate. Amy was walking on air, but as John leaned over to kiss her goodnight, she spotted her mother peering through the lounge curtains. Then her father burst out of the front door to put the empty milk bottles on the step. Her mother had obviously dispatched him at great speed.

'What spoilsports!' Amy thought as she waved to John and turned to walk up the garden path.

'Still,' she reasoned, 'I like John, and hopefully, I'll see him again, that's if my flippin' parents haven't put him off.'

The following day during the lunch break, Yvonne persuaded Amy to sneak out of school with her and spend her bus fare on sweets at the village shop. As they emerged from the shop, who should they bump into but Pam coming out of the phone box. "Ooh, here's someone else playing truant," Yvonne said with a grin, nudging Amy.

Pam smiled. "I've just had a chat with Fred," she said.

"You must be pretty keen, as you only saw him last night," Amy said casually, trying to hide her envious feelings.

"I know I'd be keen if I were in your shoes, Tibs!" Yvonne said with a laugh, offering round the bag of sweets as they walked back to school.

At work that evening, Jackie gave Amy a picture of the Swinging Blue Jeans by way of an apology. She couldn't get her a copy of the new Beatles LP because it was out of stock.

Pam was absent from school the next day as she had an interview at a local bank. "If she gets that job, our numbers will dwindle to three," Amy said gloomily as she and Yvonne walked along the corridor to registration.

"Or two if you don't include Jean since she's never here," Yvonne pointed out. "Never mind, Bat," she said, seeing her friend's sad face, "we'll stick it out to the bitter end." Amy smiled, unsure if that was a good thing.

Pam arrived at school in the morning looking pretty fed up. "I don't think the interview went too well," she told the others as they removed their coats, berets and scarves in the New Building cloakroom. "I've been giving the matter a lot of thought, and I think I will probably be better off staying on at school until next summer."

"That's great news, Tibs," said a relieved Amy, "without you, school would be even more boring, and if you were working, we wouldn't be able to see so much of each other."

"Well, I'm glad you've come to your senses at last," Yvonne added.

Pam forced a smile. "Yeah, you're right, money's not that important, I suppose."

Pam and Yvonne walked into town with Amy after school to help her choose a pair of stockings for her date with Bob.

"You never know, this Bob might turn out to be the love of your life," Yvonne said with a grin.

"Huh, I doubt it. I'm not really looking forward to this blind date."

"Just enjoy yourself, Bat," Pam said. "You can tell us all about it tomorrow."

Jackie came into the locker room at work, waving Amy's new Beatles LP triumphantly above her head. "They're back in stock!" she yelled.

"That's fantastic!" shouted Amy, grabbing it. She glanced eagerly through the song titles. "These look great - I can't wait to play it."

That evening, Amy wore her hair up in a half-bun when she left to meet Bob outside the cinema. He was early, impatiently pacing up and down, and looked relieved when Amy turned up. She was none too keen on his little goatee beard that waggled up and down as he spoke.

She enjoyed the film, 'Dr No', and afterwards, he drove her home in his little, old-fashioned sit-up-and-beg car, which seemed to suit him perfectly. It couldn't manage more than thirty miles an hour, so the journey dragged on somewhat until he eventually drew up outside her house. "How would you like to go to a live Brian Rix show in London tomorrow night?" he asked tentatively. "The coach leaves at six o'clock."

Amy sighed. "I'll be working, so I won't be able to make it, which is a shame because I love Brian Rix farces."

"Never mind. Perhaps we could go to a dance on Saturday night instead?" he suggested a little more boldly, so Amy agreed. He behaved like a perfect gentleman, opening the car door for her. He didn't even try to kiss her goodnight, which impressed her but also puzzled her. Maybe he was a bit too old-fashioned in his ways.

Friday lunchtime, Amy, Pam and Yvonne enjoyed a boisterous time in the jive session. They attempted to dance a Mod jive as a threesome but got into a tangle. Yvonne slipped, and they all ended up in a heap on the floor, laughing helplessly, but Yvonne managed to control her bladder for once.

After her hour at Woolies, Amy had to hurry up the hill out of town to get to her music lesson on time. Mrs Falco assured her she was ready for her exam on Saturday morning, but Amy wished she felt as confident.

She arrived home to an empty house. A note of explanation mentioned a casserole in the oven. Her family were visiting Great Auntie Gertie for the evening, including Ray!

"It's not fair," Amy groaned, "just when I can play my new Beatles LP as loud as I want, I have to spend the evening practising for this rotten exam tomorrow. I bet they did this on purpose!"

In the morning, Dad gave his very nervous daughter a lift to her music exam at the convent school on the other side of town. She had arranged to take the day off from working in Woolies. The exam turned out to be every bit as bad as Amy had feared. The upright piano stood alone in a large hall in front of a row of grim-faced, bespectacled judges. Luckily, she knew the set pieces by heart so that when her nerves caused her mind to blank out, her fingers switched into automatic mode and she somehow muddled through.

She came out convinced that she had not only failed but failed miserably. She cheered herself up by going into town for a spending spree, even though it was only doing Christmas shopping.

Bob collected Amy that evening to take her to the dance. He hadn't mentioned where the dance was being held, which was hardly surprising as it turned out to be at the local loony bin.

"If I had known you intended to take me to a dance at the nut house, there's no way you'd have got me here," she told him frostily as they walked into a large, brightly-lit hall. A penguin-suited band were crammed onto a small stage at one end. Bob had tickets for the dance because he worked there as a nursing assistant. Amy felt on edge all evening and gave every odd-looking stranger a wide berth.

Bob tried to reassure her. "There's really nothing to worry about. No patients are allowed in here, only the workers." Amy relaxed a little and even began to enjoy herself despite the dances being mainly waltzes and fox trots. It made quite a change from the Mod jive, even though she couldn't dance the waltz to save her life. Bob was in his element and behaved impeccably.

When they arrived at Amy's house, he helped her out of the car again. "You have been charming company," he said, taking her arm and walking her to the front gate but still making no attempt to kiss her. He arranged to see her on Tuesday evening and then drove off, leaving her feeling bemused.

Amy played her new LP while she altered her shift the following day. She took it in at the waist and added a high neck. As she stitched, she reflected on the previous evening and concluded that she and Bob had very little in common. 'I don't think there's much future for us, especially if things warm up between John Preston and me,' she thought.

As she walked to the bus stop on her way to school in the morning, she noticed an old banger trailing along the road behind her. She hurried to the bus stop and was thankful the bus arrived as she got there.

In the cloakroom, Pam came in and announced that she didn't intend to see Fred anymore. "I've become bored with him," she said, "all he ever wants to do is stay indoors. I have to nag to get him to take me to the flicks or the Scala."

"I'm sure I could suffer staying indoors with him, given a chance," Amy said dreamily.

"But Fred is so nice," Yvonne protested. "You don't know when you're well off."

"There's no point if I find him boring, so I shan't be coming to the Scala tonight, Bat, as I shall be busy finishing with Fred."

"But I can't go on my own, so that spells disaster for me because I won't be able to see the lovely John!" Amy exclaimed in dismay. "I just hope your conscience can bear it," she added bitterly and stomped off to registration.

At work that evening, Amy asked Jenny to tell Bob that she wouldn't be able to see him the following evening. "To be honest, Jenny, I don't feel like seeing him anymore. We have nothing in common because he's not my type."

Jenny looked irritated. She gave a sigh. "OK, I'll tell him, but I think you should see him again. He's a very nice person when you get to know him."

Amy spent the evening writing a lengthy letter to Kathleen. She doubted whether it would cheer her up as she wrote it under a cloud of gloom. She felt depressed at missing out on seeing John.

Pam arrived at morning registration and confessed that she had had a change of heart. "I think I'll go out with Fred until after Christmas, so I can get a Christmas present from him."

"I didn't realise you were so mercenary, Tibs," Amy said, feigning a shocked expression.

Pam went to the phone box at lunchtime. She wanted to patch things up with Fred. Meanwhile, Amy perched on the mounting block outside the stables in the Manor courtyard and wrote a 'dear John' letter to Bob, packing him up.

Just as she finished, Yvonne came galloping over. "Hey, Bat, we need to do something to cheer ourselves up. How about we skip school on Friday and go to Woolwich on a shopping spree instead?"

Amy grinned. "Sounds just what I need right now," she said, stuffing the letter into her bag. The bell rang for afternoon lessons, so they strolled across the road and met up with Pam returning from the phone box.

"It's all back on with Fred," she said with a smile.

"I've got a good mind to tell him the real reason you've made it up with him," Yvonne taunted.

"Oh, you wouldn't dare!" Pam said, looking worried.

"What's my silence worth then?"

Pam fished around in her satchel. "Here, have this - it's all I've got." She thrust half a tube of Polos and a sherbet fountain into Yvonne's hands.

Yvonne grinned. "My silence has been bought!"

As Amy walked into the locker room at Woolies that evening, Jackie rushed over, excited and keen to tell her some news. "I was at the Scala last night and saw John, so I went over to chat. I casually asked him about you, and guess what he said!"

"Well, what was it?" Amy demanded impatiently.

"He told me he thinks you're nice and said, he likes you."

"Wow, that's great! I wish I'd known you were going to the Scala. I could have met you there." This news made Amy's day, and she went off with her head in the clouds. She remembered to give Jenny the letter for Bob and then went to collect her wages as the piano exam had prevented her from collecting them on Saturday. Before she had reached the staff door, who should come wandering along and complicate matters but Bob!

"I got your message yesterday, Amy. I was disappointed to hear you'll be busy this evening, but I'll wait and give you a lift home." Amy reluctantly accepted and noticed he was driving a different car when she met him after work. She recognised it as the one that had trailed her the previous morning.

"Were you following me in this car yesterday morning?" she asked suspiciously.

Bob looked sheepish. "Yes, that was me. I was trying to attract your attention to offer you a lift, but the car was playing up and would only move at a snail's pace, so I couldn't catch you up." He drew up outside her house and suggested they meet on Thursday instead. Amy didn't dare tell him then and there that she didn't want to see him anymore, so she agreed, knowing he would receive her letter in the morning.

During 6G2's music lesson the following day, Mrs Snake discussed how they could entertain the first years at the end-of-term concert. Various ideas were bandied around, but the favourite seemed to be a play.

Amy had sensed a cold developing all day. Feeling pretty rotten, she went to bed at nine o'clock.

She awoke feeling snuffly in the morning and then had to walk to the bus stop in the pouring rain. Her class went into the gym for double games as the rain continued unabated. Miss Catting announced they would practise ballroom dancing, but the girls soon became bored swanning around the gym. They persuaded a good-humoured Miss Catting, to let them do the twist and some Mod dances. The gym session ended with everyone having a great time. Even Miss Catting joined in and attempted a gangly version of the twist, with her arms flailing around wildly.

"She can be quite good fun if you can prize her away from her hockey stick," Amy whispered to a giggling Pam, amused by Miss Catting's antics.

Yvonne walked into town with Amy after school. On the way, they finalised the arrangements for playing truant on Friday. They spent their bus money on a cream bun each, and then Yvonne cheekily asked Amy to lend her the bus fare home.

At work, Jenny told Amy that Bob got her letter that morning.

"That's a relief. At least he won't be turning up on my doorstep this evening," she said.

Jenny shook her head disapprovingly. "I feel sorry for poor Bob. I don't think you have given him much of a chance."

"He just isn't my type, Jenny," Amy insisted.

At home, she put some clothes into a bag and stuffed it into her satchel, ready for the morning.

Undaunted, that Friday was the 13th, Amy left home, ostensibly for school, and then caught the bus to Yvonne's house, pleased that her cold hadn't developed. A light snow was falling – the first snow of the winter but didn't lie on the ground.

Yvonne's parents had left for work, so Amy changed out of her school uniform, and they caught the bus to Woolwich. They entered into the Christmas spirit by wearing plastic mistletoe in their hair. Amy bought a couple of presents: two Pyrex mugs with holders for her Aunt Ruth and Uncle Henry and a pair of long green socks for Pam, as she had admired hers. She saw a lovely black and white tweed dress with a leather collar but was disappointed that she couldn't afford it.

Yvonne had brought quite a lot of money with her, so she bought a red thong dress, a grey jumper and a pair of black shoes. They went into a cafe for lunch and ordered an enormous plateful of egg and chips each. A couple of cheeky lads at an adjacent table, tried to chat them up.

"They're a bit too young for us," Yvonne said quietly.

"They're probably after a kiss under our mistletoe," Amy whispered with a giggle.

After a bit more shopping, they caught the train back to Yvonne's, and Amy changed into her school togs again. "It beats going to school, eh, Bat?" Yvonne said with a grin as she saw Amy off on her bus to work.

Amy arrived at her music lesson and was told by a proud Mrs Falco that she had achieved a first-class pass in her exam. This news left Amy completely flabbergasted. "I really don't know how I managed that!" she gasped in disbelief.

"Don't be so modest - your music is coming along very well."

But Amy wasn't convinced, and there was no way she could be persuaded to enter another exam for a higher grade.

There was a letter from Kathleen waiting for her when she arrived home. She didn't have much news and sounded a little homesick. She mentioned how she was looking forward to the Christmas holidays and promised to visit Amy as soon as possible.

Pam arrived after tea to borrow Mrs Brown's sewing machine to sew a dress she was making. She sat at the dining room table, concentrating on a straight seam while Amy washed her hair at the kitchen sink. She came in with a towel wrapped around her head and perched on the table.

She told Pam all about her day in Woolwich with Yvonne. "I wish I'd come with you after all," Pam said wistfully, snipping the thread and examining her handiwork closely. “But someone had to show willing and put in an appearance at school,” she said with a martyred air, making Amy giggle.

Yvonne arrived at Amy’s the following evening wearing her new thong dress. “Red is definitely your colour,” Amy said emphatically. She lounged on the bed, watching Yvonne parade up and down, showing it off in the confined space of Amy’s bedroom between the door and the window.

Yvonne sighed and flopped down on the bed beside her. “I’m fed up. At two o’clock tomorrow, I’ve got to go into hospital for an operation on my varicose veins.”

“Never mind, Yvonne, you should try and forget that for now. How about I play my Beatles LP so we can practise the Mod jive?” Amy suggested trying to cheer her up. She jumped up and dragged Yvonne downstairs for a dance session which ended with Amy nursing sore toes from being trodden on.

At Sunday morning breakfast, Dad came in and announced that the mice now numbered over forty.

Mum glared at her son. “You must get rid of them,” she shouted, waving the bread knife menacingly under his nose. “Or else we will end up overrun. You mark my words.”

“I thought you were going to give them to a pet shop,” Amy remarked through a mouthful of scrambled egg.

“They said they didn’t need any mice. I’ll put an advert in the newsagent’s window,” Ray muttered, looking fed up.

“You’d better do it sooner rather than later,” Mum threatened.

Amy stayed off school on Monday by pretending that her cold was still hanging around. Dad wrote an absence note with Amy's help which, unbeknown to him, would also cover her for her truancy on Friday.

Ray came home looking pleased with himself. He had bought a small cheap transistor radio to cheer himself up, but when he tried it out, he discovered it didn't pick up Luxemburg very well, which really peeved him. "Now I'll have to take it back and change it for a better one," he moaned.

Amy didn't fancy traipsing to work that evening, so she wrote out her Christmas cards instead.

A letter arrived in the morning post from Yvonne. She sounded pretty fed up and begged Amy to visit her, even though the hospital was at Woolwich.

At school, Pam met Amy in the cloakroom and told her there had been a phone call for her yesterday. "It was probably Yvonne's mum," Amy said and showed her the letter she had received from Yvonne.

Amy and Pam sneaked into the village at lunchtime to phone Yvonne's mum. Amy had been right. She had rung the school to ask if Amy could visit Yvonne on Monday evening.

"I'll try and get to the hospital this evening," she told Yvonne's mum, "but I'm not promising, so don't say anything to Yvonne."

They bought some sweets at the pub on their way back to school and returned without being spotted by a teacher.

Amy approached her father as soon as he came home from work, and he agreed to drive her to the hospital. Ray opted to accompany them just for the ride. He stayed in the car while Amy and her dad made their way to the top floor, searching for Yvonne's ward. They couldn't find a lift, so they walked up the stairs and arrived in the ward, out of breath. Yvonne's mum and stepdad were already there. Yvonne had gone to the theatre for an operation on her varicose veins that afternoon, and already she was back to her usual bubbly self. She was so pleased to see Amy even though all she had brought her were a few sweets she had left over from lunchtime as she hadn't had time to get anything else.

After visiting time ended, Yvonne's mum and stepdad insisted on showing them around their brand new caravanette in the car park. They were very proud of the neat, compact design. "We're planning on taking lots of holidays. It should be very comfortable for the two of us," Yvonne's mum declared.

Amy noted that their plans didn't seem to include Yvonne.

"You must come back to our house for coffee," gushed Yvonne's mum.

Dad rarely drank coffee, and Yvonne's parents weren't his idea of compatible company. "I'm sorry, but we can't because I've left Ray waiting in the car, and they have to be up for school in the morning," he said, bustling Amy out of the caravanette's door.

Amy rummaged around in her satchel during morning registration hunting for her homework and found two squashed fags. She and Pam sneaked off to the Manor toilets to smoke them instead of going to music and French lessons. They didn't have a light, so Amy crept into the spacious Manor entrance hall and lit one on the large open fire burning in the ornate hearth, managing to burn her hand in the process. They soon wished they hadn't bothered because they tasted dry and stale.

Lunch comprised of a delicious Christmas dinner with turkey and all the trimmings. Afterwards, the staff had a booze up in the staffroom while the girls were forced to sit, bored stiff, through the third year's feeble production of Cinderella.

Amy didn't feel like going to work after school, so she went home, washed her fringe and spent the evening listening to Luxemburg.

The last day of school arrived, and everyone was in high spirits. 6G2 entertained the first years in the gym with an impromptu comedy version of Beauty and the Beast. Yvonne was supposed to play the beast, but because she was in hospital, Amy found herself roped in and thrust into a grotesque costume. Luckily, she didn't have to speak, only make strange noises on cue. The first years thoroughly enjoyed themselves, and 6G2 found it far more fun than watching boring old black-and-white films in the main hall with the rest of the school.

Amy had brought her two Beatles LPs and her transistor to play during the lunch break in their form room. Pam gave Amy a Christmas present of a bottle of Black Rose cologne, which smelt somewhat dubious, and Amy gave Pam the green socks, which seemed to please her. 6G2 had clubbed together and collected fifteen shillings and sixpence to buy Mrs Host a bottle of Tweed perfume. They had asked Miss Catting which scent she liked best. Mrs Host was thrilled they had taken the trouble to discover her favourite perfume. The girls were slightly disappointed that Mrs Butler hadn't come to see them.

"I expect her new baby is keeping her busy now," Pam reasoned.

"Still, it would have been nice to see her and the baby," Amy said wistfully.

After lunch, everyone had to attend the carol service before being allowed to leave early, which didn't help Amy as she had to go to work. In town, she stopped to post a birthday card to Mrs Falco. She wasn't sure of the exact date of her birthday but knew it wasn't long before Christmas. At Woolies, Miss Morris asked Amy if she would work all the next day. She agreed, pleased to be getting the extra money which would make up for not working on the Saturday of her music exam.

During her lunch hour at work the next day, Amy went Christmas shopping with Jackie. She bought a plant for Mrs Falco, Dusty Springfield's record of 'I only want to be with you' for Yvonne as it was her favourite, plus some wrapping paper and greeting tags. She came out of work half an hour early to get to her music lesson on time, but she didn't give Mrs Falco her plant as she hadn't had time to wrap it up.

The last Saturday before Christmas, Woolies was the busiest Amy had ever seen it. She saw Pam briefly, during her lunch hour when they met up for a coffee in the Wimpy Bar. Pam showed her the leather wallet she had bought for Fred, costing 23/11d.

"You must be mad spending all that money," Amy told her, "or else you're in love after all."

Pam grinned. "You never know, I just might be," she said enigmatically. With their coffees drunk, they parted to return to their respective jobs.

Luggett approached Amy as everyone was changing out of their green overalls at the end of the day. "Would you like to come shopping with me at Woolwich on Monday morning? Only I don't really fancy going on my own."

"Yeah, why not. I saw a tweed dress there that I took quite a liking to. If it's still there, I shall treat myself to it."

Dad couldn't take Amy to the hospital the following day to see Yvonne as he had promised to take Mum over to the Hamilton's for tea, so that evening, she caught a train instead. She gave Yvonne the Dusty Springfield record, which pleased her even though she couldn't play it until she got home. Her new boyfriend, Trevor, was there, but he preferred to be called Tell. He soon had them laughing helplessly at his jokes. When visiting time ended, Yvonne insisted that Tell should see Amy safely onto her train.

But he had other plans. First, he took her to a pub and bought her four double rum and blacks. "I think you're trying to get me tiddly," she said, with a giggle, as she finished the fourth drink. "I've got to dash, or I'll miss my train."

She staggered to her feet, and Tell grabbed her arm. "I must see you safely home. Yvonne would never forgive me if I didn't." Amy's head was spinning a little, so she didn't bother to argue. She was grateful for the company and his steadying arm. When they arrived at her house, Mum and Dad were still out, so she invited him indoors for coffee. This proved to be a mistake. He started putting his arm around her and tried to kiss her as they sat on the settee. Amy pushed him away.

"But I really like you, Amy," he protested. "I'm surprised Yvonne hasn't introduced us before tonight. How about we go out together tomorrow?"

"Have you forgotten you're Yvonne's boyfriend?" Amy reminded him firmly, trying to prise his arm from around her waist.

"She doesn't need to know about us."

"Look, I'm very flattered, and you seem a nice enough bloke, but I wouldn't dream of stealing my friend's boyfriend, especially while she's lying in hospital." Amy's resolve might have weakened, but she didn't fancy him much anyway. She chucked him out at midnight after he had missed his last bus home, so a long two-hour walk lay ahead.

She got up early on Monday morning and met Luggett at the station to catch the train to Woolwich. She was disappointed to find the tweed dress she wanted had been sold, so instead, she bought a black dress with a black and white checked bib and a grey cardigan. Luggett did the last of her shopping, and then they returned to work at 11.15 am. They received the inevitable reprimand from Miss Morris because they hadn't asked permission to take time off to go shopping.

Back at the nappy counter, she told Jenny what Miss Morris had said. "It's not as if we get paid when we're not here," Amy complained, feeling miffed.

That evening, Dad gave Amy a lift to Mrs Falco's so she could give her the carefully wrapped plant. Mrs Falco beamed with delight at receiving the unexpected present.

Then Dad drove Amy to Aunt Ruth's house to deliver more presents, and she insisted they stop for a cup of tea. Amy could hardly believe her eyes when her aunt offered her a fag in front of her dad. She took it and lit it up, feeling very self-conscious, but to her amazement, Dad didn't say a word! As they were leaving, Dad invited his sister and Uncle Henry for tea on Christmas Day.

Amy worked all the next day as it was Christmas Eve, but she was disappointed not to get paid. Jenny and the other full-time women had clubbed together and bought her a present of stockings and deodorant. She wondered if they were trying to tell her something. Mrs Young, the nice supervisor, surprised her by giving her a box of chocolates.

Amy arrived home to find a withered, little Christmas tree leaning against the shed. The local grocer had given it to Dad as he had been helping him with Christmas deliveries in his spare time. Obviously, the tree was an unwanted one, left over. As it was too late to buy any decorations for it, it was destined to sit bare and neglected in the shed over Christmas, which annoyed Amy. 'This is so typical of the meanness of my parents!'

That evening, Pam turned up unexpectedly with Fred and some of his mates in a car. They had come to take Amy to a party being held in a large room over a pub not far from Pam's house. Amy quickly changed and got ready while Pam sat on the bed, waiting.

"I rang Yvonne's mum and she said Yvonne is out of hospital."

"That's good news. Maybe she'll keep Tell under better control now." Amy told Pam briefly about the trouble she had had with him.

Pam gave a long sigh. "Men!" she exclaimed. "Which reminds me, I'm really bored with Fred, so I'm going to pack him up tonight. It's no good, I can't wait until after Christmas."

"Oh, Pam, you're heartless! You can't do that to Fred just before Christmas. I feel so sorry for him. And what about the present you bought for him – it cost a lot of money."

Pam shrugged. "Oh, I'll still give him the wallet – I'm not that mean."

Later at the party, Amy saw Fred wandering around looking lost and miserable. She guessed that Pam had finally finished with him. She desperately wanted to go and give him a big hug, but her courage failed her. Instead, she accepted a dance with a fairly dishy Mod called Little Mick. He explained that his name distinguished him from his tall mate, Big Mick.

During the evening, John Preston turned up. He spotted Amy and came over. "How are you, and how's your mother?" he asked with a cheeky grin. Then Little Mick appeared at Amy's side, and John looked a bit peeved at seeing her with someone else, so he quickly departed before Amy had a chance to disown Little Mick. Later on, Little Mick badgered Amy for her address, but she refused to give it to him. She was still annoyed at losing the opportunity to dance with John. She searched for him, but he seemed to have disappeared from the party.

Pam spent the evening with a tall, good-looking guy called Derek, who gave her and Amy a lift home at two in the morning.

After breakfast on Christmas Day, the family sat around the space where the Christmas tree should have stood and opened their presents. Amy got a manicure set from Aunt Nora, a basket containing hair rollers, bath salts and perfumed clothes hangers from Aunt Ruth and chocolates and biscuits from Grandad. She received a practical record cabinet from her parents, and Ray was over the moon to get a Scalectrix set.

Mum received her traditional present from Wales of a handmade floral pinny. Gran had sent her one every year, but since last Christmas, Aunt Dot had inherited the dubious honour. Mum fitted in well with the pinny brigade in the Crescent, who all sported brand-new pinnies by the new year.

"There's something reassuring and dependable about a pinny," Mum insisted. "A wife in a pinny isn't going to be off looking for something different and exciting to fill her day. She's content indoors with her homely chores of cleaning and motherhood." Some in the Crescent even topped the look off with a scarf tied tightly around the head to keep the hair safely tucked away out of sight, but Mum didn't go quite that far.

Sunday afternoon was the time for Mum to swap her workaday pinny for a crisp apron which could be discreetly discarded if visitors should arrive. Mum had often darkly predicted that when pinnies were shunned and no longer worn, marriages would begin to fall apart; of this, she was convinced. Try as she might, Amy could never visualise herself as an obedient, pinny-clad housewife of the future.

Amy was permitted a small sweet sherry before dinner. 'Whoopee!' she thought sarcastically, sipping it without really enjoying it.

After the Queen's speech, Coral called in to give Amy her present of a hair spray. Aunt Ruth and Uncle Henry arrived for tea, and Aunt Ruth offered Amy a fag in front of her mother. She took it and puffed at it uneasily, sensing her mother's outraged eyes boring into her. Mum didn't dare to openly reproach her sister-in-law. After a couple of Pink Ladies, Aunt Ruth dragged a reluctant Amy over to the piano for an attempt at a duet. They didn't manage to keep in tune or together and spent the next hour practising various pieces and creating sheer torture for everyone else. 'What a typically boring way to spend Christmas Day,' Amy thought as she fell into bed that night.

The Hamilton's arrived for tea on Boxing Day. At 5.30 pm, right in the middle of teatime, Fluff and her two younger sisters turned up, but they wisely didn't hang around once they realised Mum was none too pleased with their timing. Amy gave Fluff her present, and Fluff gave Amy hers – a set of Nivea creams. After Fluff had left, Amy discovered that the gift tag was addressed to Pam.

She lazed in bed all the following morning until 1.30 pm as there was no good reason for getting up. After lunch, Pam arrived to borrow Mrs Brown's sewing machine again to put the sleeves in her dress. She stayed for tea, and then she and Amy walked into town to sit in the Wimpy Bar drinking coffee.

Amy gazed into her coffee cup and sighed. "I'm fed up, Tibs."

"Yeah, me too. How about tomorrow evening, we try the Inferno Club?"

Amy brightened up. "That's not a bad idea. I've heard some of the girls at school raving about it."

"Well, it's time we spread our wings over pastures new. I'm getting a bit tired of the same old places," Pam said, getting up to leave.

"You're right, Tibs, a new place is just what we need and maybe some new faces too!"

They were disappointed not to see anyone they knew in town. Amy walked to the bus stop with Pam and waited with her until her bus came, and then she strolled home.

Saturday, Amy was back working in Woolies and finally got paid. She met Pam after work, and they walked up the hill to her house for tea before getting themselves ready for the evening ahead.

They caught the train to Welling and found the Inferno Club just around the corner from the station. It looked like an old barn with a stage at one end, and a snack bar tucked away in a corner at the other end. There was a ladder leading up into a hay loft which was strictly out of bounds. The owner was a jolly little man who perched on a stool in the snack bar, chatting with everyone. The place was packed and very hot, but they had a great time. They chatted with a couple of boys who asked them to dance and then invited the girls to a party the following Friday.

"I can't see us being able to go," Amy whispered to Pam. "I know my mother will say no if I ask her."

Just as they were leaving, a fight broke out in the yard, outside. A boy staggered past with blood down the front of his shirt, but he didn't look badly hurt. The fighting soon stopped when someone shouted that the police had been called.

Pam and Amy didn't hang around. They hurried to the station and caught their train home. Pam alighted at the station one stop before Amy's. "I think we should go to the Inferno on New Year's Eve," she called out as Amy waved to her out of the window.

Amy didn't have the energy to walk home up the hill when she reached her station, so she waited for a bus. Suddenly, around the corner, came Alan Starling and some of his mates on their scooters. They stopped, and Alan offered her a lift home, so she gladly accepted. The sound of half a dozen scooters roaring to a halt outside her house soon had Mum peering through the curtains. Amy climbed off the pillion, thanked Alan, and then they sped off on their scooters again.

Sunday had been set aside for a family outing to visit Aunt Nora, Mum's eldest sister. Amy was gobsmacked when her aunt gave her a fag in front of her parents. 'What is happening to my aunts?' she wondered. 'Perhaps they think I've reached an age when I can smoke respectably in adult company?' But they obviously hadn't sought her mother's approval because she copped an earful from her on the way home while Dad tactfully said nothing. He just puffed away on a roll-up and concentrated on his driving.

Amy lounged in bed the following morning. After lunch, she went over to Pam's house for tea. Afterwards, they left for the Scala. They stopped on the way for a drink at the pub and bought ten cigarettes.

Dishy Graham was at the Scala and asked Amy to dance twice during the evening. He invited her and Pam to the Railway Tavern for a drink, so they went in his car. In the bar, over a quick drink, he had them giggling at his jokes. Then they headed back to the Scala.

Mad Graham was on the dance floor chatting animatedly with a girl, waving his arms around, trying to illustrate what he was saying. They spotted Fred lurking in a corner near the exit with Colin. Pam didn't want to speak to him, so she gave Amy the Christmas present to take to him. He looked taken aback but was pleased to receive it. Colin had obviously been drinking because he lunged at Amy, picked her up and swung her around until they almost fell down the steps onto the dance floor. Amy pushed him away, none too pleased with his behaviour.

Just as she and Pam were leaving, she nudged Pam. "Look, there's Little Mick vanishing into the gents."

"D'you want to hang around until he comes out to have a chat with him?"

Amy thought for a moment then decided. "No, not particularly."

Dishy Graham was waiting outside, so he offered the girls a lift home in his car. He already had three of his mates in the back seat. They accepted but found it a bit of a squash. Amy thought about Graham as she got ready for bed and concluded that she did rather like him.

On New Year's Eve, Amy ironed her clothes, ready for the evening. Pam came over, and again they caught the train to the Inferno. They found it packed out, just as before. The same two boys chatted and danced with them for most of the evening though the girls didn't particularly fancy either of them. They finally managed to get rid of them by promising to go to the party with them on Friday. Pam jotted down their phone number, intending to ring the boys on Thursday evening to tell them they wouldn't be able to make it.

The boys saw the girls leaving and insisted on accompanying them to the station and seeing them safely onto the train home.

The night was still young, and being New Year's Eve, the girls headed for the Scala to try and gate-crash their New Year's Eve dance. They chatted up the doorman, and he eventually softened and allowed them to go in for free.

Inside they found a merry crowd, wearing silly hats and chucking streamers everywhere. The noise they were making almost drowned the group playing frantically on stage. Most of the boys were drunk and staggered around, trying to kiss everyone they bumped into.

"I don't fancy hanging about to be kissed by drunken yobs," Pam said, pulling a face.

"Let's not bother waiting for midnight, Tibs," Amy said, grabbing Pam's arm to pull her out of the path of a stumbling drunk. "There's no-one here we know anyway."

They left and walked to their bus stops in the next street. Pam's bus arrived first. The friends wished each other a Happy New Year, then Pam jumped onboard, and the bus pulled away. Amy's bus stop was around the corner. After five minutes, she was also heading home on her bus. She was pleased that she would be in time to see a special edition of Ready Steady Go from 11.15 to 12.15 am, with the main attraction, an appearance by the Beatles.

She found the house in darkness, as the rest of the family had already gone to bed. They were too tired to see in the new year.

After drooling over the Beatles, she switched the television off, made a cup of coffee and then sat quietly thinking. Had she stuck to the resolutions she made exactly one year ago?

'Well, I got a Saturday job, and I've managed to keep it, even though it's been hard work, long hours and grotty pay. I failed to get rid of my freckles, but at least I tried. As for Ray, I only thumped him when he really asked for it.

This year there will be big changes coming when I leave school and start work, so I wonder what new resolutions I ought to make.......?'

Printed in the United States
by Baker & Taylor Publisher Services